coninginne van schotlant

MARY
Queen of Scots

ENDPAPERS The execution
of Mary Queen of Scots, a
contemporary Dutch
drawing, artist unknown.

TITLE-PAGE Mary Queen
of Scots, a portrait at
Chatsworth attributed to
Zuccaro.

MARY
Queen of Scots

ANTONIA FRASER

ILLUSTRATED EDITION

Weidenfeld and Nicolson London

In memory of Tony Godwin who believed in this book

AUTHOR'S NOTE
This new illustrated edition of *Mary Queen of Scots* appears nine years after it was first published: I am most grateful to Christopher Falkus of Weidenfeld's for his help and advice in preparing it.

Abridged edition first published in 1978 by George Weidenfeld and Nicolson, 11 St John's Hill, London SW11

ISBN 0 297 77522 7

Colour separation by Newsele Litho Ltd.
Printed in Great Britain by Cox and Wyman Ltd.
London, Fakenham and Reading

Contents

PART ONE
The Young Queen

1 All Men Lamented

'All men lamented that the realm was left without a male to succeed.'

JOHN KNOX

The winter of 1542 was marked by tempestuous weather throughout the British Isles: in the north, on the borders of Scotland and England, there were heavy snow-falls in December and frost so savage that by January the ships were frozen into the harbour at Newcastle. These stark conditions found a bleak parallel in the political climate which then prevailed between the two countries. Scotland groaned under the humilation of a recent defeat at English hands at the battle of Solway Moss. As a result of the battle, the Scottish nobility, which had barely recovered from the defeat of Flodden a generation before, were stricken yet again by the deaths of their leaders in their prime; of those who survived, many prominent members were prisoners in English hands, while the rest met the experience of defeat by quarrelling among themselves, showing their strongest loyalty to the principle of self-aggrandizement, rather than to the troubled monarchy. The Scottish national Church, although still officially Catholic for the next seventeen years, was already torn between those who wished to reform its manifold abuses from within, and those who wished to follow England's example, by breaking away foot and branch from the tree of Rome. The king of this divided country, James v, having led his people to defeat, lay dying with his face to the wall, the victim in this as much of his own passionate nature as of the circumstances which had conspired against him. When James died on 14 December 1542, the most stalwart prince might have shrunk from the Herculean task of succeeding him.

The position of the Stewart monarchs in the fifteenth and sixteenth centuries was peculiarly perilous in dynastic terms, for a number of reasons. In the first place, chance had resulted in a total of seven royal minorities – there had been no adult succession since the fourteenth century – which had an inevitable effect of weakening the power of the crown and increasing that of the nobility. Secondly, the Stewarts had a special reason for needing to separate themselves from the nobility, and raise themselves above it into a cohesive royal family, by the nature of their origins. These were neither obscure nor royal. On the contrary, the Stewarts were no more than *primus inter pares* among the body of the Scottish nobles. They had formerly been stewards, as their name denotes, first of all to the ruling family of Brittany, and later, more splendidly, great stewards to the kings of Scotland. It was Walter, sixth great steward, who by marrying Marjorie Bruce, daughter of Robert I, fathered Robert II, king of Scots, and thus founded the Stewart royal line.

PREVIOUS PAGE A crayon portrait of Mary Queen of Scots in 1552 at the age of nine, probably commissioned by Catherine de Medicis.

The Scottish succession from 1371–1603, showing Mary Queen of Scots in the centre of the second branch of the tree.

James v of Scotland, father
of Mary Queen of Scots,
who died at the early age
of thirty, leaving his
daughter as queen at the
tender age of six days.
Artist unknown.

The ramifications and interconnections of the Stewart family were
henceforward focused on the throne. The many intermarriages, common to all Scottish noble families of this period, meant that by the 1540s
there were descended from younger sons or daughters of the kings a
number of rival Stewart families – the Lennox Stewarts, who later came
to use the French spelling of Stuart and thus handed it officially on to the
royal line through the marriage of Mary to Henry Stuart, Lord Darnley;
the Atholl Stewarts, the Stewarts of Traquair, the Stewarts of Blantyre,
and the Stewarts of Ochiltree. Even those dignitaries whose name was
not actually Stewart often stood in close relationship to the crown
through marriage or descent; throughout her reign Mary correctly
addressed as 'cousin' the earls of Arran, Huntly and Argyll, heads respectively of the families of Hamilton, Gordon and Campbell. Kinship
as a concept was all-important in the Scotland of the period: unfortunately kinship to the monarchy was universally held to strengthen the
position of the family concerned, rather than add to the resources of the
monarchy.

Anxious to cut his way free from this prickly dynastic hedge and to find new sources of income for the bankrupt kingdom he had inherited, James v had embarked on a prolonged search for a wealthy foreign bride. Eventually in 1538 he had married Mary of Guise, the eldest daughter of the large and flourishing family of Claude, duke of Guise and his wife Antoinette of Bourbon. Moreover, in view of the predatory attitude of his uncle, Henry VIII, towards Scotland, James had decided upon the traditional Scottish alliance with the French king, in order to bolster himself with French aid against any possible English claims of suzerainty. But this foreign policy proved in the final analysis disastrous for it alienated Scotland's powerful neighbour. By the summer of 1542 Henry was determined to bring the Scots to heel and to this end English forces were mobilized in the north.

Queen Mary, having already lost two sons in early infancy, was once again expecting a child, and, as she awaited the birth of the longed-for heir, her husband rallied his army for the final crisis of his reign.

On 24 November the Scottish forces encountered the English at Solway Moss and were driven back in a disorderly rout; 1,200 Scots were captured, among them many of the leading nobles.

The king, in a state of appalling mental anguish, retired to his palace at Falkland. Incapable of digesting his personal humiliation and the humiliations of his country, he underwent a complete nervous collapse. He lay on his bed, sometimes railing at the cruel fate which had led to his defeat, at other times silent and melancholy, meditating on the wastes of despair. Into this sad sick-room came a messenger who brought the news that the queen had been confined and had given birth to a daughter. The fact that he now had an heir did little to alleviate the king's sorrow and six days later he was dead at the age of thirty.

The daughter and only surviving (legitimate) child of James, who now succeeded to the throne of Scotland, had been born at the palace of Linlithgow, West Lothian, on the Feast of the Immaculate Conception of the Virgin Mary, 8 December. She was baptized Mary, by tradition in the Church of St Michael at the gates of the palace.

For the first ten days of her life, all the rumours spread about Mary Stuart were of an exceptionally frail baby. It certainly seems likely that she was born prematurely, the confinement of Queen Mary being brought on by anxiety over her husband: a report by English observers sent to London on 12 December stated that 'the said Queen was delivered before her time of a daughter, a very weak child, and not likely to live as it is thought'.

Perhaps with the English the wish was father to the thought, since the death of the infant queen would have increased the confusion of Scotland still further, to the point of the possible extinction of the government. The secret wishes of the Scots on the other hand are probably expressed by the rumour of the time that the child was actually a boy. The position of a country with a child heiress at its head was widely regarded as disastrous in the sixteenth century. As Knox put it, 'All men lamented that the realm was left without a male to succeed'. The reason is not difficult to seek. In 1542, the successful reign of Queen Elizabeth I lay very much in the future. The birth of an heiress generally led to the swallowing-up of the country concerned, as happened in the case of Burgundy, Spain, Bohemia and Hungary with Habsburgs, and with England in the time of Mary Tudor. To the disadvantages of Mary Stuart's situation at birth, herself frail in health, the country divided and facing the prospect of a long minority, was therefore added the disadvantage of being of the weaker and therefore of the wrong sex.

The palace of Linlithgow where Mary was born – in the room in the north-west corner, overlooking the loch – and where she was destined to spend the first seven months of her life, was a traditional lying-in place of queens. James v himself had been born there. It was he who had enriched it by many improvements and it was certainly considered to be a splendid palace by the standards of the time: Mary of Guise compared it approvingly to the castles of the Loire, and Sir David Lyndsay called it a 'palace of pleasance' worthy to be put beside those of Portugal and France. However, in December 1542, above this serene place and its youthful incumbent, hovered a series of political thunder clouds.

With an outward delicacy of feeling which probably sprang in fact from shrewd political calculation, it was now thought unseemly for the English commander to pursue an attack against the kingdom of a dead man. Lisle, the English commander, reported as much to King Henry: 'I have thought good to stay the stroke of your sword until your majesty's pleasure be farther known to me in that behalf,' and he included in his forbearance 'the young suckling', the late king's daughter. Thus, curiously enough, the premature death of King James, which had such dire results for Scotland in producing another long minority, had the short-term effect of staying the avenging hand of the English army after Solway Moss. As a result the first year of his daughter Mary's existence, instead of being threatened by English armies, was dominated by two questions of important bearing on her subsequent history – who was to govern the kingdom during her infancy, and whom she was destined to marry.

Of these two issues, it was the first which demanded immediate settlement. If Scotland was to survive as an independent nation the office of governor had to be filled at once. Despite this urgency, a fierce controversy at once arose on the subject, to add to the country's troubles. It arose out of the clash of the hereditary claim of the earl of Arran, head of the house of Hamilton, to be sole governor, with the rival claim of Cardinal Beaton, which he based on a forged will supposed to have been made by the late king. The prize was a rich one. The prestige and importance of the governor, or regent, was considered to be equivalent to that of the king himself; and the political powers were interwoven with the material rewards of office. It was tradition for the governor to take over the palaces, jewels and treasure of the late king during the minority of his successor and he was responsible for the administration of the crown revenues.

As it happened, the man with the hereditary right to this important office at this critical juncture in Scottish history, James, second earl of Arran and later first duke of Châtelherault, was singularly unfitted to hold it. Mary of Guise described him succinctly as the most inconstant man in the world: the most charitable verdict is that of a chaplain who

The palace of Linlithgow, West Lothian, now in ruins, where Mary Queen of Scots was born on 8 December 1542. It was a splendid palace by standards of the time. Mary spent the first seven months of her life here. In the foreground is the parish church of St Michael where she is said to have been baptized.

called him 'a good soft God's man', presumably referring to the fact that for the past five years Arran had been a supporter of the reformed religion. Yet this vacillating figure, by the very fact that he was the head of the house of Hamilton, was destined for the most prominent position among the Scottish nobles.

Arran's grandfather, James, first Lord Hamilton, had been married to Princess Mary Stewart, sister of James III (see table of the Scottish royal succession on p. 198–9). If the child Queen Mary died, Arran could fairly claim the Scottish throne, as the next heir by blood. It was true that there was a complication: there was some doubt whether Arran's father had ever been properly divorced from his second wife and it was therefore conceivable that Arran, as the fruit of the third marriage, was illegitimate; in which case, the Lennox Stewarts who descended perfectly correctly from Princess Mary and Lord Hamilton – but from the daughter, not a son – were the true heirs to the throne. This in turn meant that the earl of Lennox, not the earl of Arran, had the hereditary claim to be governor of Scotland, and second person in the realm. Despite this Lennox shadow across the Hamilton claim, a fact to be borne in mind when considering the perennially explosive relations between the two families during this period, the Hamiltons still managed to retain their position as heirs or next heirs to the Scottish throne for nearly a hundred years.

There was nothing indecisive about the character of David Beaton, cardinal-archbishop of St Andrews, the man who now opposed Arran's claim with the will of the late king, apparently made in his favour. The evidence that Beaton actually forged the will seems conclusive, but in view of the weakness of Scotland at the time, it may be argued that Cardinal Beaton was at least making a bid to give his country some sort of strong government to combat England's rapacity. By now a man of over fifty, he had considerable knowledge of Europe, having studied in Paris, and was a diplomatist of some experience. Certainly the cardinal's

A portrait of Henry VIII by Hans Holbein the Younger. He was anxious to marry Mary to his son, the future Edward VI, and in 1544 began the 'Rough Wooing' – a programme of devastation of Scottish territory – which was to alienate the Scots and finish all hopes of an alliance by marriage.

pro-French Catholic policy represented the only alternative to subjugation under the yoke of Henry VIII. Moreover, as a prelate without any family that he might be bound to favour, he at least showed some signs of identifying his personal policies with those of Scotland, in contrast to the rest of the venal Scottish nobility.

Despite Cardinal Beaton's strength of purpose, the deciding factor in the contest for the governorship proved to be the return of those Scottish nobles captured at Solway Moss: after a sojourn in London, they were now dispatched north again by Henry VIII, like so many Trojan horses, as emissaries of his policy. While in London, they had been induced to sign a series of articles which pledged them to help Henry bring about the marriage of Mary and Prince Edward, and generally advance the cause of England in Scotland, in return for which they were given suitable pensions of English money.

In January Arran was confirmed in his office of governor and a few days later Cardinal Beaton was arrested: it seemed certain that the rulers of Scotland during Queen Mary's minority were to be a Protestant pro-English faction. Equally, the matrimonial future of the young queen

PARVVLE PATRISSA, PATRIÆ VIRTVTIS ET HÆRES
ESTO, NIHIL MAIVS MAXIMVS ORBIS HABET.
GNATVM VIX POSSVNT COELVM ET NATVRA DEDISSE,
HVIVS QVEM PATRIS, VICTVS HONORET HONOS.
ÆQVATO TANTVM, TANTI TV FACTA PARENTIS,
VOTA HOMINVM, VIX QVO PROGREDIANTVR, HABENT
VINCITO, VICISTI, QVOT REGES PRISCVS ADORAT
ORBIS, NEC TE QVI VINCERE POSSIT, ERIT.

seemed to lie in the direction of England. Henry's son, Prince Edward, then aged five, seemed the ideal spouse to unite Scotland and England firmly forever under English suzerainty, and Henry furthermore intended to bring up the Scottish queen actually at the English court, in order to check any possible fluttering for liberty in the Scottish dovecots. This marriage, which, if Edward VI had lived, would have antedated the peaceful union of England and Scotland by half a century, would not necessarily have been such a terrible prospect for Scotland, had it not been for the savagely bullying attitude which Henry VIII persisted in adopting towards his neighbour. It must be recalled that at this date Mary's future husband, the dauphin of France, had not yet been born and his mother, Catherine de Medicis, wife of the heir to the French throne, appeared to be barren, having been married ten years without producing any children at all. Thus there was no French prince in prospect whose merits could be weighed against those of Prince Edward.

On 1 July the Treaties of Greenwich were drawn up, providing for the marriage of Edward and Mary. These treaties respected Scotland's independence as a country and provided for the return of Mary as a childless

Edward, Prince of Wales, a portrait by Hans Holbein. He was five years older than Mary, and, at first, seemed the ideal husband to unite England and Scotland under English suzerainty.

widow if Edward died; the main point on which the Scots insisted and on which Henry disagreed was that the child should not actually leave Scotland until she was ten years old. Henry remained avuncularly anxious to oversee her upbringing personally at the English court – or perhaps he did not trust the Scots to implement their promises in ten years' time. But in any case the point was never put to the test, since already by the summer of 1543 the internal situation in Scotland had changed radically. Opinion, although Henry VIII might be ignorant of the fact, was no longer predominantly favourable to the Protestant and pro-English cause. Cardinal Beaton had eluded captivity and was once more in a position to galvanize Catholic pro-French opinion. Two new arrivals on the Scottish scene – the governor's bastard half-brother, John Hamilton, abbot of Paisley, and Mathew, earl of Lennox, himself – only helped to poison Arran's mind further against the English alliance. John Hamilton pointed out that by abandoning the cause of Rome, Arran put himself in a vulnerable position in which his father's divorce might be questioned; Lennox, as head of the rival Stewarts, represented a positive alternative to Arran as governor. Under the circumstances Arran's vacillating wits were no match for the machinations of the cardinal. French subsidies began to enter Scotland, to vie with the English ones, and the very day after the Treaties of Greenwich had been signed, Sir Ralph Sadler reported to Henry that French ships had been seen lying off the coast of Scotland.

Henry reacted to this news predictably, demanding that the queen be moved away from Linlithgow, which he thought altogether too accessible to the French if they landed. In point of fact, to the Scots Linlithgow no longer seemed a suitable place in which to guard their queen, although it was fear of abduction by the English, rather than by the French, which now prompted them to move her.

Mary's new home, Stirling Castle, had, in the time of Edward I's invasion, been considered the strongest castle in Scotland. In spite of its subsequent ornamentation, the castle had remained essentially unaltered since the days of Edward I. Its attractions included the splendour of the great hall of James V, which in 1618 John Taylor compared favourably with Westminster Hall, and the palace, a jewel of the Scottish Renaissance, today still showing King James's initials in the carved panels over its windows. But in 1543 it was the fortress aspect of the castle, high over the town of Stirling, higher still over the plain, and standing at the gateway of the impenetrable territory of the Highlands, which commended it to the lords who there incarcerated their queen for safety.

Henry VIII still felt secure enough in the terms of the treaty he had just signed to imagine that he could put his envoy, Sir Ralph Sadler, in charge of the queen in her new abode. But the time when Henry would have any say in Scotland's affairs was rapidly passing. The king made a series of frantic efforts to maintain his ascendancy over Arran but his arrest of some Scottish merchant ships sailing to France, and the impounding of the merchants and their goods, aroused popular indignation. Sadler warned him that the temper of the country was turning against him. After torments of indecision, Arran finally decided to throw in his lot with Beaton and the pro-French party, his mind probably made up in the end by the promise of the little queen's hand for his own son. On 8 September, in the church of the Franciscans at Stirling, 'the unhappy man', as Knox disgustedly termed him, did penance for his apostasy and received the Catholic sacrament. The day after Arran's change of faith, on 9 September 1543, Mary Stuart was solemnly crowned in Stirling Castle chapel at the age of nine months.

Edward Seymour, Duke of Somerset, was later to become Lord Protector during Edward VI's reign.

The defection of Arran marked the first turning-point in the life of Mary Queen of Scots. It decided, among other things, that Henry would no longer woo the Scots with gifts, but attempt to constrain them by force. Arran and Cardinal Beaton took no immediate steps to break with England, but the knowledge that they had cut themselves free from close entanglement with Protestant England encouraged both the papacy and the French king to renew their support to Scotland. The appearance of a papal legate, with a papal subsidy, and of French envoys at the Scottish court, presaged the final change of policy announced by the Scottish Parliament in December 1543. By the treaty of 15 December the 'auld bands' between the Scots and the French were now once more confirmed. A secondary effect of Arran's *volte-face* was the turning-away of Lennox from the party of Scottish government. Lennox was unable to endure the fact that, despite his changes of allegiance, his rival Arran still retained his position as governor of Scotland. The classical policy of the Lennox Stewarts was to ally themselves with the enemies of the Hamiltons. Lennox now turned his eyes towards England, and offered himself as a bridegroom to Lady Margaret Douglas, daughter of Margaret Tudor by her second marriage to the earl of Angus, niece of Henry VIII, and, in time to come, the mother of Henry Stuart, Lord Darnley.

Thus by the time Mary Stuart was one year old, the pieces on the traditional chess board which lay between Scotland and England had been rearranged to form an altogether different pattern from that which was in evidence when she first succeeded to the throne. In twelve months the possibility of the peaceful annexation of Scotland by England, through the marriage of Mary and Edward, and the direction of Scottish affairs by King Henry, had receded with amazing rapidity. With the renewal of the French alliance, and the birth of a son to Catherine de Medicis and the future Henry II of France in January 1544, the prospect of a very different education and marriage unfolded before the child queen.

Four and a half years were to elapse before the young queen of Scots was finally dispatched to the safety of France. They were years in which the policy of Henry VIII towards Scotland did little to correct the impression he had already given, of a vindictive bully once his will was gainsaid. In May 1544 Henry's commander Hertford set out on a planned programme of devastation of Scottish territory, by which the king paradoxically attempted to win the loyalties of the Scots. His instructions to Hertford strike a note of ruthlessness which chills the spirit, and the English records make it clear that their armies were remarkably successful in carrying out this 'scorched earth' policy.

In this atmosphere of violence the weight of the queen dowager's counsels were felt for the first time in the shifting scales of Scottish national policy. It is safe to assume that Queen Mary's secret wishes were

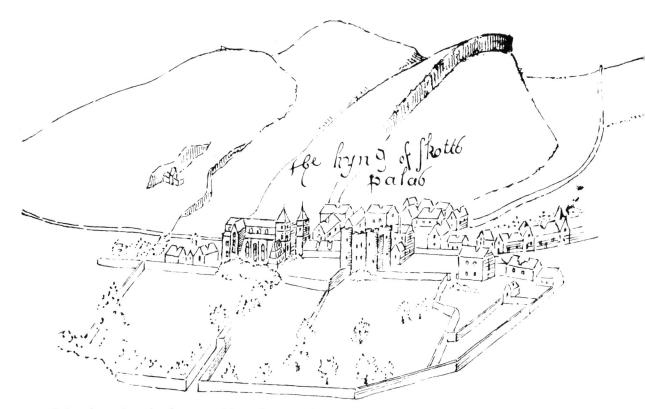

The king of Scotts palac (handwritten on image)

Edinburgh Castle, a detail from a contemporary sketch of Edinburgh seen from the north. Edinburgh Castle withstood the siege of Henry VIII's men, led by the Earl of Hertford, in 1544 when the English had already laid waste to the town.

steadily in favour of a French marriage – France was her own country, the country of her able family, and the country with enough resources to quell the English, on behalf of the Scots, if necessary. The climate of Scottish opinion was not yet ready for such a match: it needed further action on behalf of England to point the lesson that a French alliance, however confining to their independence, was at least preferable to extinction at the hands of their neighbours. Mary of Guise had also two specific hazards to overcome – Arran's desire for the marriage of her daughter and his own son, and the cardinal's steady opposition to the idea of a French marriage, as marked as had been his opposition to an English one, for the same nationalist reasons.

But Cardinal Beaton's days were numbered. Quite apart from its political confusion, Scotland's religious life was in a ferment. Not only had high office in the Church become a valuable part of royal patronage, but in a poor country such as Scotland, with a primitive economy, the Church presented a picture of disproportionate wealth. It was felt that while monks and friars idled and were supported by the community, the true objects of social pity – 'the blind, crooked, bed-ridden, widows, orphans and all other poor, so visited by the hand of God as may not work', in the words of one contemporary complaint – were being neglected. The majority of the parish churches in the country had been assigned or appropriated to bishoprics or monasteries, and other churches had no priest at all. The provincial council of 1549 enacted a significant amount of statues denouncing concubinage among the priesthood, or the promotion and endowing of illegitimate children. Repeated enactments by provincial councils urging the clergy to preach to the people showed that the problem was both pressing and that it was not being cured.

Against this background, it is easy to understand the success of any

18

anti-clerical movement: by 1543 the flames of unrest were being fed by a continuous fuel of books, pamphlets and broadsides advocating the reformed religion. Many were spiritual in content; the others were mere lampoons. The same parallel exists in those who were drawn to the new religion. Many were men of the most ascetic nature, who felt they could no longer stretch their wings under the tutelage of the corrupt Scottish Catholic Church; others were merely animated by a strong dislike of the Catholic clergy. In time past the Scottish nobles had often endowed the Church with land, in order that they might be prayed for in perpetuity: their reactions, once it was explained to them by the reformers that these prayers were not necessarily an assured passport to heaven, were predictably angry; the nobility considered that the land should be rightfully returned to them. In March 1546 George Wishart, a leading Protestant preacher of outstanding gentle character, in an age not over-endowed with the pure in heart, was burned to death in the forecourt of the castle of St Andrews. Cardinal Beaton and his bishops watched from cushioned seats on the castle walls. Three months later, a band of nobles broke into St Andrews and seized the cardinal. After holding him at sword point and asking him to repent the shedding of Wishart's blood, they did him to death.

Within a year the death of Francis I and the accession of his son Henry II to the throne of France had made the climate of opinion in France newly favourable to notions of French aid for Scotland: Henry II was anxious to conciliate his powerful Guise subjects, whose sister and niece were evidently in such a dangerous situation there. The death of Henry VIII, on the other hand, in January 1547, had no effect in reducing the savagery of the English attitude towards Scotland. In late August of that year, the former Hertford, now Protector Somerset, mounted an expedition towards Scotland which was to rival in ferocity anything the late king had commissioned.

The decisive English victory at Pinkie Cleugh on 10 September made it abundantly clear to many of the Scots that a French alliance, at the price of a French marriage for their queen, was their best hope of extricating themselves from the morass of defeat and disunity in which they now found themselves. A council was held in November 1547 at which the queen's removal to France was discussed, as well as the necessity of placing Scottish strongholds in the hands of the French. By the end of December French troops had begun to arrive in Scotland, and on 27 January a contract was signed between Arran and Henry II by which Arran bound himself to assemble the Scottish Parliament in order to give consent to the marriage of the queen with Henry's son, her deliverance to France, and the handing over of the crucial fortresses. In return Arran was to receive a French duchy.

Parliament finally gave its assent to the marriage to Mary and Francis in July 1548, and at the end of the month, after a tearful farewell to her mother, Mary set sail for France. With her went the suite which was considered suitable for her new estate in France. It included two of her royal half-brothers – Robert and John Stewart – her guardian, Lord Erskine, her governess, Lady Fleming, and a train of noblemen's sons and daughters, all about Mary's age.

2 The Most Perfect Child

'The little Queen of Scots is the most perfect child that I have ever seen'
KING HENRY II OF FRANCE

OPPOSITE Mary Queen of Scots as Dauphiness of France at the age of sixteen, a time when her charm and beauty were greatly praised by all who met her at the French court. By Jean Clouet.

BELOW Antoinette, Duchesse de Guise, Mary's Grandmother, who was delighted to receive Mary into her care upon her arrival in France. With characteristic austerity, she concerned herself principally with Mary's Moral welfare.

From the moment of her arrival in France, and indeed for the next twelve years, Mary Stuart was the focus of excited happy interest. Antoinette of Guise was in ecstasies at the appearance of her granddaughter, and wrote immediately to Mary of Guise in Scotland to express the measure of her approval. The duchess was, however, a great deal less enthusiastic over Mary's Scottish train, whom she described as thoroughly ill-looking and *farouche*. She clearly shared the general desire of the French, whether on the part of the Guises or the court, to have the complete education of this child and thoroughly expunge from her all traces of her Scottish past, which it was felt would ill equip her for her glorious future role as queen of France. The possibility that she might also one day have to act as queen regnant to her native land of Scotland was felt to be definitely subordinate. No qualms were therefore felt at the prospect of cutting the little Scottish queen off immediately from her Scottish attendants. Mary of Guise, however, with superior foresight, had sent instructions that Lady Fleming was to continue as her governess.

Mary was now propelled into the royal nursery. It is difficult to believe that any set of young princes in the history of Europe had been so fussed over, so lavished with care and attention, as the seven children of Henry II and Catherine de Medicis. The letters of their mother are replete with maternal anxieties of the sort most generally associated with mothers who have no nurses, rather than with a queen, who might be supposed to have at least the duties of the court to distract her. This devotion, this concentrated attention to the minutiae of a child's existence, was fully shared, during her childhood, by Mary, who received in addition the extra care of her Guise relations: so concerned were they over her welfare that her uncle, the cardinal of Lorraine, that great prince of the Church, appeared as worried over her toothache and her swollen face as about matters of national policy. Her grandmother, dedicated to the cause of her moral welfare, and her uncle, bestowing on her in youth the tenderness of a father, combined with the king of France himself, and the governors of his children, to make Mary Stuart's unbringing one of rigorous supervision.

The first crucial encounter for Mary at the French court was with her intended husband, the Dauphin Francis. It is to be presumed that if these two children, aged nearly six and nearly five respectively, had heartily disliked each other on sight, the Scottish–French marriage alliance would

Catherine de Medicis, who welcomed Mary into her family and treated her like one of her own children. By Jean Clouet.

still have proceeded. Nevertheless, the French courtiers hung over the meeting of the two royal children like so many sentimental cupids: whatever the contrast between the bouncing and healthy little girl and the timid, sickly boy a year her junior, whose health was already a matter of much concern, the meeting was pronounced to be a great success.

Since we are reliably informed that Mary Stuart could speak only Scots when she arrived in France, she had evidently picked up enough French in the short interval since her arrival, with the facility of childhood, to communicate with a fellow-child. Later, she was to be described as speaking French with perfect grace and elegance; although she did not lose her Scots, French became the language which Mary naturally wrote and spoke for the rest of her life. Possibly it was the hope of bringing this about which had influenced Henry in his decision to dismiss the Scottish suite. It thus happened that the most intimate female friend of Mary Stuart's childhood and adolescence was Elisabeth of France, younger by two and a quarter years. With Elisabeth, Mary had in common the elevating but separating gift of royal blood; the fact that she also shared the same nurtured golden childhood made Elisabeth the female human being of whom Mary felt herself afterwards to be most fond, and of whom she retained the most nostalgic memories in later life.

As yet, Mary had not encountered the father of the young family into which she had been adopted. This meeting finally took place in November. Henry, now a man of thirty, swarthy and melancholy of visage, seldom smiling, obsessed either with the troubles of his government or with the physical exercise for which he had a mania, took a genuine tender delight in children. Of Mary, he wrote quite simply that she was the most perfect child he had ever seen.

It is often said that a secure childhood makes the best foundation for a happy life. In marked contrast to her cousin Elizabeth Tudor, Mary Stuart enjoyed an exceptionally cosseted youth. It is left to the judgement of history to decide whether it did, in fact, adequately prepare her for the extreme stresses with which the course of her later life confronted her. What is certain is that the next six years of her life have a dream-like quality, in which she appears to have been cut off from the rough events of politics by a cocoon of servants and other satellites, whose only duty was to nurture the royal nurslings in as great a state of luxury as possible. Her life divided into two parts – at court with the princes and princesses, and with her Guise relations. The ambitious Guises were, however, fully aware of the value of maintaining their little half-royal cuckoo well and truly in the royal nest, and made no difficulties at the prospect of having her brought up, for the time being, so much at court.

At this time the establishment of the royal children was by no means a fixed entity: it was essential that a household of such dimensions should be moved every few months in order that the castle which it had inhabited might be literally spring-cleaned. Mary's life consisted largely of a series of glamorous journeyings from one sumptuous royal palace to another. With the royal children went the enormous quantities of servants thought necessary to maintain their estate and a mountain of luggage, in part accounted for by the extensive royal wardrobes.

It was thought right that Mary should be more richly attired than the princesses, to mark her future position as their brother's bride. Her accounts reveal both the abundance and the formality of a royal child's wardrobe: yards of shot red and yellow taffeta for dresses, dresses of gold damask, dresses of black edged with silver, canvas and buckram to stiffen the dresses, white Florentine serge stockings, a *vasquine* or type of farthingale to hold out the dresses, shot taffeta petticoats and orange taffeta petticoats lined with red serge. Her accessories were equally elaborate: there is mention of bonnets of silver thread and black silk, orange wool to be dyed scarlet for stockings, furs to trim her clothes. Shoes are plentiful – ten pairs of ordinary shoes in the accounts of 1551, three white, three purple, two black and two red, and also white, yellow, red and black velvet shoes. There are bills for exquisite embroideries on the clothes – rose leaves of gold thread for caps, and a bill for the embroidery of a device on a favour of white taffeta which Mary gave to the dauphin. There are bills for leather gloves of dogskin and deerskin. Three brass chests were needed to hold her jewels, which included a chain of pearls and green enamel, a gold ring with a ruby in it, and jewelled buttons of many different colours and shapes.

In the midst of this concern for her material well-being, the need for more spiritual attainments was not neglected. Education was taken seriously at this Renaissance court although Mary Stuart as a child neither had, nor was trained to have, a brain of the calibre of, for example, an Elizabeth Tudor. She was, however, by nature bright, quick, and eager to learn. In true Renaissance fashion, she was given an all-round education: she learnt not only Latin, but Italian, Spanish and some Greek; she learnt to draw; she learnt to dance, an art at which she was universally agreed to excel both in childhood and in later life; she learnt to sing and to play the lute. Graceful, athletic, she was above all anxious to please those around her.

Mary Stuart's letters to Mary of Guise bear witness to the enormous interest which the mother took in the smallest details of her daughter's upbringing, despite the distance which separated them. The sphere in which she appears to have exerted the strongest influence of all is that of her daughter's religious education: Mary of Guise laid down that her daughter was to hear daily Mass and she was given a French chaplain of her own, as well as retaining her Scottish one.

Happily, Duchess Antoinette was able to report to Mary of Guise that her daughter was extremely devout. When the duchess and the cardinal felt that it was time for the child to make her first Holy Communion, Mary wrote to her mother eagerly of her desire to do so. She requested the necessary permission, not only because her grandmother and her uncle thought it right, but also because she herself fervently desired to 'receive God'. Mary signed herself: 'Your very humble and obedient daughter, Marie.'

In 1550 Mary of Guise herself came to France to judge the progress of her very humble and obedient daughter. The visit represented the central point of Mary's childhood; overjoyed at the prospect, she wrote ecstatically to her grandmother:

Madame, I have been very glad to be able to send these present lines for the purpose of telling you the joyful news I have received from the Queen my

Mother, who has promised me by her letter dated April 23rd that she will be here very soon to see you and me, which is to me the greatest happiness which I could wish for in this world, and indeed I am so overjoyed about it, that all I am thinking about now is to do my whole duty in all things and to study to be very good, in order to satisfy her desire to see in me all that you and she hope for . . .

Evidently Mary had conceived a sort of hero-worship for her mother, a superior being, an image of strength, reliability and comfort, whom she wished to do her best to impress.

Mary of Guise arrived in September and nothing seems to have marred the love which existed between mother and daughter by the time the former sailed back to Scotland a year later; having had what turned out to be the last sight of her daughter in her lifetime, she left behind such strongly growing roots of love in her daughter's heart that the young Mary had a virtual nervous breakdown with grief at the news of her death in 1560, even though she had not actually seen her for nine years.

The atmosphere of the visit was marred however by the flagrant love affair which sprang up at this point between Henry II and Mary's governess, Lady Fleming. The liaison resulted in Lady Fleming giving birth to a son, Henry, later known as the Bastard of Angoulême, whose famous agility in later life at Scottish dances at the French court bore permanent witness to his hybrid heredity. Lady Fleming was punished for her indiscretion by being sent home to Scotland, and Mary was given a new governess in the shape of Mme de Parois.

The substitution of Mme de Parois for the errant Lady Fleming marked a further step in the obliteration of Mary's Scottish personality. Mary still loved to dress herself up in Scottish national costume, but for all her enthusiasm for her native country or its customs, Scottish clothes were by now for her definitely a form of fancy dress. Patriotism, wilfulness or the desire to please might lead her to don them: nothing could alter the fact that with the passing of every year, the progress of Mary towards becoming a Frenchwoman – a child of the smooth land of France rather than of the rugged land of Scotland – became still more marked.

By the end of 1553, when she entered her twelfth year, Mary Stuart's charmed childhood was drawing to a close in favour of a more troubled adolescence. The time had now come for her to have her own household. On 1 January 1554 Mary entered into her new estate, and to celebrate the occasion she invited her uncle, the cardinal of Lorraine, to supper that evening.

The choice was significant. Previously the Guises had been content to let their nursling spend much of her time in the royal household. But from now onwards it was important that her character should be formed in accordance with their wishes, and that she should receive her early lessons in statecraft from the people who stood to gain so much from her future high position in France – the Guises.

Every letter to her mother at this time bears some sort of witness to the detailed supervision which the cardinal was now giving to her upbringing. Under his careful tutelage, Mary's views on statecraft were carefully nurtured and she was encouraged to take an interest in Scottish affairs. In her letters to her mother on the subject, she shows aptitude and

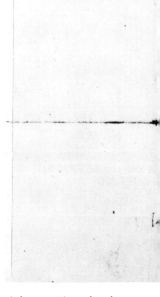

A letter written by the eleven-year-old Mary to her mother in Scotland, in which she describes her desire to take her first Communion the following Easter, as suggested by her grandmother and her uncle Cardinal Charles.

...noien de vous pouuoir escrire de
...stre si long temps sans en
...qui le Gouuerneur sest mis
...uins les places principales du
...tous les iours vostre...
... meurs sont retournes...
...me ma grand mere pour...
...oncle monsieur le cardinal
...e supplie tres humblement
...Ie ne vueil oblier vous dire
...seruice au Roy.
...me tres humbles...
...reuleur vous donner en long...

...le estre obeisante fille

application, rather than any marked independence of judgement, and at every juncture quotes or refers back to the opinions of her uncle. Scottish affairs were also the more vivid to Mary now that her mother had succeeded the ineffective Arran as regent.

After a robust childhood, Mary Stuart's general health began to show cause for concern in adolescence. When she was thirteen, her uncle thought it necessary to write angrily to her mother in order to contradict reports that Mary was generally ailing. He stated that the verdict of the doctors was that she would outlive all her relations, although she sometimes got a certain heartburn, or plain indigestion, due to a hearty appetite, which would certainly lead to her over-eating if the cardinal did not watch her carefully. The truth was that all her life Mary Stuart was to suffer from gastric troubles of which these were only the first ominous symptoms. In the summer and autumn of 1556 she fell ill with a series of fevers, possibly the precursor of the tertian fevers which haunted her the rest of her life, and for all his angry denials to outsiders, the cardinal's letters to Mary of Guise in Scotland show that he felt extreme concern at the time.

The history of Europe in the early part of the 1550s was dominated by the rivalry between the Habsburg Empire and France. In 1556 peace was temporarily established by the Truce of Vaucelles. The cardinal was away in Rome at the time and Henry II was swayed in his absence by the advice of the great rival of the Guises, the Constable Anne de Montmorency. On his return the cardinal determined to undo the peace, since he had at last persuaded the pope to enter into an alliance with France against the imperialists. War was resumed once more. The importunity of Philip of Spain to his wife, Mary Tudor, queen of England, eventually succeeded in bringing England into the war on the side of Spain. In 1557 Philip defeated the constable's army and captured Saint-Quentin; he seemed set to march on Paris. Having already earned himself a brilliant reputation on the battlefield, it was Duke Francis of Guise, the cardinal's brother, who now came to the rescue of the French people. By turning the tables of the war and recapturing Calais after its 220 years in English hands, Francis of Guise not only confounded the anti-Guise faction but also elevated the prestige of his family to new heights.

The victory of Francis of Guise at Calais and the rise of the bright star of the Guises had an important effect on the fortunes of his niece Mary. She was now, in the spring of 1558, over fifteen, and the dauphin was just fourteen. By the standards of the age, Mary was marriageable; Francis only marginally so. But Henry II now had two strong motives, both political, to persuade him towards the finalization of this marriage which had been arranged in theory nearly ten years previously. The words of the Venetian ambassador Giacomo Sorenzo, writing on 9 November 1557, sum up the situation:

The causes for hastening this marriage are apparently two; the first to enable them more surely to avail themselves of the forces of Scotland against the kingdom of England for next year, and the next for the gratification of the Duke and Cardinal of Guise, the said Queen's uncles, who by the hastening of this marriage, choose to secure themselves against any other matrimonial alliance which might be proposed to his most Christian Majesty in some negotiation for peace, the entire establishment of their greatness having to depend on this; for which reason the Constable by all means in his power continually sought to prevent it.

Henry sent to Scotland, to remind the Scottish Parliament that the time had come to implement their promises. Commissioners were duly appointed in Scotland to come to France, in order to carry out the marriage negotiations.

As a result, the betrothal of the young pair took place on 19 August 1558, in the great hall of the new Louvre, with the cardinal of Lorraine joining their hands together. A magnificent ball followed, at which Henry II danced with the bride-elect, Antoine of Navarre with Catherine of Medicis, the dauphin with his aunt, Madame Marguerite, and the duke of Lorraine with Princess Claude, whom he later married. By the terms of the betrothal contract, the dauphin declared that of 'his own free will and with the fullest consent of the King and Queen his father and mother, and being duly authorized by them to take the Queen of Scotland for his wife and consort, he promised to espouse her on the following Sunday April 24th'.

Despite the formality of the language, and the political considerations which had prompted his elders to hurry towards the match, the young groom does seem to have felt genuine affection for his bride. His mother, Catherine de Medicis, and Mary Stuart seem indeed to have been the only two human beings for whom this pathetic, wizened creature felt true emotion. Sickly in childhood, he had become difficult and sullen in adolescence; his physique was scarcely developed and his height was stunted; furthermore, there is considerable doubt whether he ever actually reached puberty before his untimely death, when he was not quite seventeen. The dauphin showed little enthusiasm or aptitude for learning, although his enthusiasm for the chase astonished the courtiers, considering his frail physique. Obviously, for better or for worse, he soon became conscious of his high position: in 1552 he was described as having a considerable sense of his own importance. A taciturn and stubborn character, he suffered from a chronic respiratory infection resulting from his difficult birth, which cannot have added to his appeal, since it prompted his mother at one point to write to his governor and urge that the dauphin should blow his nose more, for the good of his health.

However, this rather unattractive and self-important invalid evidently exhibited real signs of love towards his future bride. Capello, another Venetian ambassador, wrote that he adored 'la Reginata de Scozia' who was destined to be his wife, and whom Capello called an exceptionally pretty child. He paints a touching picture of the pair of them drawing apart into a corner of the court, in order to exchange kisses and secrets. They played childish games of chance together: on one occasion Mary won seventy-four sols, and on another lost forty-five. In short, she was the companion to whom he was accustomed, and she was in addition, young, romantic and beautiful – increasingly so, in the eyes of the courtiers. It would have been odd indeed if the dauphin had not loved and admired this exquisite and radiant bride being presented to him who was in addition a comforting friend from his childhood.

What were Mary's own feelings for her bridegroom? First of all it must be said that it is not difficult for the young to be fond of those who are fond of them, and openly display fondness. Furthermore, as a character Mary responded exceptionally easily to love all her life. She was used to being loved in the widest sense since her childhood; she desired to continue being loved, since it was a state she enjoyed; where she saw love, or thought she saw it, she found it easy to bestow her own generous affections in return. To those who have never known the transports of romantic love, companionship and the feeling of general approval are agreeable substitutes: Mary felt that she loved her bridegroom in the most worthy manner, although his infantile physique and immaturity make it unlikely that he actually aroused in her any of the feelings with which most adults endow the word.

While the two protagonists of the match were thus perfectly content to be united, there were certain political arrangements to be made. The marriage treaty provided terms with which the Scottish delegates were adequately satisfied: the young queen bound herself to preserve the ancient freedoms, liberties and privileges of Scotland; so long as she was out of the country, it was to be governed by the regency of the queen mother, and the French king and the dauphin both bound themselves and their successors, in case of Mary's death without children, to support the succession to the Scottish throne of the nearest heir by blood – still the head of the house of Hamilton, the duke of Châtelherault. Mary was given a satisfactory jointure. It was further agreed that the dauphin should bear the title of king of Scotland and that, on his accession to the French throne, the two kingdoms should be united under one crown. Up till the death of Henry, Francis and Mary were to be known as the king-dauphin and the queen-dauphiness. In the case of the death of her husband, Mary was to be allowed to choose whether she remained in France or returned to her kingdom: as a widowed queen, Mary was to receive a fortune of 600,000 *livres*; should there be male issue, the eldest surviving child should inherit both crowns, whereas if the couple bore only daughters, the eldest daughter would inherit the Scottish crown alone, owing to the workings of the Salic Law in France. The Scottish Estates agreed that the dauphin should be granted the crown matri-monial, and the state documents of Scotland were henceforth to be signed by both Francis and Mary jointly: Francis's signature, however, always appeared on the left hand and Mary's on the right – the left hand in this case, as dexter in heraldry, being the more important position because it was read first.

All these terms were nothing more than those the standards of the time dictated, when a female heiress married the representative of a more powerful kingdom. But in April 1558 Mary Stuart could scarcely have been blamed for thinking more of the gorgeous pageantry of her forthcoming wedding celebrations than of these political arrangements.

The French court, in true Renaissance fashion, desired its principals to shine out luminously against a background of endless pageantry; never were its wishes more splendidly gratified than in the marriage cere-monies of Francis, dauphin of France, and Mary Queen of Scots. The wedding itself took place on Sunday, 24 April at the cathedral of Notre Dame. The contemporary *Discours du Grand et Magnifique Triomphe faict du Mariage* gives a full description of the festivities, in which the writer himself seems to be frequently awed by the magnificence of what he is recounting. Notre Dame was embellished with a special structure outside in the antique manner, to make a kind of open-air theatre, and an arch twelve feet high inside. The royal *fleur-de-lys* was embroidered everywhere, and positively studded the canopy in front of the church.

The first sight to meet the eyes of the eagerly waiting crowds were the Swiss guards, resplendent in their liveries, who entered the theatre to the sound of tambourins and fifes. Then came Francis, duke of Guise, hero of France, uncle of the bride, and in the absence of the Constable de Montmorency, in captivity in Brussels since the defeat of Saint-Quentin, actually in charge of the proceedings. Then came a procession, headed by a series of musicians all dressed in yellow and red, with trumpets, sackbuts, flageolets, violins and other musical instruments. Then followed a hundred gentlemen-in-waiting of the king. Then came the princes of the blood, gorgeously apparelled, to the wonder, and presumably satisfaction, of the onlookers. Then came *abbés* and bishops bearing rich crosses and wearing jewelled mitres, and after them the princes of the Church, even more magnificently dressed, including the cardinals of Bourbon, Lorraine and Guise, and the cardinal legate of France.

Now entered the King-Dauphin Francis, led by the King Antoine of Navarre and his two younger brothers: Charles, duke of Orleans, and Henry, duke of Angoulême. Finally entered the centrepiece of the occasion, Mary, queen-dauphiness, led by Henry II and her cousin, the duke of Lorraine. Mary Stuart, on this the first of her three wedding-days, was dressed in a robe as white as lilies, so sumptuous and rich that the pen of the contemporary observer fell from his hand at the thought of describing it. Since white was traditionally the mourning colour of the queens of France, Mary had defied tradition to wear it on her wedding-day; it certainly remained a favourite shade with her throughout her youth, and even in later years she loved to have something white about her face and neck. On this occasion, her immensely long train was borne by two young girls; tall and elegant, she herself must have glittered like the goddess of a pageant, with diamonds round her neck, and on her head a golden crown garnished with pearls, rubies, sapphires and other precious stones, as well as one huge carbuncle worth over 500,000 crowns.

The young queen was followed by Catherine de Medicis, led by the prince of Condé, Mme Marguerite, the king's sister, the duchess of Berry and other princesses and ladies dressed with such grandeur that once again their robes could hardly be described for fear of repetition. At a given moment, the king drew a ring off his finger and gave it to the cardinal of Bourbon, who thus espoused the pair.

All the while, with typical concern for the reactions of the populace, the duke of Guise was touring the whole theatre with two heralds, making sure that the nobles were not blocking the view of the people in the streets or at the windows. When he was satisfied, the heralds cried out loudly: '*Largesse! Largesse!*' and threw a mass of gold and silver pieces to

the crowd, at which there was an immediate tumult and clamour as the
people scrambled over each other to help themselves – so much so that
some fainted and others lost their cloaks in their greed. Meanwhile all the
nobility entered the church itself in the same order as before, to find
another resplendent royal canopy, as well as gold carpets, within. The
bishop of Paris then said Mass with King Henry and Queen Catherine on
one side of the altar, the King-Dauphin Francis and Queen-Dauphiness
Mary on the other; during the offertory, further sums of gold and silver
were distributed outside. When Mass was over, the fine display of
nobility paraded all over again, with Henry taking the greatest care to
show himself to his people.

A long Lucullan banquet followed and then a ball. At the ball Henry
danced with Mary, Francis with his mother, the king of Navarre with the
Princess Elisabeth, the duke of Lorraine with the Princess Claude, and so
on down the royal scale. This was only the beginning: when the ball was
over at four or five in the afternoon, the entire court then processed to the
palace of the Parliament, the gentlemen on horseback and the ladies in
litters. In order to give the maximum pleasure to the people, they
travelled by a different route, and the crowds who rushed in vast numbers to watch them pass, almost blocking their progress by their density,

were rewarded by a sight of the new queen-dauphiness in a golden litter with her mother-in-law Catherine, and the new king-dauphin following on horseback with his gentlemen, their horses adorned with crimson velvet trappings.

A new order of entertainment now followed, organized by the duke of Guise as grand master of the ceremonies: indeed, the marriage celebrations thus entrusted to him gave Duke Francis a renewed opportunity to shine in the popular eye. The president, counsellors and officers of the Parliament were all present at the supper which now ensued, their scarlet robes mingling with glittering robes of the court. After supper, a second celebratory ball was held, even more splendid than the first, and punctuated by an endless series of masks and mummeries, in which the royal family themselves took part. Twelve artificial horses made of gold and silver cloth were brought into the ball-room: the dauphin's brother, Charles and Henry, the Guise children and other princelings then mounted the horses, and proceeded to draw along a series of coaches with them which contained a number of bejewelled occupants singing melodiously. After this spectacle, in which the fact that the gem-studded passengers were intended to be pilgrims struck the only conceivable note of austerity, six ships were drawn into the ball-room; their silver sails were so ingeniously made that they seemed to be billowing in an imaginary wind, and the ships themselves gave the impression of truly floating on the ball-room floor. Each of these magic barques had room for two voyagers, and after touring the ball-room, the noble gentlemen at the helm selected the ladies of their choice, and helped them into their boats. Once again, however, in spite of the delicate fantasy of the scene, choice was dictated more by court ceremony than by the promptings of romance. The duke of Lorraine chose Mme Claude, the king of Navarre chose his wife, the duke of Nemours chose Mme Marguerite, King Henry chose his daughter-in-law, and Francis chose his mother. The further magnificence of the occasion proved once again to beggar description – for, as the author of the *Discours* observed, no one could really decide which was lighting up the ball-room more brightly, the *flambeaux* or the flash of the royal jewels.

Throughout the wedding ceremonies, Mary had fulfilled to perfection the role for which she had been trained since childhood. Her new husband loved her and he was the dauphin of France. Mary thoroughly enjoyed her elevated rank as queen-dauphiness, for which she felt herself to be eminently fitted, being unable to remember a time when she was not treated with deference as a queen in her own right. When she needed advice, her uncles were to hand, anxious to supply it. She enjoyed the feminine friendship of her sister-in-law Elisabeth. She was young. She was beautiful. She was admired. An ecstatic letter to her mother in Scotland, written on her actual wedding-day, is almost incoherent with happiness at her new state and mentions how much honour not only Francis but her new father-in-law and mother-in-law continually show her.

Scotland itself seemed far away. Although on her wedding-day the great cannon of Edinburgh Castle was fired, not many reverberations of either this or any other Scottish explosion were liable to be heard at the

French court, of which Mary was the most lucent ornament. The first few months of her new existence as queen-dauphiness were among the happiest and most carefree in a lifespan which did not turn out to include many such oases: this was indeed the time when Mary, like Faust, might have addressed the passing moment: 'Linger awhile, you are so fair.'

The legendary beauty of Mary Stuart has been much vaunted. Whether she was a beauty by our standards or not, Mary Stuart was certainly rated a beauty by the standards of her own time: even the venomous Knox, never inclined to pass compliments to those with whose convictions he disagreed, described her as 'pleasing', and recorded that the people of Edinburgh called out 'Heaven bless that sweet face' as she passed on her way. Her effect on the men around her was certainly that of a beautiful woman. Mary's little brother-in-law Charles was so much in love with her that he used to gaze at her portrait with longing and desired to marry her himself after the untimely death of Francis. In Scotland Mary's beauty as well as her position is said to have captured the hearts of the dashing Sir John Gordon and the youthful, handsome George Douglas. Her first English jailer, Sir Francis Knollys, although unpromising material for female wiles, was considerably seduced by the charming personality of his captive. When she was twenty-three, the Venetian ambassador wrote of her being a princess who was 'personally the most beautiful in Europe'. There seems no reason to doubt that this was the general verdict of Europe during her lifetime, and that Mary Queen of Scots was a romantic figure to her own age, no less than to subsequent generations.

Her most marked physical characteristic must have been her height. In an age when the average height of the men was considerably less than it is today, Mary Stuart was probably about five feet eleven inches tall, that is to say taller than all but the tallest women today. At her French wedding she is said to have stood shoulder to shoulder with her Guise uncles: obviously she inherited this height from her mother, Mary of Guise, who in her day was celebrated for her upstanding stature. Even at the date of her execution, when Mary was humped by age and rheumatics, an English eye-witness still noted that she was 'of stature tall', and the figure on her tomb in Westminster Abbey, modelled from details taken immediately after her death, is five feet eleven inches long. Mary's height and the slenderness of her youth combined to give an appearance of graceful elongation: it also made her an excellent dancer and a good athlete, who could hunt, hawk and even ride at the head of an army in a manner calculated to dazzle the public eye at a time when the personal image of a sovereign was of marked consequence.

The portraits of Mary Stuart show that she had a small well-turned head, beautiful long hands, bright golden-red hair, amber-coloured eyes and an incomparable complexion. Nor must it be forgotten that to these physical attributes she added the essential human ingredient of charm, a charm so powerful that even Knox was openly afraid of its effects on her Scottish subjects – and perhaps, in his heart of hearts, also upon himself. It was the charm of Mary Stuart, that charm which is at once the most dangerous and the most desirable of all human qualities, which put the finishing touches to her beauty in the eyes of her beholders.

Towards the end of 1558 an event occurred of profound importance in
the history of Mary Stuart. On 17 November Mary Tudor, queen of
England, died leaving no children. Her throne was inherited by her
half-sister Elizabeth, an unmarried woman of twenty-five. Until such
time as Elizabeth herself should marry and beget heirs, Mary was thus
the next heiress to the English throne, by virtue of her descent from her
great-grandfather Henry VII of England (see table of English succession).
But the actual situation was more complicated than this simple statement
reveals. Elizabeth was the daughter of Henry VIII and his second wife
Anne Boleyn; as Henry's divorce from his first wife Catharine of Aragon
had never been recognized by the Catholic Church, so Henry's marriage
to Anne was considered void by Catholic standards, and so Elizabeth
herself was held by strict Catholic standards to be illegitimate and thus
incapable of inheriting the English throne. By this process of reasoning,
Mary Stuart should rightly have inherited the throne of Mary Tudor.
The actions of Henry VIII himself did not help to clear up the confusion:

in 1536 the English Parliament itself had debarred Elizabeth from the succession as illegitimate, and the act which restored her to the succession in 1544 did not remove the stain of bastardy. Yet by the will of Henry VIII the throne was also debarred from going to a foreigner – which by English standards also ousted Mary herself from the succession. The troubles over this will and Mary's claim to have her place in the English succession after Elizabeth lay in the future. At the moment of Mary Tudor's death, the troubles were all the other way about, and involved Elizabeth's right to be queen in the first place.

Immediately on the death of Mary Tudor, Henry II of France formally caused his daughter-in-law to be proclaimed queen of England, Ireland and Scotland, and caused the king-dauphin and queen-dauphiness to assume the royal arms of England, in addition to those of France and Scotland. Up till the death of Queen Mary Tudor, England had been firmly allied to Spain through Mary's marriage to the Spanish king; Henry now hoped to redress the balance by making a French claim to English dominion. This eminently political action on the part of the French king was to be flung in Mary's face for the rest of her life. Yet it seems certain that Mary, trained in obedience since childhood, had little say in the matter and even less opportunity for judging the wisdom of her father-in-law's decisions. 'They have made the Queen-Dauphiness go into mourning for the late Queen of England,' commented the Venetian ambassador, who was in no doubt as to where the initiative for these moves came from.

The year 1559, which became one of death at the French court, seemed destined at its outset to be a year of weddings. The Peace of Cateau-Cambrésis, signed in April between England and France on one side and France and Spain on the other, provided that all the French conquests in Italy made during the last eighty years should be surrendered, and made arrangements for two royal weddings. Mme Marguerite, the long unmarried sister of Henry II, was to wed the duke of Savoy; Princess Elisabeth, at the age of fourteen, faced the prospect of marriage to Philip of Spain, freed for matrimony once more by the death of Mary Tudor. Mary Stuart's last summer as dauphiness was spent in planning for the wedding of the beloved companion of her childhood, to be celebrated with the full regal panoply to which the French court was so well suited.

In June the two weddings were celebrated with endless tournaments and festivities. But the celebrations were overshadowed suddenly when the king was mortally wounded in a joust. Splinters from his opponent's lance pierced Henry's right eye and throat and he lay for nine days in a state of virtual unconsciousness. At 1 am on 10 July he died with grossly swollen hands and feet, all showing signs of a virulent infection.

Francis II was now king of France at the age of fifteen and a half, and Mary Stuart queen at the age of sixteen. In one blow of a lance, the fortunes of the Guises had changed. Their niece was now in the very seat of power. The stage was now set for their triumph, however short-lived. By making the young king, as one historian of the Guise family has put it, 'their nephew by alliance, their pupil by necessity', Mary Stuart had fulfilled the ultimate expectations of her family.

A contemporary depiction of the tournament at which Henry II of France was pierced in the eye by a splinter from a lance, another splinter entering his throat. He died nine days later of a virulent infection.

3 The White Lily of France

'Alba rosis albis nunc insere lilia ...'

Nuptial song on the marriage of Francis and Mary, referring to the union of the white lilies of France and the white roses of the Yorkists

On 18 September 1559, the young Francis was solemnly crowned king of France at Rheims: his consort Mary had already been crowned queen of Scotland in babyhood and, unlike previous queens of France, had thus no need of further coronation to confirm her royal state. The weather was wet and windy, and there was no great display of pageantry on this occasion, owing to the recent and shocking death of Henry II. The day after the ceremony, court mourning was resumed for a year to mark the late king's death. Although the ancient crown of St Denis had been placed on his head, the real power of France was very far from lying within the puny grasp of Francis II. The English ambassador Throckmorton analysed the situation as follows – the old French queen, Catherine, had the authority of regent, although she was not in fact regent in name; in the meantime the state was governed by the cardinal of Lorraine and the duke of Guise jointly, the duke having charge of the war, and the cardinal the ordering of all other affairs.

The Peace of Cateau-Cambrésis had not come in time to save France from cruel inflation, induced by the economic demands of war. At the same time the kingdom was being rapidly dissected by the presence of two religions, as French Calvinism became the natural target for discontent with the central authority. Even if the country had not had such grave economic problems, some sort of regency, *de facto* if not *de jure*, would have been necessary for the young Francis. His intelligence was scarcely more developed than his physique. In youth he had loved to hunt more than he had loved to learn, and later not enough pressure had been exerted to redress the balance. The result was that his mind, without being actually feeble, as his body was, had never really developed to the point when the possibilities of power and government excited him. As a king he lacked the necessary self-restraint to attend to the business of government when pleasure offered, his tutors having concentrated more on the importance of the actual role he would play, than the importance of the duties which were attached to it. The enemies of the Guises accused them of encouraging their nephew in his pursuit of pleasure in order to have the government of the realm to themselves. But there was no need to carry out such a policy of corruption: their work had already been done for them by the over-protective upbringing of Catherine de Medicis, who had, with all her loving, maternal care, developed only self-importance, not self-discipline, in her son.

OPPOSITE Mary and Francis, enlarged from a miniature in the Book of Hours belonging to Catherine de Medicis.

On 18 September 1559 Francis was crowned king of France in Rheims Cathedral. Mary was already Queen of Scots, so there was no need of further coronation to confirm her royal state.

The Guises were also accused of wishing to establish a Guise dynasty on the throne of France, but they had an infinitely more practical plan to uphold the existing semi-Guise dynasty, in the persons of Francis and Mary, who were dominated by Guise influence and whose children with their share of Guise blood would one day rule after them. The only flaw in this plan was that there was as yet no dynasty, no clutch of Valois-Guise children to lay up security for the future – only an adolescent boy and girl, both of them cursed with precarious health.

The question of the consummation of the marriage of Francis and Mary, owing to the delicate nature of the subject, rests in the sphere of probabilities rather than that of certainties. Yet it is of obvious importance in tracing the development of Mary's character not only in France, but later in Scotland in the course of her confrontation with Darnley. The true facts of the situation are somewhat obscured because contemporary commentators understandably concentrated their observations on the simple issue of whether Mary was likely to conceive a child by Francis or not; whereas in the history of Mary, it is of equal interest to consider whether she had any sort of physical relationship with her first husband, or whether at the time of her return to Scotland she was still in fact a virgin. There was never apparently any doubt in the minds of those observers at the French court who had watched the young king grow up that the queen of France would not produce a child, but if she did, as the Spanish ambassador crudely put it, it would 'certainly not be the King's'. From contemporary evidence it seems quite probable that Francis suffered from the condition known medically as undescended testicles and although, to the joy of the Guises, he started to grow up somewhat once he became king, the description of his physical deformity suggests that there was no real hope of conception.

This does not altogether rule out the possibility that the marriage was in some fashion consummated. There is evidence to the effect that, despite the cynicism of the court, Mary herself believed that her marriage was a complete one. A month after the death of Henry II, when the Spanish ambassadors came to bid her adieu, they found her extremely pale; she almost swooned and had to be supported by the cardinal. The general rumour was that the queen was pregnant. Mary herself assumed the floating tunic, the conventional garb at the time for pregnant women, and the court went to Saint-Germain for the sake of better air for her health. However, by the end of September, these interesting rumours perished for lack of further support. Mary abandoned her floating tunics and there was no further mention of a royal pregnancy.

To what then do we attribute these summer vapours of the young queen? The general hope of the court, and the passionate desire of the Guises, was that Mary should conceive a child. This desire, which she herself heartily shared, must have been communicated to her most strongly. In this case, it seems likely that Mary transformed in her mind the feeble passion of the king into a true consummation of her marriage – indeed at the age of sixteen, the natural ignorance of youth must have made it all the easier for her to do so. In the same way she transformed in her mind the symptoms of ill-health into the symptoms of pregnancy. Whether or not Mary was technically a virgin when she arrived in Scotland, she was certainly mentally one, in that her physical relations with Francis can hardly have given her any real idea of the meaning of physical love.

Troublesome as was the internal situation in France, the situation in Scotland was not much better – and here again religious differences mingled with those of civil policy. French troops had been sent in increasing numbers to the assistance of the queen regent. In their turn the Scottish insurgents, being Protestant lords of the congregation, had received aid from Protestant England. When in October 1559, the duke of Châtelherault joined the party of congregation, he presented them with a titular leader who had a claim to the Scottish throne. With his own problems of civil unrest, Francis was unable to provide further military help, and the more sensible course of negotiation was therefore decided upon. By the Treaty of Edinburgh, which was concluded on 6 July 1560, it was agreed that both English and French troops would withdraw from Scotland, and that Francis and Mary, by giving up the use of the English arms, should thus recognize Elizabeth's title. Lord St John was sent as an emissary by England to ask Francis and Mary to ratify the treaty.

This ratification, however, was destined never to take place. On 11 August the Scottish Parliament promulgated a Protestant confession of faith, and five days later abolished the pope's jurisdiction, and prohibited the celebration of Mass under the pain of death for the third offence. The Scottish Reformation was a strictly parliamentary affair; although constitutionally speaking, the enactment which produced the Reformation needed the queen's assent, in fact it never received it. Yet at one manifestation of the parliamentary will, the whole image of the Scottish monarchy had been altered in the minds of the Scottish people.

This long-term effect, however, was certainly not visible to Mary at the time. From the distance of the French court, it was difficult to realize that Queen Elizabeth had been constituted the protector of Protestantism

Mary of Guise's death in 1560 came as a hard blow to her daughter, who suffered one of the physical collapses which were the effect great sorrow had on her. This late portrait is attributed to Corneille de Lyon.

Catherine de Medicis taught Mary much of the art of politics, and together with her and Francis formed a royal triumvirate at the top of the pyramid of the court during the brief reign of Francis.

in Scotland, whether she liked it or not, and that logically the Protestant Scots would turn to England rather than France for help in the future. Still more difficult was it to envisage that if Mary ever returned to her native country, her French Catholic connections would inevitably go against her, that a country which had newly reformed its own religion by act of Parliament without the assent of the sovereign would regard the combination of her monarchical power, French upbringing and religious convictions as threatening to its *status quo*.

In the spring of 1560, however, the Scottish insurgency made its chief impression on Mary as a series of appalling troubles which faced her mother, who was by now seriously ill. This gallant woman who faced an alien people, and attempted to do at least the best she could in the cause of peaceful administration, was severely stricken with dropsy. Only a few weeks before the final settlement of the Treaty of Edinburgh she died, horribly swollen and in great pain.

The news of the death of Mary of Guise was known in France on 18 June, but was kept from her daughter until 28 June: with good reason, as it turned out, for Mary Stuart's grief when she finally did receive the news was heart-rending and she underwent one of the physical collapses which inordinate sorrow was apt to induce in her. Michiel, the Venetian ambassador, reported:

The death of the Queen Regent of Scotland was concealed from the most Christian Queen till the day before yesterday, when it was at length told her by the Cardinal of Lorraine; for which her Majesty showed and still shows such signs of grief, that during the greater part of yesterday she passed from one agony to another.

Mary's love for her mother spurred her forward in her knowledge of Scottish politics; her appreciation of French and English politics was spurred on by her own increasing estimation of her position as queen of France and heiress – or rightful possessor – of the English throne. Throckmorton's view of Mary Stuart has a particular interest. As English ambassador he had a definite motive for noting the twists and turns of her character as it developed: not only did she claim the English crown for her own, but she was also more plausibly the heiress to the throne. Life was uncertain, and Elizabeth was childless and unmarried; if Mary did not actually acquire the English throne by force, she might easily do so by inheritance. It thus behoved Throckmorton to keep a watchful eye on the nature and qualities of this young girl, whom the random chance of fate might one day establish as his own mistress.

It is significant that the Mary Stuart of Throckmorton's dispatches is a more intelligent and mature girl than the beautiful, wilful, delicate creature of, for example, the Venetian ambassador's reports to his own Italian court. Mary showed a hint of imperiousness in her words to Throckmorton concerning her refusal, with Francis, to ratify the Treaty of Edinburgh. 'My subjects in Scotland do their duty in nothing,' she told him, 'nor have they performed their part in one thing that belongeth to them. I am their Queen and so they call me, but they use me not so ... They must be taught to know their duties.' Earlier, when Throckmorton had had an interview with the royalties in February 1560, Mary had said little at first, but when the Queen Mother Catherine had made an observation to the effect that she wished to be on good terms with Elizabeth, Mary had intervened. 'Yes,' she said, 'the Queen my good sister may be assured to have a better neighbour of me being her cousin, than of the rebels, and so I pray you signify.' The point may not have been a good one in terms of power politics – since Elizabeth might well prefer rebels across the border to an active young queen, however friendly, however cousinly – but it was one worth making from Mary's point of view, and shows that her political intelligence was beginning to emerge from the cocoon of the cardinal's tutelage.

The cardinal had been the instructor of her youth, but as queen of France Mary had a new mentor in the art of politics – her mother-in-law Catherine de Medicis. It was no coincidence that Throckmorton had found the two queens sitting beside each other in February 1560. The records show that during the seventeen months in which Francis II reigned as king of France, Queen Catherine and Queen Mary were constantly in each other's company, and in fact Queen Catherine, far from being excluded from the source of power by the death of her husband, formed a royal triumvirate at the top of the pyramid of the court. A great deal has been made of the story that Mary openly despised Catherine for her lowly birth, and described her contemptuously as nothing but the daughter of a merchant. Whether or not Mary, with the imprudence of youth, made this unwise remark, and whatever her mother-in-law's private feelings, outwardly Catherine exhibited positively maternal kindness towards Mary during her period as queen of France.

Moreover Mary did not fail to be influenced by the personality of her mother-in-law. From Catherine she learnt two thoroughly feminine lessons – that the consideration of the child or unborn child, the continuance of the dynasty, should be placed above all others, and that the most effective weapons in a queen's hands were those of diplomatic intrigue. The second lesson did not fall on particularly fertile ground: Mary, unlike Catherine, was not by nature a talented or adept intriguer. Yet she was to become an enthusiastic one, and the effect of Catherine's early lessons can certainly be discerned in Mary's later career.

As the Guises' fortunes had been transformed by the sudden death of Henry II, so just seventeen months later the fragility of ambitious hopes founded on the life of a solitary human being was demonstrated once more. Francis's health had always been the Achilles heel of the Guises' plans. On Saturday, 16 November, he returned from a day's hunting in the country, complaining of a violent ear-ache and a large swelling appeared behind his left ear, caused by chronic inflammation of the middle ear.

Mary spent the last weeks of her husband's life in patient, silent nursing in his darkened chamber. Unlike their niece, the Guises bore the king's affliction with little patience: their mental agonies at the prospect opened before them by his illness seemed almost as acute as the king's physical sufferings. In their frenzy, they attacked the doctors for not doing more for the king than they would have done for a common beggar; and in their pursuit of remedies they turned to the stone of alchemy. But neither Mary's patient nursing, nor that of Catherine, nor the rages of the Guises, nor their manifold remedies, affected in any way the ineluctable progress of the king's illness. The inflammation spread upwards into the lobe of the brain and on 5 December, a month off his seventeenth birthday, Francis II died.

Mary's position was transformed by her husband's death; at the age of just eighteen she was no longer queen but queen dowager of France. Her entire position in Scotland, which had been founded on the umbrella-like protection which the French crown had extended to those Scots which it favoured, was likely to be in jeopardy now that her husband no longer sat on the French throne. But it is doubtful whether these political considerations were uppermost in the young queen's mind during the days before her husband's death and the days of mourning afterwards. On the contrary, the evidence shows that, almost alone of the central figures at the French court, Mary abandoned herself to passionate grief at the death of the king, a grief founded on the deep affection which she had felt for him, rather than the possible upset of her political plans.

By tradition the mourning period of a queen of France lasted for forty days. However, once the first fortnight was over, and Mary's storm of sorrow had abated, it was inevitable that she should consider her future in the world. There were two corner-stones on which this could be founded: a second marriage, and her return to Scotland. The Scottish situation was, however, rendered extremely uncertain by the fact that any sort of royal government had been in virtual abeyance since the death of Mary of Guise: the country was now ruled by a Protestant regime containing both John Knox and the queen's half-brother Lord James Stewart, under the titular leadership of the duke of Châtelherault. Mary was virtually an unknown quantity in Scotland and what little was known of her was feared: she was not only a Catholic but also a foreigner in Scottish eyes by reason of her French upbringing and marriage. It therefore seemed highly unlikely that Mary would be received back in Scotland unless some foreign army propelled her there: for this reason her return to Scotland was regarded as being bound up with and dependent on her second marriage.

A whole week before Francis's death, Throckmorton reported that there were plenty of discourses to be heard already of the French queen's second marriage and he cited the names of Don Carlos of Spain, Philip II's heir, the Archduke Charles of Austria, and the earl of Arran, Châtelherault's heir. After the death of Francis, an increasing number of other names were mentioned, including the kings of Denmark and Sweden, and the young Lord Darnley, with his desirable inheritance of English royal blood. There was also the possibility that Mary would marry her own brother-in-law Charles, with a papal dispensation: even the name of her own uncle, Grand Prior Francis of Guise, was canvassed. In short, by the time Mary emerged from her forty days of mourning, possible candidates could be said to include almost any currently unmarried male of roughly suitable age, whose own position could be held to benefit in any way that of the queen of Scots, either by establishing her own throne in Scotland, or by strengthening her claim to the throne of England, or even by re-establishing her on the throne of France.

The torrent of speculation made it inevitable that Mary herself would

RIGHT A bust by Germain Pilon, thought to show Mary as Queen of France.

LEFT A portrait of Charles IX by Clouet. He succeeded Francis to the throne of France, and it was even suggested that he might marry his sister-in-law by means of a papal dispensation.

BELOW LEFT Don Carlos of Spain, Philip II's heir, one of the suitors to Mary's hand, a match which was effectively opposed by Catherine de Medicis and Elizabeth I.

have to express some sort of personal predilection on the two subjects of re-marriage and Scotland, once she returned to the ways of ordinary life – unless, of course, she was content to leave her affairs and her future in the hands of her uncles as she had done in the past. This, however, she did not seem especially inclined to do. It has been suggested that the Guises lost interest in their niece once she no longer occupied the throne from which she could advance their interests: but the evidence of Mary's widowhood in France shows, on the contrary, that it was she who attempted to stretch her political wings and to struggle free as a butterfly from the chrysalis in which the Guises had lovingly contained her. In the negotiations for a second marriage the cardinal showed himself as anxious as ever to guide his niece but it was Mary who was making the first efforts to think for herself, in a way which impressed all those around her. Throckmorton reported to England that since her husband's death she had shown that she was of 'both a great wisdom for her years, modesty, and also of great judgment in the wise handling herself and her matter, which, increasing with her years, cannot but turn greatly to her commendation, reputation, and great benefit of her and her country'.

Mary was certainly a willing participant in the marriage negotiations with Don Carlos of Spain; marriage to Don Carlos, heir to the great throne of the Spanish empire, was an infinitely more glorious prospect than a highly speculative return to a distant kingdom. Mary had been trained to believe herself a worthy incumbent of thrones. Don Carlos was a Catholic and could be expected to be supported by Spanish troops. The Spanish marriage was Mary's first choice for her future after Francis's death, and the return to Scotland only assumed its full importance once the prospect of the Spanish marriage faded from the scene.

Fortunately or unfortunately, Mary Stuart was not destined to become a Spanish bride. There was an implacable, if unseen, obstacle in the way of the negotiations in the shape of the hostility of Catherine de Medicis, who feared that the house of Valois would be twice threatened by Mary's return to glory through marriage to Don Carlos. Firstly, the star of the Guises would inevitably rise again and who knew what new twists they might not give to the skein of their ambitions. Secondly, the position of Catherine's daughter Elisabeth might be threatened if Philip should die and Elisabeth be pushed aside as Catherine herself had once been. While Catherine gave Elisabeth precise instructions on how to frustrate the match from the Spanish end, she herself complicated the issue by dangling the prospect of another royal bride for Don Carlos in front of Philip's eyes – her own daughter Marguerite.

France was not the only country where Mary's Spanish match was looked on with concern. In England the prospect of Mary Stuart's marriage to a foreign prince, especially a Spanish one, was regarded as scarcely less threatening to the maintenance of English power. To Philip, confronted with the firm hostility of Catherine and Elizabeth of England, and with the prospect of Marguerite held out before him, Mary no longer seemed so alluring as a future daughter-in-law. By the end of April, Elisabeth of Spain was able to inform her mother that the Spanish negotiations with Mary had foundered finally for lack of interest on Philip's part.

Meanwhile, in the middle of March, Mary had decided to leave the French court and to set off on a prolonged round of visits to her Guise relations. Apart from her natural desire to visit the family of whom she had always been so fond, it seems likely that Mary was also anxious to discuss her future with them.

It so happened that while she was on the journey she received an envoy from the self-constituted Scottish Protestant government which, at the moment when the Spanish negotiations were foundering, opened up new possibilities in terms of a Scottish future. The emissary was her half-brother Lord James Stewart, James v's illegitimate son by Margaret Erskine. Some twelve years older than his half-sister, Lord James was a man of solemn manner and appearance; this *gravitas*, so unlike the qualities of the contemporary French nobility, was to prove highly successful in impressing the English when he dealt with them. Although more politically gifted than his contemporaries, Lord James was in fact far from immune from that practical avarice so characteristic of the Scottish nobility of this period – nor did he lack the hypocrisy which so often accompanies frequent public statements on the subject of honour. But his temperament, and above all the quality of his religious views which fitted in so well with those of the English politicians of the period, meant that he was always able to deal easily, if not honourably, with his English equivalents, and this was to give him a practical advantage in Anglo-Scottish affairs at a later stage in his half-sister's career.

His interview with Mary was not unsatisfactory to either of them, despite their widely differing points of view. Lord James had been instructed to ask the queen to embrace the Scottish Protestant faith: this she steadily refused to do. But she did state with some courage that she was prepared to come home without any other restrictions, or a personal armed escort, provided she could have use of her own religion in private. This Lord James himself had already expressed publicly to the Scots as being an acceptable demand and he convinced her that it was politically wise to give the Protestant party its head for the time being in Scotland. Mary must have been impressed as a result of this meeting with the notion that Lord James would constitute her natural adviser in Scotland, by virtue of their blood connections, as the Guises had done in France. She had emphasized to Throckmorton that she was prepared to listen to advice, and even if all Lord James's advice had not been to her liking, the basis for some tolerable *modus vivendi*, in the event of her return, had at least been reached between them.

James's advice to his sister on the subject of the Scottish Protestants accorded well with Mary's own temperament and religious convictions. In religious matters, her leaning was towards the tolerance of her mother, rather than the fanaticism of a cardinal of Guise. As a born Catholic who had known no other creed, her faith was to her like her everyday bread, something which she took for granted, and yet which was essential to her, and without which she could not imagine her existence; it was, however, in no sense an Old Testament faith, a fierce Moloch of a faith, which demanded the sacrifice of all other faiths to propitiate it, such as animated Philip II of Spain. Mary's innate clemency in matters of religion has sometimes been mistaken for lukewarm conviction. The truth was that she drew a distinction between private faith and public policy. Although Randolph wrote when she was in Scotland: 'She wishes that all men should live as they please,' Knox was quick to realize that such permissiveness did not mean, as some suggested, that the queen herself should ever be of their opinion. Mary's personal Catholicism was total, her attitude to a state religion inclined to be pragmatic.

By the time she returned to court from visiting her Guise relations, Mary had evidently made up her mind to return to Scotland, though it was not the only alternative open to her. Mary's rank in France entitled her to an honourable position at the French court; her marriage portion had given her sufficiently widespread and lucrative estates to maintain her in an adequate state; the Guise family, although somewhat blighted, were not totally destitute of power; if she remained on the Continent, it was not likely to be long before some more ardent royal suitor than Don Carlos emerged. To Mary herself must be given the credit of having personally settled for a bold course of adventure rather than the more placid, less demanding existence which it would still have been possible for her to lead in France. The truth was that, even as a young girl, Mary showed signs of having a gambling streak, and she was certainly singularly unendowed with conservatism in her nature: the familiar path was never to her automatically the most attractive while there was another more daring route to be explored. Life in France, as she had known it so gloriously, appeared to have come to an end; but on the horizon, Scotland beckoned, which might provide in time – who could tell, but Mary was an optimist – as many golden opportunities.

As it happened, at the same moment the Scots themselves were beginning to feel more warmly about their absent queen. They suddenly realized that a malleable young ruler, with a strong personal claim to succeed to the neighbouring throne, and apparently prepared to behave reasonably over religion was certainly not to be discarded in a hurry. As a result of these cogitations, Lord James wrote a letter on 10 June which constituted a virtual invitation on behalf of the Protestant lords to return. Scotland for Mary, therefore, was not a *pis aller*, but a hopeful venture, in which her Guise blood encouraged her to expect success.

Lord James was not especially put out by the fact that Mary had consistently declined to ratify the Treaty of Edinburgh: not unnaturally he shared the view that Mary had often expressed that it was a subject which could be best dealt with once she had returned to Scotland and could consult her Council. Elizabeth, however, regarded the matter somewhat differently. Throckmorton had tried repeatedly to secure the ratification but had failed. Now, when Mary applied to Elizabeth for safe conduct on her route back to Scotland, she received a point-blank refusal.

Elizabeth's refusal gave Mary Stuart her first public opportunity of rising magnificently to a crisis. She now displayed for the first time that quality of cool courage, when in the public eye, which was to be a feature of her later career. She began by expressing in polite terms to Throckmorton her regrets that she should have bothered Elizabeth by demanding a passport which she did not in fact require. She had reached France in safety, she pointed out proudly, in spite of the efforts of the English king to intercept her. Thirteen years later, she would surely once more reach her own country with her own people to help her. She now prepared to set forth across the North Sea on the 600-mile journey to her kingdom, unblessed by any passport of safe-conduct from the English queen, whose ships patrolled these seas.

Taking her leave of the king, the court and her Guise relations, Mary embarked with her retinue at Calais in the middle of August. Now that the die was cast, now that the ships were actually lying in the harbour ready to take her away from all she had known and loved and held dear for the last thirteen years of what seemed to her like her whole life, Mary's steadfast spirit temporarily deserted her. There was now no great challenge to call forth the resources of her nature, only the prospect of bidding farewell as it might be forever to France, the beloved land of her adoption.

As the galleys surged forward towards the unknown coast of Scotland, Mary gazed again and again on the fast receding coast of France, clinging pathetically to that part of the ship which was still nearest to the French shores. Mingling with the sound of the wind and the roar of the sea, a voice broken with tears could be heard, uttering its farewell, melancholy and prophetic: '*Adieu France! Adieu France! Adieu donc, ma chère France . . . Je pense ne vous revoir jamais plus.*'

PART TWO
The Personal Rule

4 Governor Good and Gracious

'Be governor both good and gracious
Be loyal and loving to thy lieges all'

LORD DARNLEY *to Mary Queen of Scots*

The journey which had begun under such dramatic auspices turned out to be comparatively uneventful and surprisingly short. On Tuesday, 19 August Mary Queen of Scots set foot once more on her native soil at the port of Leith, after an absence of just on thirteen years. Her arrival, though unexpectedly early, was greeted nevertheless, by all accounts, with enthusiasm and joy. The Scottish lords who escorted her to Holyrood Palace might be bound in loyalty to greet their sovereign, they might be fired with the intention of creating a favourable first impression, which would lead to personal advancement later, but the common people were excited by the spectacle before their eyes. Mary at the age of eighteen, tall, graceful, commanding, was everything in appearance that the popular imagination would have conjured up to fill the role of its newly arrived queen, if it had been allowed to choose. Mary professed herself to be delighted with her reception and what was more, she was able to express her pleasure to her subjects in their own language, for she had not lost her Scots despite the thirteen years spent in France.

At Holyrood Mary was installed in the magnificent towered and turreted palace which had been extended in the reign of her father in the manner of the Scottish Renaissance; here not only the debt which the style owed to French architecture as a whole, but also the fact that a number of French masons had been employed in the works, must have commended the whole building to Mary's eyes. Lying on the outskirts of the city of Edinburgh, outside the actual town walls, Holyrood enjoyed the amenities of wild country just beyond its very windows, as well as the convenience of having the capital city so close at hand.

Queen Mary now took possession of those royal apartments in the north-west corner of the palace which were to play such a significant role in her story. By the standards of the Scotland of the day, they were extremely magnificent.

For the first few days after Mary's arrival there was, in Knox's phrase, nothing but 'mirth and quietness'. But on her very first Sabbath in Scotland Mary was to discover how different her new kingdom was from her old one. On the Sunday, Mary, who had been assured by Lord James of the private practice of her religion, ordered Mass to be said in the chapel royal at Holyrood. The preparations for the service were all too familiar in a country which had only been officially Protestant for one year. An angry crowd gathered outside the chapel, while inside the queen

PREVIOUS PAGE Mary Queen of Scots, by an unknown artist.

46

Firing a Northumbrian town. A scene from Holinshed's *Chronicle* depicting the recurrent violence of the Borders.

attended a Mass which was understandably fraught with tension – the English ambassador reported that the priest was in such a state of mortal fear, that he could hardly lift the Host at the Elevation.

If the queen received a rude shock from the incident, she did not allow it to affect her determinedly tolerant religious policy. The next day she issued a proclamation in which she announced that she intended with the aid of her Estates to make a final order, which she hoped would please everyone, to pacify the differences in religion. In the meantime, she charged the whole world, in order to prevent tumult or sedition, to make no alteration or innovations in the state of religion, or to attempt anything against the form of public worship which she had found standing on her arrival in Scotland – under pain of death. She further commanded that no one should molest any of her domestic servants or those who had come with her out of France in the practice of their religion – equally under pain of death.

This proclamation may seem to us, from a modern standpoint, comparatively wise, and certainly singularly free from Catholic bigotry. It aroused, however, the venomous ire of many of the extremist Protestants, and especially that of their leading evangelist, John Knox. The next Sunday Knox took the opportunity of preaching a great denunciation of the Mass from the pulpit. While still in France, Mary had already formed the most unfavourable impression of Knox, and she told

47

John Knox, the extremist Protestant preacher who, although implacably opposed to Mary, grudgingly admitted that she had charm, a charm which he considered dangerous to the Protestant cause. Portrait by Beza from 'Les Vrais Portraits'.

OPPOSITE A miniature of Mary Queen of Scots as a young girl, by Clouet.

OVERPAGE
LEFT The double portrait of James V of Scotland and Mary of Guise, father and mother of Mary Queen of Scots, Hardwick Hall.

RIGHT Linlithgow Castle, West Lothian, where Mary was born on the Feast of the Immaculate Conception of the Virgin Mary, 8 December 1542.

Throckmorton that she believed him to be the most dangerous man in her kingdom. Now she determined to grasp the nettle; she sent for Knox to come to Holyrood.

Knox was now a man of forty-seven; having been rescued from 'the puddle of papistry', as he put it, by George Wishart in the 1540s, he had become a disciple of Calvin. The strength of his character and the force of his convictions enabled him to win over many men to Protestantism, and ensured that he remained a potent force on the Scottish scene. It was an unlucky hazard for Mary Stuart that he happened to be living in Edinburgh the first year of her residence there, to act as a demoniac chorus for all her actions, which, good or bad, he presented in the most malevolent light.

Mary's very sex was against her in Knox's opinion: whereas in the sixteenth century it was theoretically considered to be against the natural law for women to rule men, nevertheless most people were content to regard an actual woman ruler as a necessary evil which might have to be endured from time to time. Knox, however, went much further than his contemporaries and in his *First Blast of the Trumpet against the Monstrous Regiment of Women*, published in 1558, declared roundly that to promote any woman – those 'weak, frail, impatient, feeble and foolish creatures' – to any form of rule was the 'subversion of good order, of all equity and justice', as well as being contrary to God and repugnant to nature. Now he was confronted in a personal interview with one of these feeble and foolish creatures sitting on the throne of his own country of Scotland.

Mary began by attacking Knox for raising her subjects against her mother and herself, and also for writing *The Monstrous Regiment*. Knox conceded the point about her sex, and said that if she behaved well, and the realm was not brought to disaster by her femininity, he personally would not disallow her rule on those grounds alone. When Mary struggled with him over the religious issue, however, she found him much less accommodating. Finally Knox agreed to tolerate her for the time being – his phrase, which owed little to courtly flattery, was 'to be as well content to live under your Grace as Paul was to live under Nero'. But he still firmly asserted the rights of the subject to rise up against the unworthy ruler who opposed God's word.

Knox has been accused of speaking churlishly to the queen; he certainly spoke to her in a manner to which she was scarcely accustomed, but she on the other hand seems to have been stimulated rather than otherwise by his abruptness. It is true that she relapsed into tears at one moment: but the English ambassador, Randolph, thought they were tears of anger rather than grief. All her life Mary Stuart had a feminine ability to give herself suddenly up to tears when her sensibilities were affronted; she seems to have used it as a useful method of relieving her feelings; it never prevented her actions from being extremely hard-headed once she had recovered her composure. Knox quickly realized that Mary was far from being the feeble puppet which her career in France might have led him to expect. He told his friends: 'If there be not in her a proud mind, a crafty wit and an indurate heart against God and his truth, my judgement faileth me.'

Mary was still being so enthusiastically greeted by her subjects that an

IACOBVS.QVINTVS.SCOTTORVM.REX

ANNO.ÆTATIS.SVE.

28

MARIA.LOTH

TIIS VXOR

incident in the chapel royal, a rude sermon from Knox, and one brusque interview were not enough to damp her spirits. She had been received with elaborate rejoicings on her ceremonial entry into Edinburgh and, after three weeks at Holyrood, when Mary set out for a short progress around her kingdom, she was met with the same kind of enthusiasm.

The sights she saw during her progress can only have confirmed her in the conviction that it was in the best interests of peace and stability in Scotland to preserve the Protestant *status quo*. This conviction had guided her response to the curious situation apropos the structure of the Protestant Church in which she found herself on her return to Scotland. The right of the Scottish monarch to grant livings and benefices had remained unaffected by the edict of Parliament which officially changed the religion of Scotland, and, since the income from benefices could be granted if the king so wished to others than its spiritual incumbent, it had become a useful and powerful system of royal patronage. Wisely, although under no obligation to do so, Mary made provision for the ministers of the new Church, showing once again that she drew a sharp distinction between the private Mass in her chapel and the public weal in Scotland.

Randolph paid tribute to Mary's cleverness, saying that he had detected in her the fruit of the 'best-practised' cunning of France combined with the subtle brains of Scotland. Part of this cleverness was her designedly accommodating and tactful behaviour, never more so than on the subject of religion, as a result of which she was rewarded with considerable personal popularity.

The conciliation of her Scottish subjects was only one half of Mary's plan: reconciliation with Elizabeth was the other. Elizabeth had ultimately relented her fury and had granted Mary the safe-conduct she had requested. But it arrived too late, for Mary had already set sail by the time Elizabeth's letter reached France. However, once she was assured that Elizabeth had actually dispatched the safe-conduct, Mary's mood towards her cousin was as purposely friendly as her mood towards the Scots. Only thirteen days after her arrival, she commissioned William Maitland, the most experienced diplomatist out of the rather limited selection offered by the Scottish nobility, to go to England and try to treat with the English queen on the subject of succession.

The Scottish point of view on the subject of the succession had already been put to Elizabeth in a letter from Lord James, before Mary even arrived in Scotland. Ratification of the Treaty of Edinburgh was to be given in exchange for Elizabeth's acknowledgement that Mary stood next in line to the throne after herself and her lawful issue. Maitland pointed out on behalf of Mary that this meant that she could not ratify the treaty as it now stood, because its terms called on her to surrender not only her present claim to the English throne, but also all further claims after the death of Elizabeth and her problematic offspring. In reply, Elizabeth showed herself nothing if not friendly towards the queen of Scots. She even went so far as to vouchsafe the information that she herself preferred Mary to all her rivals: she knew of no better right than Mary's, and no one who was strong enough to keep Mary from the throne. At the same time she positively declined to give Mary the

OPPOSITE The Deuil Blanc portrait of Mary, by Clouet, probably painted in 1559 at the time of her mourning for her father-in-law Henry II.

ABOVE A gold three-pound
piece, minted in 1555, with
Mary's head.

ABOVE RIGHT Lady
Catherine Grey with
Edward, her elder son by
Edward Seymour, Earl of
Hertford, born in the
Tower in 1561.

acknowledgement she desired. The reason she gave was the impossible
burden which it would lay on her own relations with Mary. 'Princes
cannot like their own children, those that should succeed unto them . . .
How then shall I, think you, like my cousin, being declared my Heir
Apparent?' She also put forward a more practical reason: 'I know the
inconstancy of the people of England, how they ever mislike the present
government and have their eyes fixed upon that person that is next to
succeed.' With these revelations, Maitland had to be content. However,
Elizabeth made one concession in that she agreed to accept a certain
modification of the treaty, so that Mary should not have to sign away her
claim, beyond the period of Elizabeth's life and that of her lawful
offspring.

Elizabeth, in her personal favour towards Mary, was certainly in
contradiction to the majority of her subjects at this period. Mary was
extremely unpopular in England, being considered virtually a Frenchwoman and a Guise, as well as a Catholic, and she was especially disliked
by the English Parliament which was strongly Puritan in tone. There
were other claimants whom the English as a body might be thought to
prefer: Margaret, countess of Lennox, a granddaughter of Henry VII;
Henry Hastings, earl of Huntingdon, who was the last representative of
the Plantagenets; and Lady Catherine Grey, the younger sister of the
ill-fated Lady Jane Grey. Huntingdon and Lady Catherine were Protestants, and Margaret Douglas, though Catholic, was at least English.

Under these circumstances it is easy to understand why Mary believed
that the personal favour of Elizabeth constituted her best hope of being
recognized. Throughout the autumn Mary devoted all her efforts to
bringing about a personal meeting with Elizabeth, by which she felt
certain she could win the all-important affections of the English queen.

OPPOSITE The coronation
portrait of Elizabeth I in
her Coronation robes,
1559, by an unknown
artist. Elizabeth's
coronation was a
magnificent display of
pageantry, unlike the
inauspicious crowning of
Mary when only six days
old.

With friendly letters, gifts and even verse she wooed her, and Elizabeth rose to the bait. In December Cecil wrote to Throckmorton that he found a great desire in both queens to have an interview, although he gloomily feared the worst from two such different women meeting. The Scottish Council had agreed to the meeting in principle, although they were understandably worried about Mary's safety in view of the fact that it was less than a year since the English queen had been threatening to imprison her if she landed on English soil. There were other considerations to dampen the ardour of the Scottish Protestants. Such meetings were notoriously expensive. Not only that, but they feared that if Elizabeth was seduced by Mary's charm she might cease to keep them under her protective wing. The Scottish Catholic party were concerned that their queen, who had shown a disappointing lack of interest in their cause, should be further corrupted by a meeting with the Protestant Elizabeth and were correspondingly opposed to the whole project. The English Council were also unenthusiastic and, like their Scottish counterpart, pleaded the expense.

At the last moment, however, with that element of unhappy fatality which never seems far absent from the story of Mary Stuart, the meeting had to be put off – through no lack of keenness on the part of Elizabeth, or the objections of the English Council, but owing to the explosive situation in the rest of Europe. In March 1562 civil war broke out in France between the Catholic and the Huguenot factions. Elizabeth was forced to turn her attentions away from the proposed meeting to the conflict raging just across the Channel, for at any moment England might be called upon to intervene on behalf of the Protestant cause, if Spain supported the Catholics.

On hearing of the sudden débâcle of her plans, Mary took refuge in a violent flood of tears. But she allowed herself to be comforted by the news that Elizabeth was willing to plan the interview for the following year. With the natural optimism of her nature, she convinced herself that in the mirror of the future, that dark and cloudy surface, she could see reflected the image of success, only a year away. Little did she know that this image was merely an illusion – that the meeting between Elizabeth and Mary, which has been so often fabled by poets and dramatists, and of which the possible consequences are incalculable, but must surely have been immensely favourable to Mary, was destined never to take place.

While Mary negotiated for the throne of distant England, the volatile spirits and unruly power of her Scottish nobles presented her with certain very different problems at home, involving not only the public peace but also her own physical safety.

The mutual hatred that existed between James Hepburn, earl of Bothwell, and the Hamiltons flared up into armed confrontation in the streets of Edinburgh and only the last-minute intervention of Lord James, Argyll and Huntly, who managed to disperse the assailants, averted bloodshed. No sooner had the two sides been reconciled than Arran, Châtelherault's eccentric eldest son, laid allegations of a conspiracy to abduct the queen against Bothwell. Although Arran's sanity had long been a matter of common speculation and family concern, and

there was no proof of guilt except Arran's word, Bothwell was sternly treated. He was left to languish a prisoner in Edinburgh Castle without trial, Mary being persuaded by Lord James that it would be highly embarrassing politically to bring the incident out into the open, since if Arran was shown to have borne false witness he would have to be executed, and he was too near the throne for this to be desirable.

The rebellion of Huntly was an incident of more serious proportions. The might of the Gordons, under their magnificent but unpredictable head, George, fourth earl of Huntly, had long loomed over the north-east of Scotland. As the leading Catholic magnate, Huntly might have been a powerful ally to Mary, although he had already shown himself to be untrustworthy in defecting to the reformers, and thereby virtually wrecking the Catholic cause, after Mary of Guise had appointed him

James, 2nd earl of Arran, later 1st duke of Châtelherault, 'the most inconstant man in the world', whose change of faith in 1543 confirmed that Henry VIII's influence on affairs in Scotland was waning.

lieutenant-general of the kingdom. Now once more openly professing the faith of his fathers, Huntly incurred Mary Stuart's displeasure by making no secret of his disapproval of her cool policy towards the Scottish Catholics, and when one of his sons, Sir John Gordon, imprisoned for his part in a street brawl with Lord Ogilvie, escaped and fled northwards, Mary, encouraged by Lord James, set out on a royal progress to her northern dominions with the dual purpose of rallying the Highlanders to her side and of pursuing Sir John. She intended to

James Stewart, Earl of Moray, half-brother of Mary Queen of Scots, did much to help her govern in the first years of her reign. Portrait by H. Munro after an unknown artist.

demonstrate once and for all that the Gordons could not behave as they pleased with impunity.

As Mary travelled north, Sir John gathered a force of 1,000 horse and proceeded impudently to harry the queen's train with the deliberate intention of abducting her. When Mary reached Inverness, the keeper of the castle, Alexander Gordon, another of Huntly's numerous offspring, refused her entrance, although it was a royal and not a Gordon castle, being only committed to Huntly's charge by virtue of his position of sheriff of Inverness. This was not so much insolence as actual treason and when Mary eventually entered the castle, the keeper was hanged over the battlements for his defiance. With this brusque confirmation of Huntly's attitude towards her, Mary and Lord James now called on the earl to surrender his canon and fortresses. A prolonged game of cat-and-mouse took place before Huntly and John Gordon were 'put to the horn', outlawed. Not content to rest in the wilds of the hills to which he had retired, Huntly gathered his forces and marched against the queen at Aberdeen. In the ensuing clash the Gordons were hacked down by Lord James's forces and Huntly and his sons were captured. At this dramatic moment in his fortunes, the great northern earl fell dead from his horse in front of his captors, either from heart failure or apoplexy. His sons were executed or imprisoned and his wealth and property confiscated. The tumbling-down of Huntly's power in the north left a vacuum which Lord James, rather than the crown, was able to fill and he received the earldom of Moray and various sheriffdoms previously held by Huntly.

The Arran and Huntly episodes are of twofold interest. Firstly, they show that the abduction of Mary's person was a subject of comparatively common discussion and certainly not a novel idea in April 1567 when it was finally achieved. Secondly, they reveal how closely Mary's lot was joined with that of the new earl of Moray. At this point she was making no attempt to rule the Scottish nobles by balancing them against each other, backing each noble in turn and luring them in some fashion to destroy each other until the crown should be left triumphant. On the contrary, she was clearly backing Moray in whatever he chose to do. This policy would be satisfactory so long as the interests of Queen Mary and her half-brother coincided: should they ever diverge the queen might find that she would need the support of the other strong nobles in the kingdom, whom she was now allowing Moray to put down as he willed.

The potential powers of the Scottish crown within the constitution at this period were widespread. The problem was the implementation of these powers in a backward country, rather than the nature of the powers themselves. Apart from the obvious disadvantage of the strength of the nobles, the crown had two other great weaknesses. It had no standing army; should it be involved in action necessitating war, the crown had to depend on the locally raised hosts of other loyal nobles, with the consequent dangers of personal vendettas being involved in royal policy. Secondly the financial resources of the Scottish crown were cripplingly restricted. Although Mary Stuart received an annual income of 40,000 *livres* as her jointure as queen-dowager of France, the lands and properties of her father had been largely squandered during her minority or apportioned to the nobles. Since she did not have a right to resume these until her twenty-fifth birthday, the royal income was dependent, apart from the lease on its own lands, on wardships of minors and heiresses, export dues derived from duties on trade and ecclesiastical revenues. The method of collecting taxes in Scotland in the sixteenth century has been compared unfavourably with that of twelfth-century England, taxes being farmed out for collection to sheriffs whose offices had become hereditary. The total royal revenue in 1560 was around £40,000 Scots or about £10,000 sterling. Compared to this, that of Queen Elizabeth was £200,000, rising to £300,000 in the last ten years of her reign.

Despite these gloomy considerations, for the first years of her life in Scotland Mary Stuart made a fair attempt to recreate the conditions of the French court and to enjoy the native resources of Scotland. Fortunately she had a natural appetite for pleasures of many different types, as well as being blessed with youthful high spirits and enthusiasm, which enabled her to create pastimes where she did not find them: in particular she had a positive mania for outdoor pursuits – all her life her physical constitution demanded a daily ration of fresh air and exercise if she was to feel herself well. Although, later in her life, this caused her to suffer cruelly from the conditions of close confinement, it meant that now she was well suited to life in Scotland, where she was destined to spend nearly half her time in the saddle, progressing about her dominions. In the Scottish country-side she also had endless opportunities for hawking and hunting which she loved, and in her enthusiasm for it she met with the full accord of her subjects. Archery – for which she would wear a velvet glove – also appealed to her, and she had butts set up in her private gardens at Holyrood. She played at golf and pall-mall (croquet) and she loved to walk in the gardens surrounding her palaces, and frequently held audiences of her ambassadors there.

Mary Stuart had her resplendent side, when she appeared to her subjects as Diana the goddess of the chase; but she also had another charming and touchingly domesticated side to her character in marked contrast to this dazzling public *persona*. This paradox is stamped on many of her actions which hover between the imperious deeds of the woman born a queen, who loved to shine in the eyes of her people, and the more clinging reactions of a woman, who was after all markedly feminine, in temperament as well as in sex. She loved to embroider, and is described as sitting at her Council, placidly plying her needle, a model of the compliant female. Mary Stuart's life was also marked, in its early no less than in its later stages, by extreme attachments to her servants, particularly her own personal attendants, with whom she felt she could share her joys and woes without fear either of their presumption or their disloyalty.

Mary's court therefore had an agreeably intimate character, which spread outwards from the feminine side of its queen's own nature. There were certainly indoor pleasures enough to be enjoyed. The queen loved to dance, play at cards or at dice and enjoyed billiards, chess and back-gammon. She was a considerable linguist and her extensive library contained books in Italian, Spanish and Greek as well as French, Latin, Scots and a few English volumes. For music Mary would seem to have

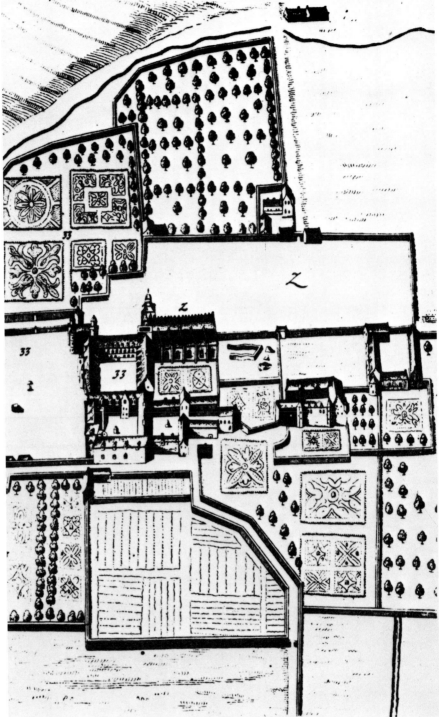

ABOVE and RIGHT The
palace of Holyrood in
1647, by J. Gordon of
Rothiemay.

had a profound feeling which, like her love of poetry, appealed to the
romantic, rather than the inquisitive, side of her nature. She herself
played on both the lute and the virginals and had a charming soft singing voice, which, like her speaking voice, won the admiration of her
listeners.

In her dress at least Mary Stuart was able to give the femininity of her
nature full reign, because to be magnificently attired was expected of a

sixteenth-century queen, by all except the most bigoted and puritanical. In childhood she had displayed a keen interest in clothes, and when she grew up, and had what virtually amounted to a constitutional duty to dress herself elegantly, she did so with innate good taste – lacking her cousin Elizabeth's inclination to bedizen herself ostentatiously, possibly because she was conscious that unlike Elizabeth she had the sort of beauty which was best set off by rich simplicity. Of course, a large proportion of her time as a young woman was spent in mourning and she did not totally cast off her mourning for Francis until she married Darnley four years later. Perhaps she understood how to make her many black accoutrements a dramatic foil for her red-golden hair, white skin and golden eyes; for the same reason white appears and reappears throughout the list of dresses in her wardrobe, there being perhaps no better setting for a glowing complexion than a white dress: the list of her robes, with their descriptions and colours, fully explains why she came to be known as '*la reine blanche*' in France.

Ordinarily, Mary wore dresses of camlet (a sort of mohair), damask or serge, stiffened in the neck with buckram, and mounted with lace and ribbons; she was also fond of loose dresses, *à l'espagnole*; her riding skirts and cloaks were of Florentine serge, often edged with black velvet or fur. Beneath her gowns were *vasquines*, stiffened petticoats or farthingales to hold out her skirts, expanded with hoops of whale bone to give a crinoline effect. Her underwear included silk doublets, and there is mention of *brassières* of both black and white silk. Her woven hose were made of silk also. Her hats and caps were of black velvet and taffetas, her veils of white.

On state and ceremonial occasions, the queen's clothes were universally glittering. The inventory of the queen's dresses made at Holyrood in February 1562 lists 131 entries, including sixty gowns of cloth of gold, cloth of silver, velvet, satin and silk. There are fourteen cloaks, five of which are in the Spanish fashion, and two royal mantles, one purple velvet and the other furred in ermine. There are thirty-four *vasquines* and sixteen *devants* or fronts (stomachers), mainly of cloth of gold, silver and satin. The dresses themselves range from the favourite white – often with silver fringes and embroidery – and preponderant black, to crimson velvet and orange damask embroidered in silver; the embroidery was so rich and detailed that it was often passed from dress to dress, and was listed separately among the jewellery.

Mary's jewels were of enormous importance of her: these, of course, represented something more than adornment, since by being treated as solid financial assets they could be held for security or sold to pay troops if necessary. Later in her life, her jewels were to enjoy a career as checkered as her own, as they were stolen, seized, sold or pawned, all to her violently expressed anguish. The inventory of her jewellery, made also in 1562, contains 180 entries. As she loved white, so the queen seems to have had an especial affection for pearls – it was noted that she was wearing two of a group of twenty-three pearls in her ears at the actual moment when the inventory was taken. But rubies she also seems to have admired, as she loved to wear crimson velvet; and among her profusion of rings, necklaces and earrings, there is mention of enamel, cornelian and turquoise, as well as, of course, gold and diamonds.

The queen paid fashionable attention to the care of her hair, and the elaborate dressing of it, according to the caprices of the time. Even in her youth, when she had lovely thick glistening hair, the dictates of the mode led her to use perukes or false hairpieces. Later in her life her glorious hair darkened, and the sorrows and illnesses of her captivity caused it to thin and go grey prematurely. Then, false pieces of hair were to be essential, but now in her heyday, she made use of them equally: there is repeated reference in her wardrobe lists to her perukes or the bags in which to keep them.

Mary had a childish love of fancy dress and dressing-up which she preserved throughout her life. It has already been mentioned that she loved to adopt Scottish national dress in France. In Scotland, with a romantic love of the Highlands, the queen adopted the custom of wearing the so-called 'Highland mantles' – these were not plaid, but loose cloaks reaching to the ground, and generally embroidered. In Scotland also, Mary loved to adopt male costume, and wander about the streets, enjoying the sort of romantic incognito among her subjects which has always been considered the perquisite of adventurous royalties. With her height and long legs, she must have made an engaging picture.

In this kind of prank, in which royalty have always indulged to escape the gilded bird-cage of their existence, it is unnecessary to discern more than natural high spirits and youthful love of pleasure. Certainly there were no sexual scandals surrounding the sovereign. Mary, who throughout her first years in Scotland was an unattached and beautiful girl, with no restraints except those of prudence to hold her back from the wildest excesses had she wished to indulge in them, was as clearly *sans reproche* in her court life, as she was *sans peur* in the hunting field. The only scandal to be seen was the scandal, in the eyes of Knox at least, of the spectacle of human enjoyment.

Mary's simple sense of fun fitted in well with the boisterous sense of humour of her Scottish subjects at this time, although this was certainly more bawdy in its most outspoken manifestations. The sixteenth-century Scots did not necessarily see the reformation of their religion as leading to the end of those hearty, crude bucolic games and sports which they had long enjoyed: they loved the favourite May game of Robin Hood, with its Abbot of Unreason and its Queen of the May. The people who enjoyed this sort of entertainment naturally loved the pageantry brought to the country by Mary and her court.

To the argument that Mary was extravagant, it may be answered that she was considerably less extravagant than her cousin Elizabeth in both her dress and her progresses. Not only was Mary used to infinitely more prodigal expenditure at the court of France, but also much of her glamour consisted in her personal charm. In any case, such display on the part of the sovereign was an essential part of personal and monarchical government. The result, as even Buchanan, later to be her harshest critic, admitted, was that this pretty, high-spirited creature, with her hunting, her hawking, her clothes, her jewels, was able to charm those members of the Scots nation who were there to be charmed.

5 The Carnal Marriage

'Nuptiae Carnales a laetitia incipiunt et in luctu terminantur'
(Carnal marriages begin with happiness and end in strife)

CECIL's *comment on the marriage of Amy Robsart and Leicester*

Mary Stuart was young, beautiful and attractive: she was also a queen and could offer an independent kingdom as a dowry to any husband. On the surface it would seem that it should not have been too difficult for her to find a suitable candidate, since she had none of the psychological problems of an Elizabeth Tudor, and was sufficiently conventionally feminine to long for a male partner on whom to depend. In theory, therefore, she had a wide choice of possible husbands: but, in practice, so many considerations had to be taken into account, that while the field was not exactly reduced – since many candidates met one or other of the requirements – it was impossible to declare a clear winner, since none of them met them all. This was true if only because many of the requirements were actually contradictory. The only point on which everyone agreed was that the choice was an important one, not in terms of Mary Stuart's happiness, but because whomever she married would inevitably expect to become king of Scotland. Francis had always been known as king of Scotland, and had also been granted the crown matrimonial: any future consort might expect to enjoy the former privilege and hope to enjoy the latter.

The first consideration was that of religion: was Mary to marry a Catholic like herself or should she perhaps attempt the more daring policy of binding together her subjects by wedding someone of their own religion? A Catholic marriage would inevitably upset the balance she was so carefully maintaining between her private religion and the public religion of her country, by emphasizing that she was very much a Catholic at heart whatever her outward tolerance to the Protestants; a Protestant marriage on the other hand would be difficult to explain to her Catholic relations and allies on the Continent, on whom she still depended.

Then there was the question of status: was she to marry an independent prince with a kingdom of his own or choose a subject within a kingdom? An independent ruler with a kingdom of his own could not fail to treat Scotland as a satellite, and could scarcely be expected to put Scottish interests above those of his own country; the raising-up of a mere subject to royal rank, on the other hand, would certainly arouse jealousy and dissension among the Scottish nobles.

Then there was the matter of the views of Queen Elizabeth on the subject. Mary's foreign policy had been directed towards getting herself

OPPOSITE A portrait of Lord Darnley and Mary Queen of Scots, the latter holding the thistle of Scotland. Darnley was proclaimed 'King Henry' by the queen on his marriage to her.

Henrie Steuart Duke of
Albanye and Marie
Quem of Scotland
1566

ABOVE Robert Dudley, Earl of Leicester, favourite of Elizabeth I, was nominated by his queen in Spring 1564 as suitor to Mary Queen of Scots' hand.

ABOVE RIGHT Margaret Douglas, Countess of Lennox, mother of Darnley and granddaughter of Henry VII, was also a claimant to the English throne.

recognized as Elizabeth's successor on the throne of England. In this endeavour, in which so far no real progress had been made, Mary's putative husband was obviously a trump card. Yet how was Mary to marry to Elizabeth's satisfaction, if Elizabeth did not express any definite choice? In the autumn of 1563 Elizabeth began to drop broad hints as to who her personal choice might be. The only trouble was that Elizabeth's choice of candidate, her own favourite, the earl of Leicester, was sufficiently eccentric to arouse serious doubts as to whether it was a genuine suggestion, or whether on the contrary she was merely trying to prevent Mary making any marriage at all. Leicester was generally considered to be Queen Elizabeth's paramour, and whatever the truth of their relationship, her familiarity with him had certainly caused scandal throughout Europe, as had the death, in the most suspicious circumstances, of his first wife, Amy Robsart, which, it was generally believed, left him free to marry Queen Elizabeth.

The disadvantages of Leicester as a husband for Mary notwithstanding, a lengthy round of fruitless negotiations was entered into, but by the beginning of 1565 Mary was still no nearer getting either a husband or the succession to the English throne. Then in February the young Lord Darnley arrived in Scotland, ostensibly to visit his father, the earl of Lennox.

It was an interesting enigma why Darnley, young, eligible and handsome, a Catholic with the royal blood of England and Scotland in his veins, should be suddenly allowed to travel to Scotland at this very moment with the express consent of Queen Elizabeth. The name of Darnley had always played a minor part in any discussion of Mary's possible suitors because of his position in both the Tudor and Stuart family trees, and because he was roughly the right age to be Mary's bridegroom.

Queen Mary could not fail to be interested in such an obvious candidate for marriage. The young man whom she saw before her was eminently handsome. In the contemporary portraits by Eworth, Darnley, at the age of eighteen, appears at first sight like a young god, with his golden hair, his perfectly shaped face and above all the magnificent legs stretching forth endlessly in their black hose. But on closer inspection the god appears to be more Pan than Apollo: there is something faun-like about his pointed ears, the beautiful slanting hazel eyes with their unreadable expression, and even a hint of cruelty in the exquisitely formed mouth with its full, rosy lips. His height and elegant physique could hardly fail to commend itself to Mary for two reasons. Firstly, beautiful as she was, Mary was nevertheless tall enough to tower over most of her previous companions. The psychological implications of this height can only be guessed at, but Darnley was certainly well over six feet one inch. Mary, for once, could feel herself not only overtopped at dancing, but also physically protected by her admirer if she so wished; as a novel sensation it could hardly have failed to be pleasant. Secondly, as Mary was also a woman of strong aesthetic instincts, she would tend to appreciate the effeminate beauty of Darnley more than the masculine vigour of some of her Scottish nobles.

The handsome youth had been well-trained in all the arts considered suitable for a gentleman of the period; he could ride a horse, hunt, dance gracefully and play the lute extremely well. The aim of his ambitious mother, Margaret Lennox, had been to make his courtly ways as winning as his outward appearance. To his internal qualities she had unfortunately paid less regard. Throughout his short life, Darnley showed remarkably little interest in any matters of the mind, and a single-minded concern for the pursuit of pleasure. The truth was that Darnley was thoroughly spoilt. He was also headstrong and ambitious; but he was ambitious only in so far as his mind could hold any concept for long enough to pursue it, since above all he desired the palm and not the race. It was the outward manifestations of power, the crown, the sceptre and the orb, which appealed to him: the realities of its practice made no appeal to his indolent and pleasure-loving temperament. Vanity was by far the strongest motive which animated him: it was vanity which made him seek out profligate companions and look for solace in the admiration of low company; it was vanity which brought about his quick, touchy temper and his fatally boastful nature; it was his vanity which made him incapable of assessing any person or situation at its true worth, since he could not help relating everything back to his own self-esteem.

None of this was apparent to Mary Queen of Scots at her first meeting with her cousin in Scotland. Her reaction was instantaneously romantic: she told Melville that 'he was the properest and best proportioned long man that ever she had seen . . .' From now on he was scarcely allowed to be away from her side.

Yet, however much Mary enjoyed the company of Darnley, she did not show any evidence of passion for him: Randolph weighed up the

An engraving of William Maitland, Mary's secretary and adviser, who married Mary Fleming.

OPPOSITE A portrait of Mary Queen of Scots painted about 1560–65, artist unknown.

OVERPAGE
LEFT Henry Lord Darnley and his younger brother Charles, painted by Hans Eworth when Darnley was seventeen.

RIGHT A portrait of Mary Queen of Scots and the future king James VI of Scotland and I of England, artist unknown.

favour she had showed him as proceeding 'of her own courteous nature' rather than anything more serious. In March Mary still seems to have regarded Darnley as one possible candidate among many. But in April the situation dramatically changed. Darnley fell ill – an illness which was to transform his fortunes and those of Mary Queen of Scots. The illness itself was of no great moment; it began with a cold and then turned to measles. Incarcerated in his sickroom in Stirling Castle, Darnley was visited with increasing frequency by the young queen. She constituted herself his nurse, and when measles was succeeded by an ague, she refused to ride forth to Perth until he was recovered and redoubled her care. Under the influence of the proximity of the sickroom, and the tenderness brought forth by the care of the weak and the suffering – and the handsome – Mary had fallen violently, recklessly and totally in love.

There can be no doubt that, whether Mary herself realized it or not, her feelings for Darnley were overwhelmingly physical. The demanding nature of her passion can easily be explained by pent-up longings which were the result of an inadequate first marriage, which had aroused few physical feelings in her and satisfied none. In the years since Francis's death she had led a life of celibacy. Her thoughts about marriage had been concentrated on the power it would bring her and she had shown little interest in the prospect of that great lover, the earl of Leicester, as a possible husband. Now at one touch of Darnley's hand, the caution, the concentration on the issue of her marriage in which Elizabeth's approval was so vital, the discretion and wisdom which all had praised in her during her four years as queen of Scotland – all were swept away in a tide of tumultuous feelings which Mary Stuart can scarcely have known she possessed.

Maitland was promptly dispatched to London to acquaint Elizabeth with the news and win her approval of the marriage – this sanction being doubly necessary because Darnley was not only a member of the English royal family through his Tudor descent but also held to be an English subject. Mary genuinely believed that she would receive this approval. Her confidence was easy to understand: Darnley had come north with the official blessing of England, and he was an English noble of the type whom Elizabeth had often observed that she wished Mary would marry. But now the honeyed trap – as Darnley turned out to be – was sprung. Mary to marry Darnley! No indeed; Elizabeth, made newly aware of the disapproval of the Scottish Protestants for a Catholic bridegroom and anxious to dissociate herself from the project, now took the line that the whole idea of the marriage was preposterous, and represented a renewed attempt on Mary's part to acquire the English throne for herself. Regardless of the fact that Darnley had gone north with her express permission, Elizabeth exploded with anger and demanded his instant return.

At this point Mary would surely have been wise to take serious thought. It was true that the approval of Philip of Spain and Charles IX of France had been sought and won but these approvals were nothing compared to the approval of Elizabeth, for after all Elizabeth could offer Mary what no other potentate had it in his power to extend – the reversion of her own throne. Over the question of Mary's marriage, hypocritically as she might behave, maddeningly as she might

THIS BE THE SONES OF Ħ RIGHT HONERABLES TERLLE OF LENOXE AD
TE LADY MARGARETZ GRACE, COVNTYES OF LENOXE AD ANGWYSE.

1563

CHARLLES STEWARDE
HIS BROTHER. ÆTATIS. 6.

HENRY STEWARDE LORD DAR̄
LEY AND DOWGLAS, ÆTATIS, 17,

Elizabeth I giving audience to two Dutch ambassadors. In this painting by an unknown artist, the Earl of Leicester and the Lord Admiral are among the councillors in the background.

procrastinate, Elizabeth was still in the position of paying the piper and therefore calling the tune. Only the rashest and most impetuous of women would have proceeded now on the same determined course without taking heed of Elizabeth's declared disapproval – but this was what love had apparently made Mary Stuart.

She was in no state to listen to the advice of even the sagest counsellor. Love was rampant in her heart for the first time, and she could hear no other voice except the dictates of her own passionate feelings. Randolph wrote to Leicester in anguish of his 'poor Queen whom ever before I esteemed so worthy, so wise, so honourable in all her doings', now so altered by love that he could hardly recognize her. To Cecil he described a queen seized with love 'all care of common wealth set apart, to the utter contempt of her best subjects'.

Darnley himself reacted predictably. In the same breath as he bewailed his once-honoured queen's infatuation, Randolph reported that Darnley was now grown so proud that he was intolerable to all honest men, and already almost forgetful of his duty to Mary – she who had adventured so much for his sake. Even those who had been his chief friends could no longer find words to defend him. Randolph made the gloomy, but as it proved singularly accurate, prophecy: 'I know not, but it is greatly to be feared that he can have no long life among these people.'

The truth was that even if Darnley had spoken with the tongues of men and of angels, Mary Stuart would have had problems in persuading her court to accept him as her bridegroom. The avowed hostility of England was fuel to the smouldering flames of Scottish hostility: Moray had viewed the match with great gloom from the start, since he had little

Elizabeth I giving audience to two Dutch ambassadors. In this painting by an unknown artist, the Earl of Leicester and the Lord Admiral are among the councillors in the background.

OPPOSITE The entrance to Holyrood Palace, Mary Queen of Scots' residence, where on 9 March 1566 Riccio was stabbed to death.

desire to see the rival Lennoxes raised up, and his own credit and influence with his sister debased. He withdrew from court at the beginning of April and the whole benefit of his advice and approval, which Mary had enjoyed for so long, was thus removed from her at one swoop. But, quite apart from Moray, there were other Scottish nobles who had ancient, feudal or hereditary reasons for disliking and fearing the Lennoxes.

All the while Mary was caught fast in the tangled bonds of passion. On

A double portrait of Mary Queen of Scots and Darnley, now hanging in Hardwick Hall.

29 July the heralds proclaimed that Darnley should henceforth be named and styled 'King of this our Kingdom'. This was Mary's ultimate proud pursuit of her own desires, since rightly she should have asked Parliament to give Darnley the coveted title of king. By bestowing it herself, she was pledging her full authority in the cause of her future husband. Finally on Sunday morning, 29 July, between five and six o'clock in the morning, a radiant Mary was conveyed to the chapel royal at Holyrood on the arm of her future father-in-law, the earl of Lennox, and the earl of

Argyll, there to await her chosen consort.

For this wedding, however, there was to be no dazzling white marriage robe for Mary Stuart, whatever the romantic passion which inspired her: she wore on the contrary a great mourning gown of black, with a wide mourning hood attached to it. This was to indicate that she came to her new husband not as a young and virgin girl, but as a widow, a queen dowager of France. Having been led into the chapel, she remained until her future husband was brought in by the same lords. They exchanged the vows of marriage according to the Catholic rite and three rings were put on Mary's finger, the middle one a gleaming diamond. Darnley then left Mary alone to hear Mass, abandoning her with a kiss, and himself going straight to her chamber to await her. With the marriage completed, Mary cast off her mourning garments to signify that she was about to embark upon 'a pleasanter life'.

There then followed the usual dancing and festivities of a nuptial celebration; if they did not compare with the grandiose ceremonies which had accompanied Mary's marriage to Francis, they were at least considered magnificent by Scottish standards. There was a banquet for the full court of nobles, the sound of trumpets, largesse scattered among the crowd and money thrown about the palace in abundance. After the dinner there was some dancing, and a brief respite for recovery, before the supper, as magnificent as had been the dinner. Finally, as Randolph reported, 'and so they go to bed'. It is to be hoped that Mary Stuart found at least this part of the ceremony to her satisfaction.

Sir William Cecil had commented on the ill-fated marriage of Leicester and Amy Robsart that carnal marriages begin with happiness and end in strife. Mary was allowed little enough time to enjoy the happiness of her own 'carnal marriage' before the first presages of strife were made apparent. Already, before her wedding, Moray had indulged in behaviour which was at best menacing, at worst plainly rebellious. Furious with Mary for her choice of Darnley as a husband, Moray's intention was to show that she was endangering the Protestant religion. But in her desire to win support for her marriage, Mary had on the contrary taken the trouble to court the favour of the reformers. Nor was Darnley himself a shining example to other members of the Catholic faith. Although a professed Catholic, he happily listened to the sermons of John Knox in St Giles Church, as well as avoiding the nuptial Mass to his own wedding. Darnley's faith appeared to have a chameleon quality about it which enabled it to assume whatever colour seemed convenient at the time. Mary's conciliatory attitude on the subject of religion showed up Moray's rebellion for what it was – jealous disaffection springing from feudally inspired hatred of the Lennoxes, with religious overtones introduced for the sake of English subsidies, rather than a genuine revolt of conscience.

In August Moray was 'put to the horn' after refusing to put in an appearance before his sister to explain his behaviour. Mary mustered troops to march against the rebels, and on 26 August she rode out of Edinburgh with Darnley swaggering at her side in gilt armour: she was swearing revenge on Moray, but the vivid emotion brought such a sparkle into her spirits that in the course of the campaign even Knox's narrative expressed admiration of her as she rode at the head of her troops: 'Albeit the most part waxed weary, yet the Queen's courage increased man-like, so much that she was ever with the foremost.'

In her absence Moray and Châtelherault entered the city; but they discovered that there was little support for them there. Mary had by now made herself extremely popular with the ordinary people – who in the course of her four years in Scotland had seen no evidence that she intended to deprive them of the practice of their new religion, and, their minds set at rest on this subject, positively enjoyed the acquisition of a young and beautiful queen, who understood better how to reach the hearts of her humbler subjects than those of her nobility. With no sign that help was to be forthcoming from Elizabeth, Moray realized his cause was hopeless and fled across the border into England.

It is difficult to explain Moray's conduct in terms of statesmanship: not only was Mary not threatening the Protestant religion at the end of July, but it was actually his rebellion which enabled Mary to send an emissary to Rome in September asking for a papal subsidy to assist her in the conflict. Mary had understandably been experiencing some difficulty in the past two years in convincing the pope that she truly had the cause of Scottish Catholicism at heart. Yet papal money continued to be a golden lure as was papal approval to one who might at any moment need foreign Catholic support: now Moray's rebellion, so publicly stated to be in the cause of Protestantism, presented the Scottish queen with a perfect opportunity to present herself in Rome as a champion of the Catholic faith. But the truth was that Moray, in his revolt, was no more championing Protestantism than Mary was championing Catholicism by attacking him. The composition of their respective parties shows how strongly feudal and family alliances still acted in Scottish politics. Moray had Châtelherault on his side, because the Hamiltons were perennially opposed to the Lennox Stewarts. Mary in turn reacted to Moray's revolt by pardoning young Lord Gordon, Huntly's son, and restoring him to his father's title, for the very good reason that the Huntlys were now the sworn enemies of Moray. Even Bothwell was allowed back into royal favour because his enmity against the Hamiltons could be relied on to keep him loyal to the queen.

The Chaseabout Raid, as Moray's abortive rebellion was called, marked a significant change in Mary's attitude to her Scottish nobles, which may not have been politically wise, but whose genesis was certainly easy to trace. In the course of four years her two major subjects had both revolted against her in the interests of their own power. She had defeated them both, married the man of her choice, and had been able to re-establish herself as a champion of the Scottish Catholic cause abroad, without in fact making as yet any significant concessions to the Catholics in Scotland. None of these experiences had taught her to trust her own nobility at any point where her interest might conflict with theirs: she therefore took the natural step of relying more and more on those who had no mighty Scottish lands and clans to back them up, no family feuds to sway them, and who did not belong to the spider's web of Scottish family relationships. Mary began to make use of a sort of middle-class

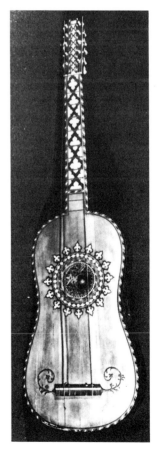

Riccio's guitar, now in the Royal College of Music, London.

A coin struck at the time of Mary's marriage to Darnley, and its obverse.

secretariat. These rising stars were 'crafty vile strangers' in Randolph's term, although Mary saw them as loyal and discreet servants. It was a move which was passionately resented by the nobles who saw themselves about to be edged out of the centre of a stage they had occupied so tempestuously and for so long.

Of these men, Davy or David Riccio, who was appointed Mary's secretary in 1564, was the most interesting character. He came of a good but impoverished Savoyard family and was of course a Catholic. The one fact on which everyone agreed – and which appears in every contemporary record whether by friend or foe – was that Riccio seemed extremely ugly by the standards of the time, his face being considered 'ill-favoured' and his stature small and hunched. Ugly as he might be, Riccio was generally conceded to be a fine musician, and music was Mary's private passion. He was also an amusing conversationalist.

To Mary, the loyalty of Riccio was at least beyond reproach, and she had a natural horror of disloyalty, especially when it accompanied ingratitude. The ingratitude of Moray seemed to her fantastic: here was a mere subject, on whom she had showered honours and goods, trying to prevent her marrying whom she pleased. Mary had *au fond* an unhypocritical and undissembling nature. Although she enjoyed the prospect and motions of intrigue, she lacked the disposition of the true intriguer. By nature frank and open, she was also passionate, quick to love, quick to hate, easy to weep, easy to laugh. This meant inevitably that she had a love of being committed: she preferred action, whatever the cost, to inaction, whatever the gain. Her fluctuating health may well have played some part in this; it was infinitely easier, in one of her nervous bouts of energy, to galvanize herself to spring forward than to rally her strength for a debilitating period of waiting. But such tendencies marked Mary off from the real plotters. Her love of commitment meant that in turn she felt bitterly betrayed when those around her seemed to neglect her interests for their own. Her fiercest hatreds were always reserved for those whom she had raised up and who now let her down – Moray came into this category and Darnley was shortly to enter into it.

Unfortunately this July marriage, begun in the high summer of love, did not preserve its warmth into the cooler temperatures of autumn and winter. At first, as Melville said, Mary was so delighted with her new acquisition, Darnley, that she did him great honour herself, and willed everyone who desired her favour to do the like and wait upon him. But after the honeymoon was over – a honeymoon spent, as it happened, virtually on the field of battle defending Darnley as a choice of husband – Mary was ready to return to the more serious business of ruling Scotland. In her work she was only too happy to have Darnley beside her – his signature, that of 'King Henry', was together with hers on every document, although Mary signed on the left (the position of honour because it was read first) and Darnley on the right (unlike Francis who had occupied the left). Yet Darnley was obviously not much interested in the process of government. He sulkily demanded the crown matrimonial (egged on by his father Lennox), and wished to spend more money than Mary, perpetually embarrassed in this respect, could easily provide: the crown matrimonial, which Francis had enjoyed, could only be granted by Parliament at the instance of Mary, but it would have ensured that Darnley's power was equal with Mary's while she lived, and continued after her death, if Darnley survived her. Darnley's way of showing himself worthy of this high honour was a strange one. He spent his time hunting, hawking and in the pursuit of pleasure, and governmental measures were often held up by his absence, since they demanded the joint signature. Eventually an iron stamp or seal was made of his signature to prevent delays and even Darnley's partisan, Buchanan, admitted that Darnley raised no objections to the practice.

At the beginning of December, Mary went to the palace of Linlithgow to convalesce after a recent indisposition. Her illness, a recurring pain in her side, may have been exacerbated by other more fruitful symptoms: she must now have been about two and a half months pregnant with the future James VI. The birth of an heir – preferably male – was of vital importance to Mary's plans; if she gave birth to a son, she would automatically be placed in a much stronger position with regard to the English succession than a mere childless queen.

The prospect of motherhood, much as she must have desired it for dynastic reasons – did not increase Mary's affection for Darnley. In view of the four-year gap in their ages, there may originally have been something quasi-maternal in Mary's feelings for the beautiful young Darnley, which she was now able to satisfy more conventionally in the prospect of impending motherhood. It is significant that her confidante Leslie, in his *Defence of her Honour*, deliberately chose to refer later to her 'very motherly care' for her husband. In addition, ill-health was obviously causing her discomfort which may in turn have caused distaste for the more physical aspects of married love. Certainly her violent infatuation for Darnley did not survive the onset of pregnancy.

The best summary of the points of difference between Mary and her husband is provided in the memoirs of Lord Herries. Mary believed 'all the honour and majesty he had came from her: that she had made choice of him for her husband by her own affection only, and against the will of many of the nobility'. Darnley, on the other hand, was complacently convinced that 'the marriage was done with the consent of the nobility who thought him worthy of the place; that the whole kingdom had their eyes upon him; they would follow and serve him upon the fields, where it was a shame a woman should command'. And as the memoirs added: 'These conceits [were] being continuously buzzed in the young man's head.' It was, however, quite one thing for Mary to get on badly with her husband, and for Darnley's young head to buzz, and quite another for this disagreement to be put to savage use by Mary's enemies. Darnley by himself was powerless, whatever his posturings. Darnley as the tool of Mary's opponents could have a cutting edge. For it was a regrettable fact that by the beginning of 1566 there were quite a number of Scottish nobles who were inclining to put themselves in the category of the queen's enemies. Their disputes with the queen had quite different origins from those of Darnley, but the combination of two forces of disaffection was capable of proving very dangerous for Mary – and fatal for her servant David Riccio.

6 Breakdown

'He misuses himself so far towards her that it is an heartbreak
for her to think that he should be her husband.'

MAITLAND, *on the relations between Mary and Darnley, October 1566*

I n January 1566 Queen Mary was in her own estimation riding high,
with her courage unimpaired and her resolution only strengthened
by the recent ordeal through which she had passed with such
success; the future, bringing with it the prospect of the birth of an
heir, looked bright to a woman whose nature combined spirit and
optimism with tenderness. But there was no denying that the opposition
which was building up against her both within and without Scotland had
an ugly aspect to it: if she had appreciated its real extent, even Mary in her
most buoyant mood might have experienced some unquiet moments
while she speculated just how and when such thunder clouds would
break into the fury of the storm.

First of all there were set steadily against her those Protestant lords
temporarily in exile, such as Moray; their primary desire was to return to
Scotland, but their hostility to Mary was given a new edge when she
threatened, in addition to banishment, to attaint them and declare their
properties forfeited at the forthcoming session of Parliament, to be held
in the spring.

Then there were the Kirk and Knox who feared to see Mary take
advantage of her new strength, since the defeat of Moray, to advance the
claims of the Catholic Church; this they also suspected she might try to
accomplish at the coming parliamentary session.

Added to these two groups were those other Protestant nobles within
the confines of Scotland, such as the earl of Morton and William Maitland, who hated to see Mary's 'base-born' advisers advanced to the
detriment of their own position. Riccio, as chief representative of this
despised and hated class, was the natural scapegoat for their hostility. He
was also the obvious suspect on whom Darnley could pour his rage and
jealousy against his wife – if such a jealousy could be focused on the
hunched figure of the little Italian. It was now the work of Mary's
opponents at court to incite the foolish, bombastic Darnley into such a
frenzy that he might be persuaded to join their own more serious
enterprises. In order to do so it was necessary to present to Darnley that
in the opinion of many Scottish nobles he, not Mary, would make the
most suitable ruler of Scotland. This was the notion which was now
'buzzed' in Darnley's excitable brain.

With extreme cynicism, the Scottish nobles, including Moray, were
now proposing a scheme which involved the coronation of the very
man against whose elevation they had rebelled in August. Darnley's

OPPOSITE Mary Queen of
Scots' house at Jedburgh,
where in October 1566 she
became so severely ill that
it was feared that she was
dying.

Catholicism was apparently no longer of account to the Protestant lords once their persons and properties were threatened.

It was now plainly suggested to Darnley that his wife was Riccio's mistress, and that the waning of his own power was due to the machinations of the Italian. Mary, conscious of her innocence, added fuel to the flames by openly finding pleasure in Riccio's company and his counsels. Could there have been any truth in the story? Neither Riccio's height nor his ugliness would have been any certain bar against a woman finding him desirable, since attraction follows its own rules. It is true that Mary herself did not appear to find men of this sort appealing – Darnley, young, elegant, beautiful and outwardly romantic was the type she apparently admired: all we know of her relations with Riccio, including her behaviour at his death, seems to fit into the pattern of ruler and confidant, rather than mistress and lover. But what really militates against the possibility of Mary having had a love affair with Riccio is the timing of it. Later the reproach was to be flung in the face of James VI that he was actually 'Davy's son'. In order for the accusation to be true the queen would have to have been indulging in a secret love affair with Riccio throughout the same summer in which she was so obviously infatuated with Darnley. It seems that the worst that Mary can be accused of is a certain lack of prudence, which was very much part of her character, rather than some more positive indiscretion.

The character of Darnley was like a tinderbox on which it was all too easy for the disaffected nobles to strike a flame using Riccio as a flint. Darnley's drunkenness was beginning to constitute a public problem and when Mary tried to restrain him, he insulted her. Nor was his drunkenness his only weakness: he searched for his pleasures in many different corners of human experience; on the one hand there were rumours of love affairs with court ladies; on the other, in a letter to Cecil in February, Sir William Drury hinted at something so vicious which had taken place at a festivity at Inch-Keith, too disgraceful to be named in a letter, that Mary now slept apart from her husband.

Despite the anxiety caused by Darnley's behaviour, Mary persisted in her plan to hold a Parliament in March at which the Protestant lords who had rebelled would be attainted and their properties forfeited. She turned a deaf ear to any suggestion that they should be pardoned, with the exception of Châtelherault, who had been forgiven on condition he went into exile for five years. Under these circumstances the two-pronged conspiracy to restore these lords and give Darnley the crown matrimonial went forward. In a letter to Leicester, Randolph hinted at 'things intended against her own [Mary's] person', for let us not forget what was surely ever-present in the minds of Lennox and Darnley, that if Mary vanished from the scene and her unborn child never saw the light of day, Darnley had an excellent chance of becoming king of Scotland in his own right. It was a propitious moment for the Lennox Stewarts, since the head of the Hamiltons was abroad in disgrace.

A bond was now drawn up and signed by the conspirators; these included Morton, George Douglas the Postulate, his illegitimate half-brother, Ruthven, Lindsay and Argyll, as well as Moray, who signed it at Newcastle. The declared intentions of the signatories were the acquisition of the crown matrimonial for Darnley, the upholding of the Protestant religion and the return of the exiles. The lords were careful to obtain Darnley's signature in order that he should be as thoroughly implicated as themselves; but in all the clauses of the bond there was no mention of any sort of violence or of David Riccio. Only one item had a faintly menacing ring: 'So shall they not spare life or limb in setting forward all that may bend to the advancement of his [Darnley's] honour.'

In the meantime the behaviour of Riccio, like that of Darnley, played into the hands of the conspirators, for Riccio's arrogance matched Darnley's vanity. An astrologer tried to tell him of the dangers of his situation and of his unpopularity, and warned him to 'beware of the bastard'; Riccio assumed this referred to Moray and confidently replied: 'I will take good care that he never sets foot in Scotland again' – forgetting that the description could apply to a number of other people in sixteenth-century Scotland. Similarly, Mary brushed aside Sir James Melville's warnings of rumours and 'dark speeches' that he had heard.

On Thursday 7 March, Parliament assembled, and the following Tuesday was fixed as the day on which the bill of attainder against Moray would be passed. The fixing of this date automatically induced the climax of the conspirators' plans. On the evening of Saturday 9 March, the queen was holding a small supper party in her apartments at the palace of Holyrood; advancing pregnancy and ill-health had made her increasingly disinclined to go about in Edinburgh, preferring the company of her intimates at home. Those present with her all fell into this cosy category – her half-brother Lord Robert Stewart, her half-sister and confidante Jean, countess of Argyll, her equerry Arthur Erskine, her page Anthony Standen, and of course her secretary and musician, David Riccio. Perhaps there was to be music later, or perhaps this was to be one of those evenings, which Darnley so much resented, when the queen and Riccio played at cards until one or two in the morning. At any rate the atmosphere was innocuous and domestic rather than exciting.

Mary's apartments in Holyrood lay in the north-west corner of the palace, on the second floor; the rooms were four in number – a large presence chamber at the head of the main staircase, a bed-chamber of considerable size lying directly off it, and off that again two very small rooms in each corner, not more than twelve foot square, one a type of dressing-room, the other a supper-room. Beneath these apartments, on the first floor of the palace, lay Darnley's rooms. The two sets of apartments were connected by a narrow privy staircase which came out in the queen's bedroom, close to the entrance to the supper-chamber. The heart of Mary's apartments was indeed a curious place from which to pluck one of her own servants, since there were the guards surrounding the queen's person to be taken into account. How much simpler it would have been to kill a mere servant in some other less public place. The fact that the murder was deliberately planned to take place in the presence of the queen when she was nearly six months pregnant points to some malevolent intentions towards her own person as well as the elimination of a presumptuous servant.

As supper was being served, to the great surprise of those present, the figure of Darnley suddenly appeared up the privy staircase; although he

Patrick, Lord Ruthven, 'a highly unsavoury character', who led the assassins of David Riccio, Mary's secretary.

was by now a comparative stranger to these domestic occasions, he was still welcomed as the king. But a few minutes later there was a far more astonishing apparition on the staircase – Lord Ruthven, burning-eyed and pale from the illness of which he was generally thought to be dying on his sick-bed. So amazing was his emergence at the queen's supper party, that the first reaction of those present was that he was actually delirious. However, his first words left the queen in no doubt as to what had brought this death's head to her feast. 'Let it please your Majesty', said Ruthven, 'that yonder man David come forth of your privy-chamber where he hath been overlong.' Mary replied with astonishment that Riccio was there at her own royal wish and asked Ruthven whether he had taken leave of his senses. To this Ruthven merely answered that Riccio had offended against the queen's honour. On hearing these words, the queen turned quickly and angrily to her husband, realizing the Judas-like quality of his visit, and asked him if this was his doing. Ruthven then launched into a long and rambling denunciation of Mary's relations with Riccio, reproaching her for her favour to him, and for her banishment of the Protestant lords. Riccio had shrunk back into the large window at the end of the little room, and when Ruthven made a lunge towards him, Mary's attendants, who seem to have been stunned into inaction, at last made some sort of protest. 'Lay not hands on me, for I will not be handled,' cried Ruthven, with his hand on his dagger: this was the signal for his followers to rush into the room from the privy staircase, pistols and daggers at the ready. In the ensuing confusion the table was knocked over, and Lady Argyll was just able to save the last candle from being extinguished by snatching it up as it fell (although presumably the flickering light from the fireplace still filled the little room). Riccio clung to the queen's skirts until he was dragged, screaming and kicking, from the room, across the bedroom, through the presence chamber to the head of the stairs. His pathetic voice could be heard calling as he went:

'Justizia, justizia! Sauvez ma vie, madame, sauvez ma vie!'

Here he was done to death by dagger wounds variously estimated at between fifty-three and sixty: a savage butchery for a small body. Mary was convinced later that the first blow had been struck over her shoulder: at all events, the first knife wound was made by George Douglas, Morton's illegitimate brother, thus fulfilling the prophecy concerning the bastard; he carefully used Darnley's own dagger for the bloody deed in order to involve him still further in the crime.

For the rest of her life, Mary Stuart was to believe that her own life had been threatened in the course of the tumult in the supper-room and that Darnley had intended to compass her own destruction and that of her unborn child. It is indeed impossible to understand her later attitude to Darnley without taking into account this steadfast inner conviction. But the quality of Mary Stuart's spirit, her courage and daring, was proof

A sketch of the tiny supper room in Holyrood Palace from which David Riccio was dragged to be stabbed brutally to death. Through the open door lies the Queen's bedroom.

85

even against such an appalling experience, despite her condition.

When Ruthven, Darnley and the others had departed, Mary sent one of her ladies for news of Riccio's fate. When she was told that he was dead, she wept for a moment, but then she dried her tears and exclaimed: 'No more tears now; I will think upon revenge.'

So far the conspirators seemed to be in complete command of the situation, except for the annoying fact that their other intended victims, Bothwell and Huntly, had escaped by jumping out of a back window of the palace. It had been intended to slay these two as well as Riccio, as being all adherents of the queen. This very night, when the conspirators' triumph seemed certain, was crucial in the history of Mary Stuart. At some point in the course of it she took the bold decision to choke down her feelings of revulsion for Darnley and win him over to her side, reasoning that the character of Darnley might now be the weakness of the conspirators' cause, as it had once been the weakness of her own. Therefore, when at daybreak the next morning, Sunday, Darnley went once more to her chamber, he found his wife calm rather than reproachful, and during that day she won back her facile husband by convincing him that his own prospects were as bleak as hers under the new regime. It was a triumph of a stronger character over a weaker one.

Armed with the knowledge of Darnley's new treachery, Mary was able to greet the conspirators the next day with composure and even charm. She promised pardon and that she would overlook recent hideous events. Moray, apprised of what was about to take place, had set off from Newcastle: he arrived back in Edinburgh on the Monday, the day before his attainder had been due to be passed by Parliament. Mary, unaware of Moray's complicity in the plot, and remembering their intimacy of old, flung herself into his arms, crying: 'Oh my brother, if you had been here, they had not used me thus.' The lords remained suspicious of Mary's true feelings, despite her promise of pardon, and she was compelled to feign the pangs of labour in order to preserve secrecy about her intentions. On the Monday evening Mary carried the second stage of her plan into effect by sending for Stewart of Traquair, the captain of the royal guard, Erskine her equerry, and Standen, one of her pages; she begged them in the name of chivalry to assist her not only as a defenceless woman, but also as the mother of the future king of Scotland. These gallant gentlemen proved susceptible to her appeal, and promised to stand by her escape, in the manner she now outlined.

At midnight the queen and Darnley made their way down the privy staircase, up which the assassins had filed only fifty-two hours before, and out through the servants' quarters of Holyrood. Outside to meet the royal couple were Erskine, Traquair, Standen and two or three loyal soldiers with horses. Mary mounted pillion behind Erskine and in a short while, under the friendly cover of darkness, they were clear of the town.

The plan was to go to Dunbar Castle. The ride was of necessity fast, and as furious as possible. Even so, Darnley, in a panic of fear at being hunted down by the men he had so recently betrayed, kept spurring his own horse and flogging that of the queen, shouting: 'Come on! Come on! By God's blood, they will murder both you and me if they can catch us.' Mary pleaded with him to have regard to her condition, at which

Darnley only flew into a rage and exclaimed brutally that if this baby died, they could have more. By the time they reached Dunbar Castle, on the coast, twenty-five miles from Edinburgh as the crow flies, the long night was almost over. For a woman in an advanced state of pregnancy, a five-hour marathon of this nature must have been a gruelling ordeal. Even now, the queen's formidable courage did not desert her, and she set about the task of consolidating the advantage which her liberty had given her.

The escape of Bothwell and Huntly proved decisive. Atholl, Fleming and Seton also came to her at Dunbar. Men began to flock to the queen's side, stirred up by these loyal agents. On 18 March she was able to re-enter Edinburgh victoriously at the head of 8,000 men, only nine days after the murder which had caused her to flee from the city so precipitately.

Darnley rode beside her, like a sulky page. At the news of his defection, his fellow-plotters had fled from Edinburgh on the morning of 17 March, realizing that their rebellion no longer had any focal point. Moray alone remained in Edinburgh since he had cunningly arrived in the city too late to be implicated in the bloody events of the night of 9 March.

It was easy enough, once Mary was back in Edinburgh, to rescue the body of Riccio from its common grave, and have it reburied according to the Catholic rite in her own royal chapel. Yet the murder of the Italian had marked a turning-point in the affairs of Mary Queen of Scots, and the memories of the affair were not so easily laid in peace and forgotten as his poor lacerated corpse.

The most obvious result was Mary's abiding hatred of Darnley. She had either concealed this in order to facilitate her escape from Holyrood, or else she did not at this point realize the full extent of her husband's complicity. Either way, the conspirators now took the understandable if vindictive step of sending the bond to the queen, so that she should see for herself the full extent of her husband's treachery. Yet once more Mary was obliged to put a good face upon the situation for the time being, and issue a public statement of his innocence. It was not within the compass of her thoughts to take any action against her husband before the birth of her child, since Darnley was quite capable of casting doubts upon the child's legitimacy, if it suited his purpose. In his reflective moments Darnley must have realized that he was now a marked man. Of the powers that then existed in Scotland – the queen, Moray and his associates, Bothwell and the loyalist nobles, he had betrayed them all or tried to attack them at one or other point in his career. Should these potential enemies flag, there was also a whole new ferocious band of them headed by Morton, now in England, who might not stay there forever.

As Mary's relations with Darnley settled down into an uneasy truce until the birth of her child, it was natural that she should come to rely increasingly for political advice on those nobles who had proved themselves loyal to her throughout the two crises which she had faced in the past year. Into this category fell notably James Hepburn, earl of

Bothwell, who seemed to display that combination of resource, loyalty and strength which Mary had so persistently sought among her Scottish nobles. Bothwell was now reconciled with Moray and allied by marriage to Huntly, having married his sister Jean Gordon, and he seemed set in Mary's estimation to form a useful loyal member of the Scottish polity. Yet Bothwell in his character seemed to sum up those very paradoxical contrasts which made it so difficult, for anyone not brought up among them, to understand the nature and behaviour of the Scottish nobles. In the past Mary had been baffled and angered by Huntly, puzzled and hurt by Moray. Now she was once again, by the unwitting fault of her French upbringing, to make a mistake of judgement and see in Bothwell the mirage – it was no more than that – of a strong, wise protector, able to solve her problems by holding down the other nobles under his heel.

Bothwell was not a stupid man; he had been well educated and was well travelled. He came of the great border family of Hepburns, and, like all his class, was keenly interested in the acquisition of official positions, such as lieutenant of the borders, which would extend his family's power. Yet the effect of Bothwell's concentration on the possibilities of the main chance had in fact given him a far better record of loyalty to the central government than most of his contemporaries. As a feudal baron, and primarily a soldier, he was apt to choose the quick, if bloody,

Edinburgh Castle, to which Mary was able to return victoriously, nine days after the murder of Riccio, at the head of 8,000 men.

solution to any problem. It was true that during his brief spell as the queen's husband Bothwell showed signs of a certain administrative ability, as a soldier can sometimes make a successful politician in a crisis, but his personal qualities negated his usefulness in any delicate situation, and made him the last person to unite successfully that essentially disunited and suspicious body, the Scottish nobility. For one thing, Bothwell's violence and boastfulness scarcely led to popularity, and he was certainly not a man who was prepared to try using charm to gain his objectives. In appearance Bothwell lacked the hermaphrodite beauty of a Darnley; he was but of middle stature and the only known portrait traditionally said to be of him shows a face which is certainly not conventionally handsome. It is the face of a man who might well prove attractive to certain types of women, because it is strong and vital, yet from another point of view it gives the impression of one to whom the defence of the rights of the weak would seem a thorough waste of time.

At the beginning of June Mary began to make preparations for the birth of her child. At the wish of her Council, she had been lodged in Edinburgh Castle since early April; the great castle frowning on its rock over the town below was evidently felt to be a safer locality for this important event than Holyrood, so recently demonstrated to have the flimsiest defences. It would also be understandable if Mary herself had

'Queen Mary's Room' in Edinburgh Castle where the future James I of England and VI of Scotland was born 19 June 1566.

The cradle used by Mary Queen of Scots for her son, James.

been reluctant to give birth to her child in the same apartments where her servant had been butchered. On 3 June the queen took to her lying-in chamber ceremoniously, according to the custom of the time, to await the confinement, and on Wednesday, 19 June, after a long, painful and difficult labour, the baby prince was born; despite the length of the labour, he was an impressively healthy child.

The birth of a male heir was signalled with immense rejoicings in Edinburgh, and five hundred bonfires were lit to illuminate the city and the surrounding hills with their festive flames. The whole artillery of the castle was discharged and lords, nobles and people gathered together in St Giles Church to thank God for the honour of having an heir to their kingdom, the fact that St Giles was the main Protestant church demonstrating the great legacy of goodwill which awaited any queen who gave birth to a healthy prince in this era. Sir James Melville rode off to London to break the news to Queen Elizabeth. The English queen reacted with her famous outcry, the primitive complaint of the childless woman for a more favoured sister: 'Alack, the Queen of Scots is lighter of a bonny son, and I am but of barren stock.' It was true that the birth of James duly enhanced Mary's merits as a candidate for the English throne, but it also inevitably moved the child's own father, Darnley, further down the line of succession for both the English and Scottish thrones. Queen Mary, aware of the temperament with which she was dealing, took care to display the baby to him publicly and announce: 'My Lord, God has given you and me a son, begotten by none but you.' She went on, uncovering the child's face: 'Here I protest to God as I shall answer to him at the great day of Judgement, that this is your son and no other man's son. I am desirous that all here bear witness.' She added, as though to clinch the matter by a note of contempt for her husband: 'For he is so much your own son, that I fear it will be the worse for him hereafter'. Having thus, as she hoped, preserved her child from the stigma of illegitimacy, Mary devoted the rest of her time in Edinburgh Castle to his care, having the baby to sleep in her own room, and frequently watching over him at night.

The birth of James had two dramatic effects upon Mary Stuart: she no longer had any pressing motive for demonstrating a public reconciliation with Darnley, and at the same time her own extremely precarious health had its balance finally destroyed. There is no evidence that she ever really recovered it before her extremely serious illness at Jedburgh four months later, and this illness in turn led to a prolonged phase of highly nervous, almost hysterical ill-health which lasted right through until her incarceration on Lochleven the following June. But for her actions and movements during the next eight months, the critical period from the birth of James in June 1566 until the death of Darnley in February 1567, it is extremely important to distinguish between information and reports written at the time – that is to say before the death had taken place – such as ambassadors' comparatively impartial reports on the state of Scotland, and those accounts written long after the evènt specifically to prove Mary's guilt with Bothwell, such as Buchanan's *Book of the Articles*, written as an accusatory brief at the time of her trial in England.

It is a remarkable fact that there is no uncontested evidence among the letters or reports written before Darnley's death, whether French, English or Scottish, to show that Mary was involved in a sexual affair with Bothwell while her husband was still alive. The picture of the Scottish court through the autumn and winter of 1566, built by contemporary comments, is of a queen to whom her husband was becoming an increasingly distasteful problem, and a nobility to whom he was becoming an increasingly urgent one. Not one observer made any attempt during this period to connect the queen's growing scorn for Darnley with a growing affection for Bothwell, although the point would have been one which the ever-watchful ambassadors would have been delighted to make if they had felt it to be true. Of the couple, Mary and Bothwell, Mary was wracked in health, not in itself very conducive to romance, and desperate to solve her marital problems; she was also well aware by now that she had created these problems for herself originally through her physical infatuation for Darnley; the very last intention in her mind was to tread so soon again down the treacherous paths of passion. Bothwell on the other hand was steadily bent on his own personal advancement in Scottish government affairs. It is questionable whether the one had the energy, and the other the inclination for the time-wasting business of an adulterous love affair when there were so many important matters to hand.

In view of the state of her health and her convictions that Darnley had aimed at her death and that of her child, Mary's refusal to grant him his conjugal rights would be easy to understand: but of course it could scarcely be expected to lead to happier relations between them and his humiliation as a husband was one of Darnley's main points of complaint. The most likely state of affairs between them during July and August would seem to be an occasional reluctant acquiescence on the part of the queen to her husband's embraces, which did little to convince Darnley that she either loved or respected him. After Mary's illness, and especially once the matter of a divorce had been broached at Craigmillar, her abstinence from any physical relationship was certainly total: by then she clearly wished to have nothing more to do with him as a husband.

Since her return to Edinburgh after the murder of Riccio, Mary had taken the trouble to reconcile her subjects to each other and to her. In September du Croc, the French ambassador, reported to Catherine de Medicis the newly excellent relations which existed between Queen Mary and her subjects – they were 'so well reconciled with the Queen as a result of her own prudent behaviour, that nowadays there was not a single division to be seen between them'. Darnley, on the other hand, was equally ill-regarded by both parties.

In early October Mary travelled to Jedburgh, in the Scottish border country, to hold a justice eyre. While there she received news that her lieutenant on the borders, Bothwell, had been seriously wounded in a foray, and was now lying in danger of death at the castle of Hermitage. The queen did not immediately take any action, but five days later she decided to pay Bothwell a visit, not so much to express her sympathy, as for the practical reason that he was her lieutenant and one of her chief advisers, and she needed to consult with him. Bedford, reporting the incident, commented that the queen of Scots would certainly have been

sorry to lose Bothwell, but made no remotely bawdy suggestion about the loss, which was by implication a strictly political or administrative one.

On 16 October, the queen, accompanied by Moray and a large number of her court, as well as a quantity of soldiers, decided to ride over to the Hermitage, visit Bothwell, and, since this border fortress was not prepared to receive the luxurious burden of a royal stay, return to Jedburgh that same day. The day's journey meant a ride of a little over fifty miles. Although a good day's ride at the time was considered to be thirty to forty miles, it was always considered possible to ride more than fifty miles in emergencies: the ride was not an outstanding hardship to a queen accustomed to daily hunting and riding hard in the saddle all her life.

However, on her return to Jedburgh Queen Mary fell violently and seriously ill. Undoubtedly the ride contributed to the final impetus of her collapse, but she had evidently been sickening in her habitual and, as it seemed, nervous fashion for some sort of breakdown for weeks, since the situation with Darnley seemed to admit no solution. Physical and mental stress now apparently combined to produce an attack of illness so severe that many of those who observed Mary in the throes of it formed the opinion that she was unlikely to recover, even if she was not already dead. First the queen was seized by a prolonged fit of vomiting – 'more than sixty times' – so long and severe that she several times fell into unconsciousness; two days later, she could neither speak nor see, and had frequent convulsions. There was a temporary recovery, but by 25 October she had become so rapidly ill again – 'all her limbs were so contracted, her face was so distorted, her eyes closed, her mouth fast and her feet and arms stiff and cold' – that she was once more considered to be

Hermitage Castle, Roxburghshire, the castle on the borders of Scotland belonging to James Hepburn, Earl of Bothwell, where Mary visited him in October 1566 when he was lying seriously wounded after a foray.

93

on the verge of death. The situation was saved by the queen's physician who seeing some signs of life in her arms, bandaged her very tightly, including her toes and legs from the ankle upwards, and then having her mouth opened by force, poured wine down it. He then administered a clyster, the queen vomited an amount of corrupt blood, and subsequently began to recover.

Throughout this period of illness, Darnley scarcely showed himself the devoted husband. He was in the west of Scotland when Mary fell ill and did not, as Buchanan and Knox afterwards stated, come rushing to his wife's side. He paid the queen a brief visit eleven days after she first fell ill, and then returned to Glasgow.

The next episode in the mounting tragedy of Darnley took place at the end of November at the castle of Craigmillar, an enormous baronial edifice on the outskirts of Edinburgh. Mary was still in the hands of her physicians, since her illness, and was apparently in a state of deep depression. Du Croc commented that no future understanding could be expected between the queen and her husband for the two reasons of his arrogance and her suspicion. Since the murder of Riccio, Mary evidently regarded herself as permanently threatened by some possible conspiracy on the part of Darnley. But Mary's chief nobles were equally resolute in their hatred of Darnley, who had betrayed them over Riccio and was yet still left nominally able to lord it over them as king of Scotland. Experience had not curbed Darnley's arrogance: nor were nobles of the temperament of Moray, Argyll, Bothwell and Maitland likely to forgive and forget.

According to the 'Protestation' of Huntly and Argyll (written in January 1569 when Huntly and Argyll formed part of the Marian party), Moray and Maitland now broached the subject of a divorce to Argyll; Huntly was then brought in, finally Bothwell; then the queen was approached. Maitland opened up the argument by saying that means would be found for Mary to divorce Darnley, if she would only pardon Morton and the other Riccio assassins still in exile. The queen promised her consent, but said that the divorce must be legally obtained without prejudice to her son. Maitland then suggested 'other means' and in a famous phrase told the queen that 'Moray would look through his fingers'. At this the queen quickly asked them to do nothing against her honour, and Maitland replied: 'Let us guide the matter among us, and your Grace shall see nothing but good, and approved by Parliament.' This was in effect to be the case of Mary's supporters in later years, to prove her innocence over the death of Darnley. They maintained that the queen, although anxious to rid herself of Darnley, could not have known that the nobles actually intended to kill him, since Maitland had assured her that whatever happened would have parliamentary approval. But of course Mary was not, and was never intended to be, one of the executive conspirators; the details of the deed were not within the province of her concern, although it was difficult to see what 'other means' Maitland was contemplating, except perhaps a treason trial of Darnley before Parliament which would result in his execution. Mary, however, did not examine the situation so candidly in her own mind. She was a queen and a woman; as a woman she wished to be rid of an intolerable marital situation; as a queen she expected her nobles to help in a difficult governmental problem of order; there could be no benefit to her thinking too far or too early into how the nobles proposed to carry out her wishes. If Moray was quoted as intending to 'look through his fingers', Queen Mary intended to keep her own hands tightly across her eyes.

It seems virtually certain that a bond was then drawn up and signed at Craigmillar by those nobles who intended to get rid of Darnley, including Maitland, Bothwell, Argyll, Huntly and James Balfour, with Morton signing later on his return to Scotland, much as a bond was signed before the murder of Riccio. Following the parallel with the Riccio bond, it is unlikely that the murder was specifically mentioned in the document. Moray did not sign the Craigmillar bond although he certainly knew of its contents.

In December the queen was able to turn her mind from her vexatious problems with her husband to the happier matter of her son's baptism. Shortly after the birth, messages had been sent to the king of France, the duke of Savoy and the queen of England to act as godparents. Darnley objected to the inclusion of Elizabeth, because of her animosity towards him (she had never officially countenanced his marriage), but his objections were overruled by Mary who visualized a golden future for her son James if Elizabeth's goodwill could be secured. On 17 December the ceremony took place, according to the Catholic rite, in the chapel royal of Stirling Castle. The little prince, now just on six months old, was carried in the arms of the count of Brienne, proxy for the king of France, from the royal apartments to the chapel between two rows of courtiers, the whole scene lit by flaring torches. M. du Croc represented the duke of Savoy. Queen Elizabeth had sent a magnificent gold font as a present for her godson. But as Bedford, her emissary, was a leading English Puritan, he could not stand proxy for her at the font. Thus Jean, countess of Argyll, the child's aunt, acted as proxy godmother for Elizabeth and held James in her arms.

The accomplishment of the ceremony was celebrated with all the magnificence which Queen Mary could command. She clothed the nobility at her own expense for the occasion, 'some in cloth of silver, some in cloth of gold, some in cloth of tissue, every man rather above than under his degree', and afterwards there were fireworks and masques.

In all these rejoicings, there was only one mysteriously absent figure, that of the baby's father, 'King Henry' himself, although he was actually present in the castle of Stirling at the time. It has been suggested that his absence was due to his continued bad relations with Queen Elizabeth and because Bedford had been instructed not to give him his due as king of Scotland. But no such instructions have been discovered. It seems more likely that Darnley hated the idea of the English, from whose ranks he sprang, whom he had once scorned, seeing how far he had fallen in prestige at the Scottish court; it would certainly be in his character to avoid any occasion of public humiliation, real or imaginary. At the end of December, Darnley left Stirling abruptly and went to Glasgow, the traditional centre of Lennox Stewart power, where he hoped to be more royally treated.

7 The Murder of Darnley

'I'll pity thee as much' he said
'And as much favour I'll show to thee
As thou had on the Queen's chamberlain
That day you deemedst him to die'

BOTHWELL *to* Darnley, *from the ballad* Earl Bothwell

In October at Jedburgh Mary Queen of Scots had nearly died. At Glasgow in the New Year Darnley in his turn fell extremely ill. At the time it was given out that he had smallpox, but it seems more likely that he was actually suffering from syphilis. Bothwell, in his own narrative of events written during his captivity in Denmark, *Les Affaires du Conte de Boduel*, took the trouble to cross out the words *petite vérole* (smallpox) and insert *roniole* (syphilis) in his own handwriting. Darnley's skull, now in the Royal College of Surgeons in London, was analysed by Sir Daniel Wilson and discovered to be pitted with traces of 'a virulent syphilitic disease'. The queen did not immediately visit her husband, but she did show her habitual humanity: she sent him her doctor and gave orders for the royal linen to be cut into ruffs for the king's nightshirt.

Despite this kindness, clearly she was still pondering in her mind legal ways and means of ridding herself of this degenerate creature as a husband. For Darnley was still in some respects dangerous, even though he was threatened from so many quarters. He was clever enough to see that he had a possible line of attack against Mary in her determinedly *laissez-faire* policy towards the Scottish Catholic Church, and he was unscrupulous enough to contemplate blackening her reputation in the eyes of the Catholic powers abroad with the aim of elevating himself, as the champion of the Catholic faith, in Scotland. It will never be known exactly how much of this 'Catholic' plot existed in the imagination of Darnley, or indeed Darnley's enemies, and how much reality there was behind the rumours and suspicions. But certainly at the turn of the year there were whispers that Darnley was once more intriguing against his wife which were loud enough to reach the queen's ears.

On 20 January Mary set off for Glasgow to bring back her sick husband on a litter to Edinburgh, to finish off his convalescence in her own company. In view of the dispassionate contempt which she quite openly held for him, it is necessary to consider exactly what prompted her to make the journey. It is true that Mary had always displayed courteous kindness towards Darnley's sufferings; but some more compelling argument than sheer humanity must be advanced to explain her actions – and also to explain what is every bit as mysterious, why Darnley so readily agreed to follow her back.

In January some sort of conference took place at Whittingham, one of the Douglas castles, between Bothwell, Morton, newly returned to

Are to be ſould in Popes head Alley at the white hoſe
by Iohn Sudbury and Georg Humble

The moſt illuſtrious Prince Henry, Lord Darnly, King of Scotland, father
to our Soueraigne lord King Iames. He died at the age of 21. 1567.

The moſt excellent Princeſſe Marie Queene of Scotland, mother to our Soueraigne lord King Iames. She died. 1586. and intombed at Weſtminſter.

R. Elſtrack
ſculp.

A posthumous double
portrait, the caption of
which does little to
indicate the true nature of
the deaths of Darnley and
Mary.

A contemporary sketch, sent to Cecil in London, of the scene after the murder of Darnley at Kirk o'Field in February 1567. *Top left*: the figure of the infant James, Darnley's son, in his cradle, with the legend 'Judge and Avenge my cause, O Lord'. *Left centre*: the quadrangle of houses attached to St Mary, Kirk o'Field, showing the house which had contained Darnley as a heap of rubble after the explosion. *Centre*: the town hall, on to which Darnley's house backed directly. *Top right*: the figures of Darnley and his servant in the gardens, with a chair, a cloak and a dagger beside them. *Below left*: the dead body of Darnley being carried away, watched by the crowd.

Scotland, his cousin Archibald Douglas, and Maitland. The exact truth of what happened at this conference is impossible to establish, since afterwards, once the nobles concerned were on different political sides, each accused the other of having raised the subject of Darnley's murder. However, it is clear that a plan was beginning to take shape, although it is important to notice that neither party suggested that the queen had any foreknowledge of it. But there was one detail in which the queen could help them: their plan demanded that Darnley should be in Edinburgh or thereabouts, rather than Glasgow, where he was surrounded by his own Lennox Stewart adherents. It is possible that, to this end, Maitland indicated to Mary that in practical terms it was unwise to allow Darnley to remain in Glasgow where he might manage to work up an effective conspiracy against her. Equally, the queen herself may have needed no particular prompting to see that it was safer to have Darnley under her own eyes, where experience had taught her that it was easier to control him, than loose in the countryside, either plotting or breeding dissension with his wild schemes.

The question still arises exactly how Mary induced her husband to accompany her back to Edinburgh: for it is clear that once Mary arrived in Glasgow, she experienced no difficulty in persuading him to make the move. Darnley freely consented to the plan, and this despite the fact that he had heard some rumour of what had transpired at Craigmillar. The promise which Mary seems most likely to have held out to Darnley was the resumption of full marital relations on his return to health. Mary's coldness as a wife wounded his vanity as a man, and also, he felt, threatened his status as a king, there being more to the embraces of a queen than the mere feel of her arms around him. This promise would have been enough to rouse Darnley's ambitions all over again, to rekindle his hopes of future grandeur as king: in this way he went willingly out of his own feudal domain of influence into hers.

The only subject on which the queen and king now disagreed was the place where Darnley should spend the rest of his convalescence: he needed constant baths to improve his condition and his face was still shrouded with a piece of taffeta. Mary had intended to bring him to the castle of Craigmillar, a little way outside Edinburgh, that same castle where the bond had been signed. Darnley, however, declined to enter the stronghold, as his own servants testified. Perhaps he was afraid to do so. He chose instead – and once again there is general agreement that the choice was his, not the queen's – a house of moderate size on the outskirts of Edinburgh, in a quadrangle known as Kirk o'Field.

The house in which Darnley now settled for the last days of his recovery was in many ways ideally suited for the state of convalescence. It lay on a slight eminence and the site was open and healthy compared to the low-lying Holyrood; as Bishop Leslie said, the air was thought by doctors to be the most salubrious in the whole town. It was far enough from Holyrood for the king's illness not to be an embarrassment to him, yet it had the security of lying just within the town wall.

Darnley took up residence in his new dwelling on Saturday, 1 February. The last week of his life was pleasant and almost domesticated. Queen Mary felt confident that her husband had for the time being no opportunity to weave any plot against her, especially as his father Lennox, so often his evil genius in feeding his childish vanity with praise, was still in Glasgow. The courtiers settled into a routine of visiting Darnley at Kirk o'Field and then returning to the royal palace at Holyrood for the other formal ceremonies of court life. Relations at this point between Darnley and his wife were perfectly amicable. On the Wednesday the queen spent the night at Kirk o'Field. According to her own account, propinquity now led to newly friendly relations between them.

While Darnley and Mary jogged through their last week of marriage in comparative peace, Bothwell and his fellow conspirators had been hard at work to compass the death of the one and the deliverance of the other. Darnley could not be expected to stay in the lodging forever and Holyrood with its guards obviously presented more of a problem from the point of view of assassination than Kirk o'Field. ·

Sunday, 9 February was to be the last day of Darnley's convalescence. It was announced that he would return to Holyrood early on the Monday. It was also the last Sunday before the beginning of Lent, and, as such, a day of carnival and rejoicing; two events typical of the life of Queen Mary's court were planned to take place. In the morning Mary's favourite valet Bastian Pages married Christiana Hogg, and in the afternoon a formal dinner was given by the bishop of the Isles for the returning ambassador of Savoy. Afterwards, the queen and her court rode down to Kirk o'Field in order to spend the evening with Darnley.

Archibald Douglas went to Edinburgh to seek Mary's consent to the killing of her husband, according to his cousin, the Earl of Morton – Mary refused.

The queen planned to sleep Sunday evening at Kirk o'Field once more at the end of her day of revelry.

There was a crowded scene in the house, as there had been on many previous evenings during the preceding week. The royal entourage – 'the most part of nobles then in this town', said the queen – crowded into the king's chamber. The nobles played at dice while the queen chatted pleasantly to the king. There was probably some music, a song in the background to the sound of the lute or the guitar. It was the sort of evening the queen much enjoyed whether at Holyrood or any of her other Scottish palaces: she may even have appreciated the comparative adventure of sleeping at Kirk o'Field. But at ten or eleven o'clock her intention to do so that night was forestalled. Something – or someone – reminded the queen that it was the hour of Bastian's wedding masque which she had promised to attend. Queen Mary was unable by nature to resist this sort of obligation. It now seemed unnecessarily inconvenient to return once more to Darnley's lodging after the masque to sleep there, since he was coming back to Holyrood early the next morning. Darnley was sulky at the idea of the change of plan, making the petulant demur of a sick man from whom the centre of amusement was being suddenly swept away. According to Moretta, the Savoyard ambassador, the queen lightly gave him a ring as a pledge of her goodwill. Then she bid him goodbye. Down the staircase went the queen, out to the door where the horses were ready to take her back to her palace. As she stood to mount her horse, she paused for a moment puzzled. She saw in front of her her own page, a former servant of Bothwell, French Paris. 'Jesu, Paris,' said the queen. 'How begrimed you are!'

Little did the queen know that her innocent observation touched at the core of secret happenings. For at some point during the day which the queen had spent in the formal court ritual of a servant's wedding and an ambassador's dinner, Bothwell's henchmen, including Paris, had placed enough gunpowder in the vaults of the cellar of Darnley's house to blow it sky-high and reduce it to a heap of rubble.

Mary, in happy ignorance that the house in which she had just spent a relaxed evening was in fact heavily mined with gunpowder – if she had known, one can hardly believe that she would have rested in it so contentedly – now returned to Holyrood. Here she attended the masque in honour of Bastian's wedding and at about midnight she retired peacefully to sleep in her apartments. It was a cold night; there was a new moon and a little snow powdered the streets and fields around Holyrood.

It was now time for Bothwell, released from the royal presence to join his underlings at the scene of the crime to supervise the lighting of the fuses. He was not the only nobleman present. From a nearby house came Archibald Douglas and some of his men; although the Douglases were kinsmen to Darnley (through his mother Margaret, born a Douglas), they were under the leadership of Morton, and were sworn to the destruction of the man who had betrayed them over Riccio.

Meanwhile, within the doomed house, Darnley sulkily made preparations for his early departure the next morning. Then he retired for the night, with his valet sleeping in the same room, and three other servants sleeping in the adjoining gallery. There was a light burning in the window of a house across the quadrangle, otherwise all was calm and silence over Kirk o'Field.

At two o'clock in the morning, or thereabouts, the silent air was rent by an explosion of remarkable proportions. The keeper of the ordnance afterwards likened it to thunder. Paris said that the air was rent by the 'crack' and that every hair of his head stood on end. The memoirs of Herries described it thus: 'The blast was fearfull to all about, and many rose from their beds at the noise.' People in nearby houses came rushing out into the streets in fear, to find the house in which their king was lodged reduced to a pile of rubble. In the garden outside the town wall lay the dead bodies of the king and his valet. The king was still in his nightgown, and naked beneath it. Beside him was a furred cloak, a chair, a dagger and some rope. There was no mark or mutilation on either body, 'no fracture, wound or bruise' as Buchanan put it – and no sign of the work of the blast. The king and his servant had been strangled.

The paradoxical, almost ludicrous, element in the whole situation was that Bothwell had not actually killed Darnley by his mighty explosion. For Darnley in fact died at other hands than those of the earl of Bothwell. Something frightened Darnley, as he lay in the mined house, and frightened him so badly that he escaped out of the lodging in only a nightgown, and attempted to make his way across the gardens to safety. He had had no time to dress himself, and although his servant picked up a cloak, Darnley was not wearing it when he died. They had one dagger between them. The chair and rope indicate the improvised method of their escape – a chair let down by a rope out of a window. There had been no time to alert the other servants. Darnley acted with the speed of panic.

The most likely explanation of Darnley's precipitate departure would be that he was wakened by some noise and looked out of his window to see the gathering of Bothwell's men and the Douglas faction in the garden. Gunpowder would probably not have immediately sprung to mind but fire would. Burning the enemy's house over his head was a comparatively common sixteenth-century Scottish practice. The sight of Bothwell and the hostile Douglases milling outside his house would certainly have suggested some imminent danger of fire, if not assassination, to Darnley. Put at its mildest, there were no arguments to linger. But for Darnley, even once outside the house, there was no escape. The fleeing figures in their white nightgowns were discerned by some of the Douglas men who pursued them into the gardens. Here they were quietly and efficiently strangled, even as the house itself exploded in a roar of flames and dust. Some women living in the nearby houses said afterwards that they overheard Darnley's wretched last plea for mercy to the Douglas men, who were after all his relations: 'Pity me, kinsmen, for the sake of Jesus Christ, who pitied all the world . . .' The plea went unanswered. Darnley died, a boy of not yet twenty-one, as pathetically and unheroically as he had lived.

James Douglas, Earl of Morton, one of the participants in the murder of Darnley. He was later Regent for the child king, James VI.

8 The Mermaid and the Hare

'Certain stars shot madly from their spheres
To hear the sea-maid's music'

SHAKESPEARE *in* A Midsummer Night's Dream
(said to be a reference to Bothwell and Mary)

At the palace of Holyrood Queen Mary was woken from her sleep by a noise like twenty or thirty cannon. Shortly afterwards messengers brought her the news that the house at Kirk o'Field had been totally destroyed, and her husband's dead body found lying near by. Her first reactions were horror and shock – horror at what had happened and shock at the feeling that she herself had had such a narrow escape. She wrote the same day – Monday, 10 February – to her ambassador, James Beaton, in Paris, pouring forth her amazement and distress, although it is noticeable that her conventional grief for Darnley was outweighed by her conviction that the conspiracy had been aimed at her personally. 'The matter is so horrible and strange,' wrote the queen, 'as we believe the like was never heard of in any country.' The queen did not yet know who was responsible, but was certain that with 'the diligence our Council has begun already to use ... the same being discovered ... we hope to punish the same with such rigour as shall serve for example of this cruelty to all ages to come'.

It is evident that at the moment when she wrote this letter, a few hours after the crime, it had not yet struck the queen that any of her chief nobles were involved in its execution. The sheer outrageousness of the explosion had distracted her from considering the known enmities between Darnley and many of the nobility – as Bothwell must have planned that it should; nervously convinced that she herself had only escaped death by a miracle, the queen was at first more inclined to ponder on her own enemies than on Darnley's. The official letter sent to France by the lords of the Council on the same day also emphasized the danger to the queen. So far then, Bothwell's strategy had succeeded.

The royal widow behaved with perfect correctness. Darnley's body was brought to Holyrood to be embalmed, and was laid formally in state for several days, before being buried in the vaults of the chapel royal. The queen ordered the court into mourning, for which £150-worth of black was ordered. Although, according to Knox's *History*, Mary showed no outward sign of joy or sorrow when shown the corpse of Darnley, her strange composure – so unlike her usual ready tears – may well have been due to simple shock. She herself embarked heavily on the traditional forty days' mourning for her husband. Her spirits had never recovered properly from her Jedburgh illness; now her nervous health became so critically weakened by the shock of the crime that, according to Leslie, the Privy Council were earnestly exhorted by her doctors to let her get

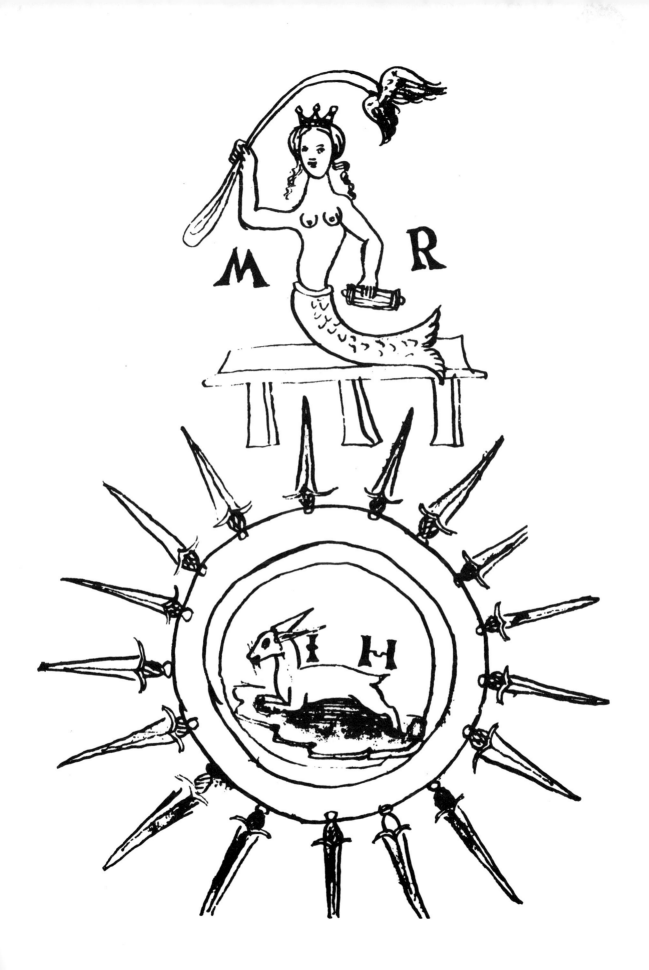

away from the tragic and gloom-laden atmosphere of Edinburgh for a while, lest incarceration in the closed chamber of the widow should cause a total breakdown. So the queen went to Seton, one of her favourite haunts close to Edinburgh, and spent three recuperative days there.

Once the distressing impact of the murder had worn off, it could not fail to occur to Mary that this was no hideous outrage by unknown assassins, but a deliberately planned *coup* on the part of those nobles who had hated Darnley, and who had openly discussed his removal with her at Craigmillar. It must now have become apparent to her that she herself had been in no personal danger, but that Darnley had paid the penalty for his treachery in the violent and bloodthirsty manner which she had by now come to associate with Scottish vengeance.

Rumours were already percolating rapidly round Edinburgh. A quantity of people, many of them servants, had been involved in the murder; it was hardly likely that an outrage of this magnitude would remain a total mystery for very long. Tongues wagged. There were dark hints and others a good deal plainer. Placards began to appear in the streets, the most virulent of which showed Queen Mary as a mermaid, naked to the waist, with a crown on her head, and Bothwell as a hare – the crest of the Hepburns – crouching in a circle of swords. The implication behind the use of the mermaid was not romantic, as might appear to modern eyes, but deliberately insulting, since the word was commonly used in the sixteenth and seventeenth centuries to denote a siren, and thus by analogy a prostitute.

This was the supreme moment for Mary to show herself the prudent and ruthless sovereign, and benefit from the actions of others to make her own position thoroughly secure. Her Achilles heel in Scotland – her husband Darnley – had been eliminated from her path by her own nobility. She had not known of the crime beforehand, and was not implicated in the details. Now her best course – a course urged on her by both Catherine de Medicis and Elizabeth – was to pursue the murderers with public vengeance, in order to establish once and for all her own innocence of any possible complicity. After all, once the nobles came to power they took good care to produce some criminals publicly, as we shall see, in order to exculpate themselves; Mary should have been at least as practical while she still had the opportunity. Even if she could not go as far as arraigning Bothwell himself, there were underlings to be sacrificed. As it was, her conduct bordered on madness. The Privy Council had, immediately after the deed, announced a reward of £2,000 for the capture of the criminals; there had been vague questionings of Darnley's servants; but beyond that no further steps were taken to secure any arrests. Neither the placards, the rumours, nor Lennox's furious denunciations of his son's murderers – about whose identity he was personally in no doubt – seemed to have the power of penetrating Mary's passive state of despair and melancholy. Since health and shock had clearly robbed her of any shred of political judgement, she was exceptionally dependent upon her advisers. But the advisers who surrounded her were all for one reason and another incapable of pointing out the true facts of the situation; never was Mary Stuart's pathetic lack of loyal, disinterested consultants more disastrous to her than in the period immediately after Kirk o'Field.

Moray's first concern was to clear himself of any possible guilt in the eyes of his English friends. He left for London at the beginning of April, anxious to put as much distance as possible between himself and the Scottish court, partly so that he should not be involved in the contentious struggle for power which he saw coming, in which the strength of the hated Bothwell seemed to be growing hourly, partly so that he could ingratiate himself in England. Of the queen's other possible advisers, Maitland had been involved in the plot, and could therefore scarcely advise her to pursue its punishment vindictively, and Bothwell was hardly likely to counsel a course so alien to his own interests. There was thus no force to conjure the queen out of her mood of lassitude and melancholia. The Scotland of her dreams and early happiness now seemed to her a cruel and barbarous country where deeds of violence succeeded each other in remorseless succession; her secretary and now her husband had been done to death within a year, not by low assassins but by the chief men of the kingdom, and the bloodshed horrified her. In her sad passivity, she allowed herself to lean increasingly on the one man close to her who still showed strength of purpose, energy and deter-mination – and was also only too anxious to direct the affairs of state. Unfortunately for Mary, that man was Bothwell, who, whatever his dominating qualities, was also the chief suspect of her husband's murder.

On 23 March, the fortieth day after Darnley's death, the queen's period of mourning officially came to an end. In fact her sorrows were only just beginning. The vociferous demands of Lennox for vengeance had reached a pitch that even Mary, advised by Bothwell, felt herself unable to ignore them. In a letter of 24 March she agreed to allow Lennox to bring a private process in front of Parliament against Bothwell as the slayer of his son. It was hardly surprising that, in two letters written at the end of March, Drury reported the queen to be in continuous ill-health – 'She has been for the most part either melancholy or sickly ever since, and especially this week upon Tuesday or Wednesday often swooned . . . the Queen breaketh very much.' On the day appointed for the trial, Bothwell rode magnificently down the Canongate, with Morton and Maitland flanking him, and his Hepburns trotting behind. Although the due processes of justice were observed at the trial, the absence of the accuser Lennox – understandably afraid to appear in Edinburgh in view of the fact that the city was swarming with Bothwell's adherents – meant that Bothwell was inevitably acquitted.

Bothwell's next move was absolutely in keeping with his character and the conditions of the time: if he was to make his power even more effective by occupying the position of king, he needed the support of at least some of his fellow-nobles. The contemporary expedient of a bond was once more called into play. In order to secure adherents for this new bond, on Saturday, 19 April, Bothwell duly entertained many of the nobles and prelates then in the capital to a lavish feast. At the end of this momentous supper party, Bothwell produced a long document, the main point of which, apart from his own innocence of the murder of Darnley, was that if the queen would accept him as a husband then the signatories were to promise themselves to promote the marriage by

The ruins of Dunbar Castle, to which Mary was 'abducted' by Bothwell. Three weeks later she was his wife.

counsel, vote and assistance. To this remarkable manifesto, known as the Ainslie bond after the name of the tavern where the supper party took place, those present, including Morton, Maitland, Argyll, Atholl and Huntly, now put their signatures. Although the motives and loyalties of some of the signatories must be considered highly suspect – for surely to Morton and Maitland King James Hepburn could be no more acceptable than King Henry Stuart had been – nevertheless Bothwell now had in his pocket the document he considered he needed for his next bold move forward.

The queen having gone to her favourite Seton again, Bothwell followed her there, accompanied by Maitland. According to Queen Mary's own story, it was here that he first paid suit to her, suggesting both that she needed a husband and that he was the best man to fill the role, since he had been selected to do so by her nobles. This direct approach threw the queen into a state of confusion. By her own account, she did not know what to do, especially when Maitland assured her of what she knew only too well, that it had become absolutely necessary that some remedy should be provided for the disorder into which public affairs had fallen for want of a head. Now her chief nobles were apparently pleading with her to accept Bothwell – 'a man of resolution well adapted to rule, the very character needed to give weight to the decisions and actions of the Council'. However, Queen Mary always asserted afterwards that she refused Bothwell's proposals at this point, on the grounds that there were too many scandals about her husband's death, despite the fact that Bothwell had been legally acquitted of complicity by Parliament.

With this refusal still uppermost in her thoughts, the queen proceeded to Stirling Castle to pay a visit to her baby, who, as custom demanded, had now been handed over into the care of his hereditary governors, the Erskines. Mary arrived on Monday, 21 April and spent the whole Tuesday enjoying the company of her child. The queen played with him in peace, happily unaware that this was the last meeting she was ever to have with her son.

Mary started back to Edinburgh with only Maitland, Huntly, James Melville and about thirty horsemen to accompany her. As the queen and her little troupe reached the Bridges of Almond, about six miles from Edinburgh, the earl of Bothwell suddenly appeared with a force of about 800 men. Bothwell rode forward, put his hand on the queen's bridle, and told her that since danger was threatening her in Edinburgh, he proposed to take her to the castle of Dunbar, out of harm's way. Some of Mary's followers reacted disagreeably to the sudden appearance of Bothwell, but the queen said gently that she would go with the Earl Bothwell rather than be the cause of bloodshed. Docilely, without more ado, she allowed herself to be conducted about forty miles across the heart of Scotland; she seemed to accept Bothwell's story so totally that she made no attempt to seek rescue from the country people as she passed. Her only positive action was to send a messenger to Edinburgh to issue a warning of possible danger. When the provost heard what had happened, a very different view was taken of the disappearance of the sovereign. The alarm bell was rung and the citizens were begged to attempt a rescue. But by this time there was little that they, or anyone could do. At midnight, the queen was within Dunbar Castle, surrounded by a force of Bothwell's men. The gates of the castle were firmly shut behind her.

This abduction – if the word can truly be applied to anything so calm and placid as these proceedings – represents a typical example of Bothwell's thinking. Even if earlier hints of Bothwell's predilection for abduction, in Arran's story, are disregarded, Bothwell clearly had the mentality which considered that a sufficiently public outrage covered in some curious way a multitude of sins. This had been his reasoning over Kirk o'Field. Now he confidently believed that an abduction would not only put an end to further consultation and discussion about the marriage – in which his reasoning was perfectly correct – but also distract public attention from his connection with Darnley's death by the very flagrancy of the act; here of course his reasoning was disastrously wrong. Was Queen Mary enlightened in advance as to her prospective fate? The intended abduction was certainly widely known about beforehand among the nobles, and contemporary evidence points strongly to the fact that the scheme had been outlined also to the queen and that she had agreed to it weakly, as a possible way out of the morass in which despair brought on by ill-health seemed to have landed her. Mary, still envisaging Bothwell as her help and support among the nobles, and not as the reprobate adventurer whom his enemies later built up in their writings, felt in no position to withstand his latest proposition; it was presented to her by Bothwell, using the same arguments which he had used to himself, as a convenient solution to her difficulties.

Once within the castle of Dunbar, Bothwell made his second planned move – an equally characteristic one, although in this case the queen was not consulted beforehand. He decided to complete his formal abduction of her person by the physical possession of her body. His intentions in this aggressive act were as before perfectly straightforward: he intended to place the queen in a situation from which she could not possibly escape marrying him. Bothwell was certainly not in love with Mary, although he may have accompanied his actions with some sort of protestation such as he thought suitable to the occasion. But in the course of the gratification of his ambitions, rape was not the sort of duty from which Bothwell was likely to shrink. Melville, who was present in the castle at the time, was quite certain that the ravishment had taken place: 'The Queen could not but marry him, seeing he had ravished her and laid with her against her will.' It is interesting to note that Bothwell's and Mary's contemporaries believed instantaneously and strongly that the abduction scheme had been a rigged one and intended to save the queen's face. But it was also widely believed that Bothwell had completed his scheme by making love to the queen, and that this was probably against her will.

It is sometimes suggested that Mary found a sexual satisfaction with Bothwell which she had not experienced with either of her previous husbands. This may or may not be true: it can certainly never be proved, since the queen herself never ventured any opinion on the subject, and to the end of her life always firmly attributed her marriage to Bothwell to reasons of state rather than the dictates of the heart. In fact, the events leading up to her marriage to Darnley point far more clearly to the workings of physical infatuation than those leading up to the Bothwell marriage. In spring 1565 Mary Stuart was a young and beautiful woman, healthy and energetic, long widowed, eager to be married; in spring 1567 she was broken in health, distraught, nervously concerned about the future of her government. Quite apart from the evidence of events, it seems extremely doubtful whether they were the sort of couple who would have been drawn to each other if political considerations had not been involved. Practical ambition had driven Bothwell to woo the queen: this elegant, coquettish, literary-minded, slightly cold woman, with her graceful figure, her red-gold hair, her laughing flirtatious ways, her demand for obedience to which she had been accustomed from her earliest years, was not the type to appeal to Bothwell, who in the past had always shown an inclination towards more earthy examples of womanhood. Of all Mary Stuart's qualities, her courage and gaiety, her ability to make quick decisions and pull herself rapidly out of an untenable situation were those most likely to appeal to Bothwell, but these had been strangely in abeyance since her virtual nervous breakdown at Jedburgh. The important fact in Bothwell's eyes was that she was queen regnant of Scotland, with the power to make her husband king consort and effective ruler of the country.

Of course it would not be essential for Bothwell to love Mary for her to respond to him: she might even have experienced some perverse satisfaction in domination by this straightforward and brutal man, so different from her other husbands. The feelings which Queen Mary felt for Bothwell can only be estimated in terms of the importance which as a woman she gave to the whole subject of sex. In early youth she naturally paid little attention to such a question, and during the period of her first widowhood also was remarkable for the discretion with which she conducted herself. Her disastrous marriage to Darnley, springing from physical attraction, gave her every reason to adopt an extremely suspicious attitude towards passion and its consequences. If, despite all these considerations, she experienced some genuine fulfilment in Bothwell's embraces, it is remarkable how little effort she made to keep in touch with her husband once she was in captivity: from the moment of her abdication onwards she seems to have lost all interest in Bothwell, as though he belonged to some previous, unsuccessful, political phase of her life. Another interesting aspect of her captivity is that she made absolutely no attempt to quench any desires of the flesh, if indeed she felt them, during the whole nineteen years; there is no rumour, which bears investigation, of the sort of liaison which would surely have occurred had she become, under Bothwell's tuition, the *grande amoureuse* of so many imaginings. On the contrary, from the age of twenty-five onwards, the queen led a life of total chastity.

Whatever Mary's inner feelings for Bothwell during the short period of their concubinage – three weeks from Dunbar to the marriage, and four weeks thereafter – their union was certainly not founded originally on the flimsy basis of passion. The queen had not one but three pressing and – as it seemed to her – good reasons for giving her consent to the marriage with Bothwell. In the first place he had succeeded in convincing her that he would at last provide her with the able and masterful consort whom she had so long sought to share with her the strains of the government of Scotland. He had subjugated her by the undoubted strength of his personality at a time when broken health had induced in her a fatally indecisive, even lethargic state of mind, so that faced with the reality of Bothwell and his positive aims, she was unable to see clearly where her own best interests lay. Secondly, Bothwell was able to show her the Ainslie bond which proved to her satisfaction that the majority of her nobility were prepared to accept him as their overlord. Mary had married Darnley defiantly against the advice of most of her nobles: she did not intend to make the same mistake twice. Thirdly, Bothwell had effectively ensured that the queen would not be able to go back on her word by the act of physical rape. The union had already been consummated; it remained to transform it into a legal marriage.

Jean, Countess of Bothwell, who made no protest when Bothwell divorced her to marry Mary, but who remained installed in his castle of Crichton.

Having secured the queen's acquiescence, Bothwell quickly arranged his divorce from his first wife, and on 6 May brought the queen back to Edinburgh. As they rode towards the castle, according to the *Diurnal of Occurrents*, a contemporary diary probably written by a minor court official, the Earl Bothwell led the queen's majesty by the bridle of her horse, as though she were a captive.

As Mary moved in a trance towards her public union with Bothwell, already the forces of aristocratic reaction were coalescing against his meteoric rise. Furious at the realization that Bothwell – one of their own number – had made himself a virtual dictator, on 1 May a party of dissidents gathered at Stirling. They vowed in yet another communal bond to strive by all means in their power to set their queen at liberty, and defend her son Prince James. In this meeting at Stirling, it is significant that the key figures were Morton, Argyll and Atholl – all three of whom only ten days before had signed the Ainslie bond promising to forward Bothwell's suit of the queen. The conspirators sent a message to Mary offering her their support against the Lord Bothwell. But since Bothwell was firmly governing all matters around her, the queen could scarcely credit that he already lost the support of the fickle Scottish lords.

The days passed with horrible speed towards her wedding-day. On Thursday, 15 May, just over three months after the death of Darnley, Mary married Bothwell in the great hall of Holyrood. A greater contrast to the two previous weddings of the queen could hardly be imagined. The very fact that the ceremony took place according to the Protestant rite showed how much the queen had lost control of her destinies. After the wedding there were no masques or 'pleasures and pastimes', as there had always been before when princes married. There was merely a wedding dinner, at which the people were allowed to watch Mary eating her meal at the head of the table, with Bothwell at the foot. There were no rich presents for Bothwell as groom as there had been for Darnley, and no lavish replenishment of the queen's wardrobe. Her sartorial preparations were confined to having an old yellow dress relined with white taffeta, an old black gown done up with gold braid and a black taffeta petticoat relined. Of all the sad events in the life of Mary Stuart in Scotland, this squalid, hurried wedding, of a rite she did not profess, without any of the preparations she so loved, is surely the most pathetic.

Judging from the comments of observers, Mary's brief married life with Bothwell brought her absolutely no personal happiness. Du Croc commented on the strange formality between the queen and her husband on their wedding-day, and later she confessed to Leslie, in floods of tears, how much she already repented of what she had done, especially her Protestant marriage ceremony. In front of others, Mary's sadness was even more fearful and more desperate; the day after the wedding, Melville heard her actually ask for a knife to kill herself, and when he remonstrated with her, the queen threatened to drown herself. The hysterical nature of Mary's reaction shows not only how far she was from feeling any kind of personal love for Bothwell but also how desperately close her nerves were to the surface and how far her self-control had vanished. As it began to dawn on her that she might have betrayed her whole reputation in order to marry a man who was no more suited than Darnley to advise her, Mary Stuart's future began to look very black indeed. Maitland told du Croc a little later that from the day of the queen's marriage there had been no end of tears and lamentations, since Bothwell was furious and jealous if she looked at anyone except him – he accused her of having a pleasure-loving nature, and liking to spend her time in frivolous worldly pursuits, like any woman. Even before the marriage Bothwell's unkindness had led to quarrels between them. His language was said to be so filthy that even Melville was constrained to leave his presence. But Bothwell in his treatment of Mary was less concerned with the niceties of their legal relationship than with the power that it brought him. The lords claimed that Bothwell kept Mary the virtual prisoner of his ambition. None of their number had been able to speak to her without Bothwell being present; so suspicious had Bothwell become that he kept the queen's chamber door perpetually guarded by his own men of war. Drury reported on 20 May that the queen's distress was the talk of the court: never, it seemed, had a woman changed so much in appearance in so short a space of time. The mermaid and the hare were evidently as ill-suited to live together as might be expected of a half-fairy sea creature and a wild animal of the earth.

Fast as events had moved before Mary's wedding, the speed only increased after the ceremony. By the end of May the clouds of war were gathering round Bothwell's head. Bothwell had many virulent enemies and the familiar network of allegiances and betrayals now brought them together. In order to blacken the case against Bothwell, and to gloss over the previous commitments of Maitland and Morton, it was necessary to give a dimension of morality to their quarrel – that Bothwell, as the king's murderer, must be brought to justice. The treachery of Sir James Balfour surpassed that of anyone else: for he, who had been closely involved in the murder of Darnley, and who had been granted the custody of Edinburgh Castle as a reward for his complicity, now secretly treated with the conspirators and agreed to support their cause, on condition that his custody of the castle was confirmed.

On 6 June Bothwell took Mary from Holyrood to the castle of Borthwick, a stark, twin-towered, fifteenth-century fortress, about twelve miles south of Edinburgh. The lord of Borthwick was an ally of Bothwell but the castle was surrounded by the insurgents and Bothwell realized that it was ill-situated to withstand a siege. He therefore slipped away through a postern gate, with only one companion, leaving Mary to hold the castle. The besiegers called up to the queen to abandon her husband and accompany them back to Edinburgh. When she proudly refused they shouted insults at her of a nature 'too evil and unseemly to be told', wrote the governor of Berwick, Sir William Drury, in a letter to London, as he described the new plight of 'this poor princess'. The poor princess had not, however, lost all her old spirit, and she disguised herself as a man and escaped out of the castle by night to the nearby Black Castle at Cakemuir. Here she met up with Bothwell and together they made their way to Dunbar.

It was at Dunbar that the ultimate treachery of Balfour revealed itself: for it was his message to the queen that she would do better to return to Edinburgh, where the guns of the castle, under his command, would support her, which brought her and Bothwell out of this comparatively safe place, before the royal forces had mustered to anything like a secure strength. All the queen's belongings and wardrobe had been left behind in Edinburgh or at Borthwick: she was now dressed in clothes hastily borrowed at Dunbar, a short red petticoat, a muffler, velvet hat and sleeves tied with bows, such as the women of Edinburgh wore. Her charm and dignity were undiminished by her costume: it was her reputation which no longer had its pristine purity in the minds of her ordinary subjects and as the royal cortège passed 'the people did not join as was expected'. By the time the queen reached Haddington she had only about 600 horsemen. Mary and Bothwell passed the night – their last together – at the palace of Seton, the house which Mary had loved so long and happily in her six years in Scotland.

On Sunday, 15 June 1567, at 2 am in the morning, the confederate lords marched out of Edinburgh. In the van of their procession was borne a white banner showing a green tree with the corpse of Darnley lying underneath it, his infant son kneeling before him, and the legend: 'Judge and avenge my cause, O Lord.' A few hours later the royal army under Bothwell also moved out and took up a commanding position on Carberry Hill. The nobles took up their position on a hill opposite. In between the two armies, neither of them exactly certain as to how they should proceed, the queen lacking troops and the nobles lacking authority, there appeared the figure of du Croc, the French ambassador, who had panted out from Edinburgh after the insurgents.

Du Croc was now deputed by the rebels to beg Mary to abandon Bothwell, at which they were to restore her to her former position, while they themselves would continue to be her loyal subjects. This Mary absolutely and furiously declined to do. She pointed out in a passion of indignation to du Croc that these same lords had signed a bond recommending the marriage with the very man they were now opposing so vehemently – 'It was by them that Bothwell had been promoted,' she kept repeating. By her own account Mary had no inkling at this point that the lords intended to charge Bothwell with the murder of Darnley: but certainly she felt absolutely no temptation to desert Bothwell. In the first place, Bothwell, with all his faults, had shown himself loyal to her throughout her adversities and his own; she felt no such confidence about the behaviour of men of the calibre of Morton, Lindsay and Ruthven.

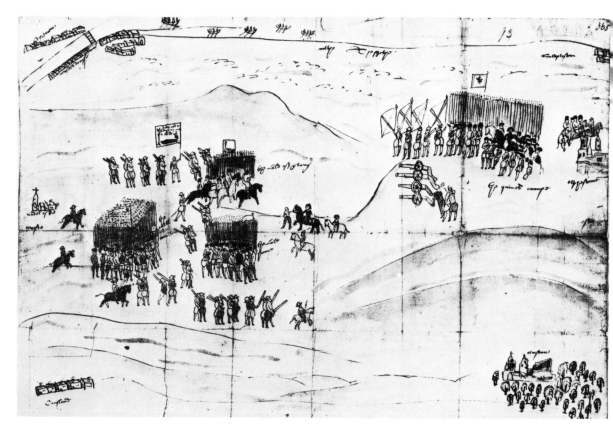

Secondly, the queen must by now have realized herself to be pregnant by Bothwell. The fact could not fail to seal their union in the mind of such a philoprogenitive woman.

As Mary refused to relinquish Bothwell, both sides now gave themselves up to a series of chivalric parleys, reminiscent of medieval warfare, in which challenges to personal combat were given and taken with great enthusiasm, but no actual battles took place. Bothwell, according to du Croc, was in high spirits – 'a great Captain, speaking with undaunted confidence, and leading his army gaily and skilfully . . .' But even as these parleyings were proceeding, the royal troops were melting away. Like an ancient hero, Bothwell stood alone while his troops vanished. It was too late to attack his enemies now and there was no sign of the Hamiltons, who it was hoped might reinforce them.

At evening the rebels decided to press their advantge with a new parley and Kirkcaldy of Grange rode forward. Aware that the royal party was suffering from a striking lack of troops, Bothwell suggested to Mary that they should retreat to Dunbar, where there was a possibility of rallying much more support to the queen's side. But Mary could not believe that the situation was so desperate. She considered that the wisest course for her to pursue in the interests of peace and the avoidance of bloodshed was to accept a safe-conduct for Bothwell, and trust herself to the confederate lords, whom she now apparently thought would investigate everything anew by Parliament. Kirkcaldy assured her that the Crown as such was not being attacked. Bothwell it was agreed would gallop off to Dunbar, either to raise further troops, or to await parliamentary developments in the capital. With renewed trust in her nobles, Mary bade farewell to the man for whom she had sacrificed so much in terms of honour and reputation. They embraced in full view of both armies. At sunset Bothwell mounted his charger, and, after five weeks of power, galloped away down the road to Dunbar. It was the last sight Mary was ever to have of him.

The queen of Scots was now thoroughly alone. And her entry into the camp of the rebels immediately and rudely jolted her confidence in the love which she still believed her subjects bore her. Here was no enthusiastic reception, no cheers, no protestations of devotion. On the contrary, the soldiers shouted crude insults at her. The queen's spirit still held. She said loudly and openly to Morton: 'How is this my lord Morton? I am told that all this is done in order to get justice against the king's murderers. I am told also that you are one of the chief of them.' Morton slunk away. But Mary Stuart needed all her courage to endure the ordeal before her. She, who all her life had been greeted publicly with adulation and enthusiasm, now heard the soldiers shout, 'Burn her, burn the whore, she is not worthy to live,' as they conveyed her along the road into Edinburgh. Amazed, almost stunned, the queen allowed tears of shock and humiliation to pour down her cheeks, as she rode forward in the clothes she had acquired at Dunbar – now 'all spoiled with clay and dirt'. For the first time she began to realize what the effect had been on the ordinary people of Scotland – the people who had once loved her – of her reckless action in marrying her husband's assassin, and of those weeks of propaganda by the enemies of Bothwell. To them she was now no longer their young and beautiful queen, but an adulteress – and an adulteress who had subsequently become the willing bride of a murderer.

In Edinburgh the queen was taken to the house of the provost. The nobles sat down to a hearty supper, but the queen retreated in a daze of horror at her experiences into her bedroom – even here, however, she could not find peace, since the guards insisted on remaining with her inside the room so that she could not even undress. Mary now lay down on the bed, still in the red petticoat in which she had come from Dunbar, and gave herself up to the wastes of despair. There seemed no hope, and certainly no honour in Scotland, since the nobles, to whom she had freely surrendered, now held her a humiliated and unconsidered captive.

By the next day Mary's self-control had utterly collapsed. She came to the window, and cried out to the people that she was being kept in prison by her subjects who had betrayed her. The sight of her brought rioting outside and more mockery and more insults. The lords pulled her back but before they did so, many of her subjects had seen the distraught woman as she showed herself at the open window – her hair hanging down around her face, her clothes torn open so that the upper half of her body was almost bare, her beauty ravaged, her courage gone. Where now was the exquisite princess who had fascinated the French court and half Europe, in this wretched, near-demented creature hanging out of the window of an Edinburgh prison, half naked, her bosom exposed, shrieking that she had been betrayed? The people of Edinburgh, their innate decency overcoming their moral disapproval, were shocked into pity and compassion at the sight. It was four weeks since Mary's marriage to Bothwell, and not quite two years since her boldly triumphant marriage to Darnley. This was the nadir of Mary Stuart.

LEFT A contemporary sketch of the field at Carberry Hill on 15 June 1567: in the centre of the picture, Mary on horseback is being led across to the army of the rebel lords by Kirkcaldy of Orange; Bothwell, also on horseback, sits directly behind the row of guns; the Red Lion of Scotland flies above the Queen's army, and above the rebel army flies the banner referring to the death of Darnley: 'Judge and Avenge my cause, O Lord.'

BELOW Borthwick Castle where, in June 1567, Mary was besieged – Bothwell having abandoned her – and from which she escaped disguised as a man.

9 Lochleven

'How the Mouse for a pleasure done to her by the Lion, after that, the Lion being
bound with a cord, the Mouse chewed the cord, and let the Lion loose ...'

AESOP's *fable of the mouse and the lion, quoted in the deposition
of a servant after Queen Mary's escape from Lochleven*

The confederate lords were aware that they were on extremely
delicate ground with regard to the queen's imprisonment, since
this imprisonment had followed ruthlessly on her own vol-
untary surrender in the interest of civil peace. Mary herself had
genuinely, if naïvely, expected a parliamentary investigation into the
murder of Darnley to follow her surrender. It was just this inquiry which
Morton, Maitland and Balfour in particular had good reason to fear.
Under these circumstances, the lords decided that it would be too
dangerous to keep the queen in ward in Edinburgh itself. The people of
the city regarded the queen's wretched state with sad astonishment: it
would certainly be easier to keep their moral disapproval of her
behaviour at fever-point during her absence, when rumours of her
depravity could be spread without fear of contradiction.

On the Monday evening, therefore, the queen was escorted hurriedly
north. She was not allowed to take any of her ladies-in-waiting with her,
but only two *femmes-de-chambre*; nor was she allowed to take any clothes,
not even a nightdress or linen. Late that night Mary reached the vast
waters of Lochleven. Here, on one of the four islands in the middle of the
loch, lay the dour castle of Sir William Douglas. Douglas was a most
trustworthy jailer from the point of view of the lords: he was the
half-brother of Moray, being the son of Moray's mother Margaret
Erskine by her legal husband Robert Douglas, and he was cousin and
heir-presumptive to Morton. The lords could certainly rely on his
interests being bonded to theirs.

The queen was now rowed across the bleak waters of the lake. On
arrival in the castle she was conducted quickly and unceremoniously to
the laird's room; it had in no way been prepared for her visit, and lacked
any sort of furniture, equipment or even a bed suitable to her rank and
condition. Mary sank once more into a stupor in which sickness, aggra-
vated by pregnancy, despair and exhaustion, all played a part. She
remained in this semi-coma for a fortnight, neither speaking to anyone
nor, as she remembered afterwards, eating or drinking, until many of
those within the house actually thought she would die.

Mary had visited the castle of Lochleven before under happier
auspices, using it as a centre from which to hunt in Kinross-shire. But by
nature, Lochleven was indeed more suited to be a prison than a pleasure
haunt. In the sixteenth century, the island on which it stood was so small
that it hardly extended beyond the walls and garden of the fortress – the

present-day slightly larger island being the result of a considerable fall in the water level of the lake in the last century. Its dominating, square main tower, from which an excellent view of the shore was to be obtained, stuck up out of the lake like a signpost pointing to its inviolability. This tower had been built in the late fourteenth century, and in it the laird and his family lived. The castle also contained another round tower, built in the corner of the courtyard, and here the queen was eventually incarcerated, on the grounds that this would make it more difficult for her to signal to the shore. The lake itself, then twelve miles across, was a bleak place even in August, with the Lomond hills lowering over it, and the flat, grey waters punctuated only by the occasional dark trees of the islands; during the winter, the winds and rain would sweep across the lake and make it a desolate place indeed. It was certainly a prison from which escape would prove a virtual impossibility without connivance from the inside.

On 16 June the warrant for the queen's imprisonment was signed by nine lords, including Morton. In view of the fact that the previous bond of the rebel lords had expressly referred to their intention of releasing Mary from the thraldom of Bothwell, and restoring her to liberty to rule as before, it was small wonder that the queen now felt herself to be totally betrayed – being in closer thraldom than ever, her liberty far more grievously curtailed than it had ever been in the days of her marriage to Bothwell.

In the meantime Bothwell himself was still at liberty. From Carberry

ABOVE The dour castle of Sir William Douglas on Lochleven, where Mary was first imprisoned by the Scottish lords. Photographed by the author.

BELOW Curtain and valances from the bed of Mary Queen of Scots, in Lochleven Castle.

Hill he had gone to Dunbar, but on hearing of the queen's imprisonment, he sallied forth from the castle, and during his remaining two months within the bounds of Scotland attempted with great energy and single-mindedness to raise some sort of support for her. At first he enjoyed a certain success, but having ignored the summons to appear in Edinburgh to answer charges of murdering Darnley and kidnapping the queen, he was formally declared an outlaw and forthwith his supporters melted away. Even so he managed to elude capture and make his way to the Orkneys, where he hoped to rally support once more. Unlike Mary, the lords now took care to pursue with relentless ferocity those of Bothwell's underlings who had been involved in the murder of Darnley. The series of executions, which continued throughout the rest of the year, was intended to distract public attention from the complicity of the new governors of Scotland, Morton, Balfour and Maitland, in the crime.

The first fortnight of Mary's incarceration was an agonizing experience, not only on account of her wretched health. Throckmorton, who had been sent north by Elizabeth to parley with the lords, heard that the queen was kept 'very straightly'; the lords did not intend that there should be any dramatic moonlight flittings from Lochleven. After a fortnight her total nervous collapse seems to have drawn to an end. Drury heard from Berwick that she was 'better digesting' her captivity, and could even take a little exercise.

The queen still absolutely refused to hear of divorcing Bothwell. Her pregnancy by Bothwell was now thoroughly established in her own mind, and she feared more than ever to compromise the legitimacy of her unborn child. Moreover, her extreme suspicion of the intention of the lords towards her own person had only been deepened by their behaviour since Carberry Hill. Although Maitland told her that if she agreed to divorce Bothwell she would be restored to liberty and freedom, Queen Mary must have doubted whether the lords would have carried out their part of the bargain. Her return could not fail to threaten their newly acquired power, as well as bringing out into the open once more the events leading up to the death of Darnley. Had the lords wished to re-establish her, they had had an excellent opportunity after Carberry Hill, instead of which they locked her up on Lochleven. The existence of the infant Prince James which had once seemed to promise so much for Mary's future, now told as strongly against her. A long royal minority, with a series of noble regents, was traditionally regarded by the Scottish aristocracy as a time for aggrandizement. It should be borne in mind that on 8 December 1567 Mary herself was approaching her twenty-fifth birthday, on which date it was possible by custom for a sovereign to call back wardships and properties given out during his or her own minority. To the Scottish nobility, the rule of the thirteen-month-old James was an infinitely preferable prospect to that of his mother, whether she divorced Bothwell or not.

It is noticeable that Throckmorton was deeply shocked by the brutal attitude of the Scots towards their sovereign. He was especially shocked to find that noble families like the Hamiltons, who had a vested interest in the succession, were ready to join the lords if Mary died. The Hamiltons were ambitious enough to see how their chances of succession would be

Sir Nicholas Throckmorton, Elizabeth I's emissary to Scotland to seek wardship of Prince James for Elizabeth after Mary's capture, and who was shocked by the brutal attitude of the Scots towards their sovereign.

greatly improved with the disappearance of Mary; there would then be only the little king to be eliminated 'and we are home'. Throckmorton was genuinely convinced that Mary's life was in danger and he believed that it was his intervention – by convincing Maitland that Mary's death, apart from being an outrage, would only clear the way for the Hamiltons – which actually saved her.

On one point the lords were adamant: Throckmorton should not visit the queen personally, despite his many requests to do so. He was thus compelled to depend on their own bulletins as to her state of mind. They assured him that Mary was still madly infatuated with Bothwell, and said in addition that she would be willing to abandon her kingdom for him and live like a simple damsel (a statement for which there was no other confirmation and on which Mary's subsequent career casts considerable doubt). More importance can be attached to her first communication to Throckmorton, which he reported on 18 July, when she sent word that she would in no way consent to a divorce from Bothwell 'giving this reason, that taking herself to be seven weeks gone with child, by renouncing him, she should acknowledge herself to be with child of a

bastard and forfeit her honour'.

It was now some eight weeks since the queen's marriage to Bothwell: in her letter she therefore suggests that the baby had been conceived subsequent to the marriage. But at some date before 24 July, no doubt as a result of privations and stress, she miscarried, and according to Nau, her secretary, who inserted the phrase very carefully as an afterthought on the page, found herself to have been bearing *'deux enfants'*. If the twins had been conceived at Dunbar, on or about 24 April, they were about three months' old at the moment of miscarriage, and the double gestation would have been easily recognizable. At eight weeks, the foetus is just over one inch in length; but at twelve to thirteen weeks, the foetus is three and a half inches long, which would have made the recognition of *'deux enfants'* perfectly possible. On balance of probabilities, it seems likely therefore that the queen conceived the twins at Dunbar at the end of April, and that by Carberry Hill, at least, if not earlier, knew for certain that she was pregnant by Bothwell.

What is virtually impossible is the suggestion, sometimes made since by historians, that the queen could have conceived twins by Bothwell in January, before Darnley's death. When Guzman, the Spanish ambassador in London, wrote to Philip II on 21 June, saying that the Scottish queen was five *months* pregnant, he probably mistook five months for five weeks, since there is no reference of any sort through March, April and May to the royal pregnancy, which would have been becoming rapidly more apparent as the queen's figure changed. This was an age in which such facts were speedily known by the accurate news service of servants' gossip. The spring months following the Kirk o'Field tragedy were among the most critical of Mary's existence, in which her every word and action were watched, checked and reported: how inconceivable is it then that an event of such moment as her growing pregnancy outside the bonds of marriage should have passed quite unnoticed until the sixth month, by observers who would certainly have grasped joyfully at such a convenient weapon to destroy, if not Mary, at least Bothwell, the child's father.

The queen's miscarriage proved a turning-point in her attitude to Bothwell, for it removed one important obstacle in the way of divorce. By 5 August Throckmorton no longer despaired of securing her consent to the divorce, as he had done previously.

It was while the queen was lying in bed after her miscarriage, by her own account 'in a state of great weakness', having lost a great deal of blood, and scarcely able to move, that Lindsay came to her and told her that he had been instructed to make her sign certain letters for the resignation of her crown. Mary now believed herself once more to be in great personal danger on this tiny island in the midst of an enormous lake, whose waters could claim any victim silently without the circumstances of their death being ever properly known. Despite her fears, the queen was outraged at the monstrousness of the request, and continued to demand that she should be taken in front of her Estates for the parliamentary inquiry which had been promised to her; but Lindsay's rough words on the subject, that she had better sign, for if she did not, she would simply compel them to cut her throat, however unwilling they

OPPOSITE James VI and I as a child, by Arnold Bronkhorst.

The Earl of Mar, governor of Stirling Castle, where Prince James was held and, at the age of thirteen months, crowned king of Scotland.

OPPOSITE ABOVE
Hermitage Castle where Mary visited Bothwell in October 1566.

OPPOSITE BELOW A miniature, by an unknown artist, traditionally said to be of Bothwell: the only known portrait of him.

OVERPAGE
The Cenotaph of Lord Darnley: the future James VI kneels beside the tomb of his father; behind are his grandparents the Earl and Countess of Lennox, and their younger son Charles. Painted by Levinus Vogelarious, sometimes known as Venetianus, and dated 1567.

might be to do so, only convinced her further of her own personal danger.

It was at this point that Robert Melville hinted to Mary that by no means everyone in the castle was as hostile to her as the laird of Lochleven himself: his brother, for example, George Douglas, a handsome, debonair young man, was already showing himself susceptible to the charms of the beautiful if unfortunate prisoner. But from the actual signing of the letter of resignation there was no escape. Mary told Nau later that Throckmorton had managed to smuggle her a note in the scabbard of a sword, telling her to sign to save her own life, as something so clearly signed under duress could never afterwards be held against her. Certainly if duress was ever held to affect questions of legality there could be no possible legality about such a document by which Mary, on a lonely island, without any advisers, signed away the crown she had inherited twenty-four and a half years ago in favour of her own son, and a regency of her half-brother, and did so surrounded by soldiers under the command of the new regent's own brother. Shortly afterwards, Mary fell seriously ill again; her skin turned yellow, and she broke out in pustules, so that she began to believe she might have been poisoned. This disease, which seems to have had something to do with the liver, was relieved by bleeding, and potion which was said to strengthen the heart.

As a result of the instruments which his mother had been compelled to sign, on 29 July James was crowned king of Scotland at the Protestant church just outside the gates of Stirling Castle, at the tender age of thirteen months. The circumstances strongly recalled those of Queen Mary's own coronation twenty-four years before: once more the Scottish crown belonged to a puny child, hedged round by a grasping nobility, whose powers seemed to have been curtailed very little in the intervening years. On the day of the coronation, the gloomy peace of Lochleven was disturbed by all the artillery of the house being dis-

NON SINE SOLE
IRIS.

charged; the queen, sending to find out what the matter was, discovered that bonfires had been lit in the garden, and that the laird was celebrating riotously at the news. He asked her mockingly why she too was not making merry at the coronation of her own son, at which Mary started to weep and went indoors.

On 22 August James Stewart, earl of Moray, recently returned to Scotland, was proclaimed regent. One side-effect of his new status was the opportunity which it gave him to take possession of Mary's rich hoard of jewellery. It was a subject on which the queen felt strongly, and continued to do so for the rest of her life: the rape of her jewels by Moray caused her as much indignation as any other single injury he did to her.

The proclamation of Moray as regent, coupled with the disappearance of Bothwell from the Scottish scene, led to a period of comparative calm on the little island of Lochleven. The queen's health gradually returned, since the enforced seclusion, however odious, did at least ensure her the rest which she so grievously needed. With health and the sinking away of hysteria returned also resolution and calm, positive thinking. By the beginning of September, she was able to write to Robert Melville far more in her old vein of practical decisiveness, as though the year from the birth of James onwards had been lived under some black and disastrous shadow, now fortunately rolled away. She asked for materials, silks to embroider, and clothes for her ladies. The question of her own clothes was now much better resolved: much of her gilded wardrobe was gone forever, seized by the confederates, and not a great deal of attention seems to have been paid to her luggage-less state. But the private *aide-mémoires* of her chamberlain, Servais de Condé, shows that even in June some clothes were of necessity brought to supplement the clothes in which she had travelled: such as a red satin petticoat furred with marten, some satin sleeves, a cloak of Holland, a pair of black silk tights, or *chausses* and, more practically, some pins and a box of sweetmeats. Later she received more clothes of the same utilitarian nature, and what must have been a welcome parcel, her perukes of false hair and other accessories to arrange her coiffure. To a queen accustomed to the lavish grandeur of royal state since childhood, this was the diet of captivity. There was certainly no mention of the gorgeous dresses of earlier inventories of the royal wardrobe. But, as captivities go, it was not particularly

Stirling Castle, where James was baptized 17 December 1566, and where Mary saw him for the last time on Tuesday 22 April 1567.

OPPOSITE The Rainbow Portrait of Elizabeth I at Hatfield House.

125

Mary Queen of Scots'
signet ring.

stringent, and on Lochleven, once her health was recovered, the queen began to develop those harmless, agreeable but petty activities with which royal prisoners while away their time – an unwitting dress rehearsal for the long years of imprisonment which lay ahead. She began to dance once more, and played at cards. She embroidered. She walked in the garden. She also looked out of the window towards the dark sedge reeds along the distant edge of the lake and, fed by the prisoners' fare of hope, pictured the moment when she too would be standing on that wind-blown shore, once more at liberty.

If the queen dreamt of freedom, in the manner of all prisoners, it is unlikely that she also dreamt of Bothwell. Melville's hint to her concerning George Douglas had borne fruit. The young man, personable and gallant, was only too happy to see in his sovereign a frail and helpless woman, the victim of a cruel fate. Her fragile beauty drawn with suffering, coupled with her romantic history, could not fail to move him further. The queen drew George Douglas's sympathies by the exertion of her famous personal charm and gentleness, but, although his heart was genuinely stirred by the presence of this romantic heroine, Mary's aim in this relationship, however much she appreciated the admiration, was quite clearly to escape from Lochleven; she now hoped to have found in George Douglas the weak link in the Douglas chain. But she was also able to extend her allure and her promise beyond even that of her own affections: for as Bothwell had now disappeared, there was in theory no reason why George Douglas should not aspire to her hand. Bothwell had been pursued to the Orkneys by his inveterate enemy, Kirkcaldy of Grange, who promised to bring him back dead, or die himself. In the event, neither death took place, for Bothwell escaped to Norway. King Frederick, joint sovereign of Denmark and Norway, quickly perceived in his uninvited guest a useful pawn in international politics, who as the husband of the queen of Scots, heiress-presumptive to the English throne, could certainly be used against the English queen. Bothwell was therefore taken prisoner and, although Moray pressed for his extradition, and Bothwell himself wrote anxiously to the king of France asking for help, he was destined to remain in a series of Danish prisons, of increasing squalor, for the rest of his life.

Throckmorton returned to England at the beginning of September, having made it clear, on the instructions of the English queen, that Queen Elizabeth did not acknowledge Queen Mary's abdication from the throne of Scotland; nor did she acknowledge the regency of Moray, despite his many friendly overtures to England. But regardless of this disapproval from across the border, the Marian party in Scotland seemed temporarily in abeyance, and by the middle of October, Moray was able to write to Cecil that Scotland was quiet.

Scotland might be quiet, and no part of it quieter than the tiny island in the middle of Lochleven which held the imprisoned queen. Nevertheless the course of Mary's fortunes did not stand still. The winter of 1567 was remarkable for an unpleasant development in her affairs. The governing lords found that circumstances dictated they should change their attitude both towards her and towards the official reasons for her imprisonment.

It was not enough to keep Mary incarcerated, having procured her abdication; the lords needed to provide some further public justification for their behaviour towards her. Originally they had claimed to be freeing Mary from Bothwell's tutelage. But now Bothwell had disappeared from the Scottish scene and Mary was in prison at Lochleven, they could hardly continue to criticize her on the score that she was unduly influenced by Bothwell. Some other reason had to be put forward to justify her continued confinement. Ignoring the deep implication of some of their own number in the murder at Kirk o'Field, in December 1567 – nearly a year after the event – Mary was herself publicly blamed for the death of Darnley.

The existence of certain documents which implicated Mary in the crime was mentioned for the first time in front of the Privy Council on 4 December. The text of these writings was not quoted, nor were the actual documents produced; but their existence was used to justify a new act of Council which stated that the official cause of Mary's detention was her involvement in her husband's death. Mary was said to have encouraged the outrage 'in so far as by divers her privy letters written and subscribed with her own hand and sent by her to James Earl Bothwell, chief executioner of the horrible murder'. At the Parliament convened by Moray on 15 December, Mary's abdication of the government was said to be 'lawful and perfect'; James's investiture and coronation was described as being valid as those of his ancestors, since it was to be considered as though his mother were actually dead. Moray's appointment as regent was confirmed, and the lords who had taken up arms at Carberry Hill were formally vindicated in that Queen Mary had been 'privy, art and part of the actual devise and deed of the fore-named murder of the King her lawful husband'. This was quite a new departure from the line which the lords had taken on the eve of Carberry Hill. Then all the talk had been of Bothwell's guilt; now for the first time the subject of Mary's guilt was introduced. It was a change of emphasis which boded no good for Mary's future.

Although Mary herself was unaware of the turn which matters were taking, the news that Moray was summoning a Parliament was enough to cast her into a state of fervour agitated by frustration. She addressed a long letter to her brother, asking that she should be allowed to vindicate herself before it, as previously arranged; she touched on her relationship with Moray, the favours she had shown him, his promises to support her, and earnestly suggested that she would submit to any law, even laying aside her queenly rank, if only she could be allowed a hearing; Queen Mary also pointed out pathetically her past virtues as a ruler – how she had never been extravagant or embezzled her subjects' money, like so many sovereigns. To this *cri de coeur*, in which can be heard the desperation of the captive who will promise anything, if only he or she can be allowed a hearing from the outside world, Moray sent only a few lines of acknowledgement.

Yet by mid-winter the graph of Scottish loyalties was rising once more in Mary's favour. For one thing, the Hamiltons were annoyed that Moray had assumed the regency, which they thought belonged rightfully to their family, as in the past. Kirkcaldy and Maitland were both

An enamelled pendant with the arms of Mary Queen of Scots below a crystal.

privately concerned lest Mary's abdication under duress might be considered illegal in the future. The Scots people, who had been told that their queen had been removed for complicity in Darnley's murder, could see for themselves that many nobles, far more intimately involved than she, were not only at liberty, but forming part of the government of the country, and Moray's persistent hunting down of the lesser criminals did not, as was intended, distract attention from this patent fact.

As spring came to Lochleven, Mary was able to smuggle out a few letters to France and England, describing her plight and appealing for aid. But it was inside rather than outside assistance which proved effective. So long as George Douglas remained on the island itself, there was not a great deal he could do to help his heroine beyond organizing her correspondence by bribing the boatman. But in the spring George Douglas quarrelled with his brother the laird (they both seem to have had their share of the peppery Douglas temper) and was ordered out of the house and off the island. This gave him the necessary opportunity to alert on the queen's behalf lords such as the faithful Seton, on whose loyalty she knew she could rely. Not only had George Douglas incurred his brother's wrath, but his rumoured plans to marry the queen seem to have also brought down the anger of Moray on his head, so that he was in a mood of fair rebellion towards his family and the established government of Scotland by the spring. Queen Mary was able to turn this to full advantage.

There was by now another spy within the castle dedicated to the queen's cause – young Willy Douglas, an orphaned cousin of the house called 'the little Douglas', who was also won over by the charm and kindness she had shown to him.

The date fixed for the escape attempt was 2 May. On that day Mary received word from George Douglas that all was ready and, while the laird was at supper, Willy Douglas dexterously removed his keys. The queen, dressed in a red kirtle borrowed from one of her women and a hood like those worn by countrywomen, boldly crossed the courtyard, although it was full of servants passing to and fro, and went out of the main gate. With the gate relocked behind them, the queen and her sole attendant, Willy Douglas, made their way down to the boat on the shore and, hidden beneath the boatman's seat, the queen was carried safely across the loch.

Mary was welcomed ashore by George Douglas and John Beaton who escorted her to Lord Seton and his followers. The country people, who recognized the queen, cheered as she passed. The music of popular acclaim must have sounded sweetly in Mary's ears after her confinement.

Queen Mary was once more at liberty after ten and a half months of captivity on a tiny island. In the meantime a countryman of lesser loyalty had rowed back to Lochleven to report her escape. The laird of Lochleven fell into such a passion of distress at the news that he tried to stab himself with his own dagger. But it is pleasant to record that those two other Douglases, George and Willy, who had placed devotion to their queen above family interest, were duly rewarded by her continual gratitude in later life and remained in her service during her English captivity.

PART THREE
The Captivity

10 In Foreign Bands

'And I'm the sovereign of Scotland
And mony a traitor there
Yet here I lay in foreign bands
And never-ending care.'

ROBERT BURNS, Queen Mary's Lament

On hearing that his sister had escaped from her prison, the Regent Moray was sore amazed, said the *Diurnal of Occurrents*; more especially because he happened to be at Glasgow when he learnt the evil news, and by now Mary had reached nearby Hamilton. The regent's first instinct was to desert the unhealthy area of western Scotland – where such loyal Marian lords as Herries and Maxwell held sway in the south, and Argyll, now also a Marian, in the north, to say nothing of the menacing prospect of the key fortress of Dumbarton, still firmly held for the queen, to the west beyond Glasgow. But prudence prevailed: the regent decided to stand firm, rather than let the whole west unite for the queen; as it turned out, he was amply repaid for the steadfast nature of his decision.

Supporters had flocked to the queen as a result of the series of proclamations in which she had once more sought her subjects' allegiance. The Marian party had by now reached impressive proportions – twice as many as that of the regent, said the queen. Estimates vary from 6,000 royalists to Moray's 4,000 to 5,000 and 3,000 repectively; but all agreed that Mary's party had considerable numerical superiority. This preponderance had the fatal effect of encouraging the queen's army to skirt Glasgow narrowly on their route to Dumbarton, in the hopes of drawing the regent into a fight and thus annihilating him. But despite being greater in number, the Marians were poorly led, and when they clashed with Moray's forces at the small village of Langside, their lines broke before the enemy. Mary's servant John Beaton told Catherine de Medicis later than Mary had mounted on her own horse and, like another Zenobia, ridden into the battle to encourage her troops to advance; she would have led them to the charge in person, but she found them all quarrelling among themselves, insensible to her eloquence and more inclined to exchange blows with each other than to attack the rebel host. Once the battle was clearly decided in favour of Moray, the queen had to ride, not like Zenobia into battle, but like any fugitive away from the scene of her defeat.

Guided by Lord Herries, the queen decided to flee south, into the south-western territories of Scotland which were still extremely Catholic in feeling as well as loyal to Mary, under the feudal sway of two Catholic magnates, Herries and Maxwell. A rough and wild journey brought Mary to the Maxwell castle of Terregles.

It was here at Terregles that the critical decision was taken to flee

PREVIOUS PAGE Mary Queen of Scots, by P. Oudry. An inscription in Latin was added after her execution to the effect that in 1568 'she came down to England under hope and estimation of help promised by Elizabeth', but was executed after Nineteen years' detention and 'earned in Heaven a crown more glorious than those three [England, Scotland and Ireland] the enjoyment of which she lost on 18 February 1587'. In fact, Mary was executed on 8 February 1587.

OPPOSITE Elizabeth I of England.

further on into England. The decision was made by the queen alone. She herself described dolefully to Archbishop Beaton in Paris how her supporters had cautioned her piteously not to trust Queen Elizabeth. The general view was that she should either stay in Scotland – where Herries guaranteed that she could hold out for at least another forty days – or go to France and hope to rally some support there. In retrospect, either course would seem to have been more sensible than seeking an English refuge. We cannot tell what considerations weighed with Mary Stuart to choose it nevertheless, what dreams of friendship and alliance with Elizabeth still possessed her; yet the siren song of Elizabeth's friendship, the mirage of the English succession, were still strong enough in this moment of decision to blot out the stable image of the proven friendship of France, where Mary had actually lived for thirteen years, and whose shores could be sought so easily from a western port of Scotland. In France Mary had the inalienable estates and incomes of a queen dowager; as a Catholic queen fleeing from a Protestant country, she had every reason to expect the support of her brother-in-law, Charles IX, to say nothing of her Guise relations. Even if Elizabeth had shown stronger support for Mary against her rebels in the short interval since Carberry Hill than the French king, the patent fact that Mary was a Catholic whereas her insurgents were mainly Protestants meant that the French would always have a vested interest to help the Scottish queen as their co-religionist.

In place of friendly France, Mary Stuart chose to fling herself upon the mercy of unknown England, a land where she had no party, no money, no estates, no relatives except her former mother-in-law, Lady Lennox, who hated her, and Queen Elizabeth herself, whom she had never met personally, and whose permission she had not even obtained to enter the country. As decisions go, it was a brave one, a romantic one even, but under the circumstances it was certainly not a wise one. No human character is static. Different circumstances develop different aspects of the same personality. Perhaps ten months in prison had served to bring out in Mary's nature that streak either of the romantic or of the gambler, which leads the subject fatally on ever to prefer hope and high adventure to the known quantity, and which Mary Stuart passed on so dramatically to many of her later Stuart descendants. From now on, like all captives, Mary Stuart was to live of necessity far more in the world of dreams, than in that of reality. Her confinement in Lochleven seemed to have already begun the process of attrition in her powers of judgement. The queen herself summed up the subject of her fatal decision in a sentence at the end of a letter to Beaton written towards the end of her life as sad as any she ever wrote: 'But I commanded my best friends to permit me to have my own way ...'

The decision once taken, Herries wrote to Lowther, the deputy governor of Carlisle, asking permission for the Scottish queen to take refuge in England. But Mary did not even wait for the return of the messenger. She was now in borrowed linen, and in clothes and a hood lent by the laird of Lochinvar. The hood was especially necessary because her head was shorn of its beautiful red-gold wealth of hair as a precaution against recognition. In this disguise she made her way west from Terregles to the

Letter of Mary Queen of Scots to Queen Elizabeth, shortly after her escape to England in May 1568; Mary protests passionately against Elizabeth's decision not to allow her into her presence to justify her behaviour.

abbey of Dundrennan, and on the afternoon of Sunday, 16 May she went down to the little port at the mouth of the abbey burn. From this undistinguished sea shore, she could actually see the coast of England across the Solway Firth. Perhaps the sight encouraged her, for at three o'clock in the afternoon the queen of Scotland embarked in a small fishing boat, with only a tiny party of loyal followers. In this humble fashion, Mary Stuart, who had been born in such magnificence in the palace of Linlithgow, a princess of Scotland, left her native country in a common fishing boat, never to return.

According to one tradition, during the four-hour journey the queen had a sudden premonition of the fate which awaited her in England, and ordered the boatmen to take her after all to France; but the winds and tide were against her, and the boat went remorselessly on towards England. Nau mentions no such vacillation: when Queen Mary arrived at the small Cumberland port of Workington at seven in the evening, she seemed as elated as ever by the heady wine of optimism. Queen Mary stumbled as she first set foot on English soil; this omen, which might have been interpreted in a sinister light, was on the contrary taken by her followers as a sign that their queen was coming to take possession of the country.

The next morning the deputy governor, Lowther, already warned by Herries's letter, arrived with a force of 400 horsemen to conduct the queen back to Carlisle, and by 18 May Mary was installed in semi-captivity at Carlisle Castle.

Lowther reported that the attire of the Scottish queen was 'very mean'. Once more in Mary's history a hurried escape from danger, in disguise, had left her with nothing in the way of a change of clothes. Noting that the Scottish queen had so little money with her that it would scarcely cover the costs of clothing she so sadly needed, Lowther gallantly ordered her expenses to be defrayed. Lowther was evidently puzzled as to exactly how he should treat this strange bird of rare plumage which had so confidently flown into the English aviary; but he was determined to err if anything on the side of courtesy, not knowing from one minute to the next whether his guest might not be summoned to London and there received with every honour by Queen Elizabeth herself.

Puzzled as Richard Lowther might have been as how to treat his royal visitor, his bewilderment was as nothing compared to the perturbation of Elizabeth's advisers in London. Here Queen Mary's arrival, romantic foolish gesture as it might be, had caused a flutter from which the English court would take time to recover. After all, how was Queen Elizabeth to treat the royal fugitive? She had not captured Queen Mary, nor sought to do so. Mary had arrived of her own free will, expressly seeking English assistance, as her own letters immediately before and after her arrival testified – a point which was to be raised again and again by Mary during her years as an English prisoner, and last of all, with pardonable bitterness, at her trial. Yet Queen Mary's request to be restored to her own throne posed Elizabeth a whole series of problems which she could hardly ignore. It was unthinkable in fact for the Protestant English queen to take arms against Scotland on behalf of her Catholic cousin; on the

Dundrennan Abbey, Kirkcudbrightshire, to which Mary fled in disguise before leaving her native country forever and throwing herself on the mercy of the English.

other hand if Elizabeth did not do so, there was nothing to stop Mary making the same request to the French, who might seize with enthusiasm upon this new opportunity for entry on to the British mainland. Therefore, to allow Mary to pass freely through England to France was hardly good politics from the English point of view. That the Scottish queen should be received at the English court, and permitted to enjoy full liberty in England was an equally obnoxious prospect from the angle of English statecraft. Mary Stuart at liberty might prove an unpleasant focus for the loyalties of the English Catholics. Mary herself might have forgotten that ten years before as dauphiness of France she had claimed to be the rightful queen of England, but Elizabeth's principal adviser Cecil had not forgotten her pretensions, and there was no guarantee that the English Catholics had either.

Taken all in all, the most politic course from the English point of view was to temporize, until sufficient assessment had been made of the interior situation of Scotland. In the long run, Elizabeth felt, it would probably be wisest to dispatch Mary back to her difficult subjects, rather than let her loose in either England or France, and furthermore there was that other consideration that subjects should not be encouraged to rebel against queens. But of course there was no question of restoring Mary by the force of an English army; the terms on which the Scots would accept Mary back would have to be discovered by cautious inquiries – and, if possible, negotiated to Elizabeth's own advantage. In the meantime it would be best to keep Mary in the north not exactly a prisoner, but not exactly free, not exactly debarred for ever from Elizabeth's presence, but

BELOW Sir William Cecil, Lord Burghley, was Elizabeth's principal adviser and saw Mary as a potential threat to the English throne.

BELOW RIGHT Bolton Castle, Yorkshire, to where it was decided to send Mary after she had fled to England.

certainly not welcomed into it. The only course which was emphatically to be debarred to Mary was that of seeking French help: Mary was to be told plainly that as Elizabeth intended to assist her herself, any attempt on the Scottish queen's part to bring in the French as well would be regarded as merely renewing old quarrels. Fortunately Mary had not arrived in England with an unbesmirched reputation: there was that unresolved matter of Darnley's death, and the scandal she had caused by marrying the chief suspect. The cloud of old scandal round Mary's head now provided a convenient excuse for putting her off from Elizabeth's presence, until she should have been cleared of all guilt. And in such work of arbitration, who would be more suitable to act as judge between Mary's cause and that of her nobles than the English queen herself?

Queen Elizabeth's next move was to send her trusted counsellor, Sir Francis Knollys, to treat with her guest-captive along these delicate lines. Knollys, now about fifty-five, was a man of the highest honour and a leading Puritan. Despite their religious differences, Mary made an immediately favourable impression upon this experienced courtier. He discovered in her a woman of innate intelligence, blessed with an eloquent tongue and full of practical good sense; to these qualities, she also joined considerable personal courage. Knollys metaphorically scratched his head as he wondered what on earth was to be done with such a spirited creature, and he questioned his correspondents in London whether it was indeed 'wise to dissemble with such a lady'.

The answer came back from the south that it was indeed wise to dissemble, since it was, for the moment, the most politically advantageous course open to the English. Knollys was therefore instructed to tell Queen Mary that she could not be received at the English court until she had been purged of the stain of her husband's murder, and this purgation could only be achieved if she submitted herself to the judgement of Elizabeth. Tears flowed from Mary's eyes at the news: in a passion of rage at the injustice, she pointed out that both Maitland and Morton had assented to the murder of Darnley 'as it could well be proved, although now they would seem to persecute the same'.

Mary's state within Carlisle Castle was on Knollys's own admission far from luxurious. There were heavy iron gratings across Mary's windows and a series of three ante-chambers packed with soldiers led to her own chamber. Whenever she walked or rode she was attended by a guard of a hundred men. Her chief lack was of waiting women: she who had been surrounded all her life by ladies of the highest rank to attend her, now had only two or three to help her, and they were 'not of the finest sort'. The arrival of Mary Seton, one of Mary's most devoted ladies, provided a welcome relief, more especially as she was an expert hairdresser. Such feminine skills were all the the more necessary since the queen had chopped off her own hair during the flight from Langside; it never grew again in its old abundance and it seems that for the rest of her life Mary was dependent on wigs and false-pieces. Despite Mary Seton's endeavours, the queen's clothing still remained a problem. Queen Elizabeth, appealed to for some help out of her own copious wardrobe, responded with gifts of such mean quality – some odd pieces of black velvet and old dresses – that the embarrassed Knollys tried to explain them away by saying that they had been intended for Mary's maids. Moray was scarcely more generous: when he dispatched three coffers of his sister's clothes from Scotland the queen noted angrily that there was but one taffeta dress amongst them, the rest merely cloaks and 'coverage for saddles' – ironically useless to a captive. She had to send for sartorial reinforcement from Lochleven. In July she did receive from her chamberlain in Scotland a number of belongings, mainly accessories including gloves, pearl buttons, tights, veils, coifs of black and white, and twelve *orillettes* or bandages, to place over the ears when asleep, no doubt to cut out from the royal consciousness the heavy tread of the soldiers in the rooms outside.

To Mary these feminine considerations of dress and hair, and even the conditions of her confinement, were secondary to her grand design to reach the presence of Queen Elizabeth. From her arrival at Workington towards the end of May, until the end of the conference at York, and its removal to London, Queen Mary wrote over twenty letters to Queen Elizabeth, most of them extremely long, well thought out, intelligent pieces of pleading, all elaborations on the same theme of Mary's need for succour to regain her Scottish throne, and her trust in Elizabeth to provide it.

Meanwhile, in Scotland, Moray and his supporters had quite independently reached the same conclusion as Elizabeth: Mary's guilt over Darnley's death and her subsequent marriage to Bothwell were the points to be stressed if Mary was to be kept where Moray would most like to see her – in an English prison. The difference between Elizabeth and Moray was that Elizabeth at this point intended ultimately to restore Mary to Scotland, and only wished to delay the process; Moray on the other hand had no wish to see Mary back on the throne on any terms whatsoever. To Moray, the viciousness of his sister was no moral issue, it was a question of his own survival as governor of Scotland. Moray was therefore determined to go much further than the English and make the mud already thrown at Mary stick so hard that there could be no question of this besmeared figure returning to reign.

It was significant that Cecil himself, in a private memorandum, could find Mary's alleged moral turpitude the only true excuse for keeping her off the Scottish throne and in an English prison. In favour of setting Mary at liberty were the following arguments: that she had come of her own accord to England, trusting in Elizabeth's frequent promises of assistance; that she herself had been illegally condemned by her subjects, who had imprisoned her and charged her with the murder of Darnley, without ever allowing her to answer for her crimes; that she was a queen subject to none, and not bound by law to answer to her subjects; lastly there were her own frequent offers to justify her behaviour personally in front of Queen Elizabeth. It was indeed a hard case to answer; it was certainly not answered by Mary's opponents at the time, nor has the passage of time and the unrolling of history made it seem any less formidable as an indictment of England's subsequent behaviour.

It was under these circumstances then, that shortly after Mary's flight to England, the first salvos in the new campaign to blacken her reputation once and for all were fired by the men who now occupied the throne from which they had ejected her. The queen's 'privy letters', which had first been heard of in the Parliament of the previous December, now made a new appearance on the political scene. Moray's secretary, John Wood, was dispatched to London with copies of the letters and instructions to show them secretly to the English establishment, in order to hint at what big guns Moray might be able to bring against his sister, if only the English would encourage him to do so.

The encouragement which Moray needed was an assurance from Elizabeth that she would not restore Mary to her throne in the event of her being found guilty of the murder. For it was of no avail to accuse Mary of murder, and prove it by fair means or foul, if she was subsequently to be restored to her throne. Her vengeance might then be expected to be fierce upon those who had accused her. At this critical juncture, it seems likely that in response to Moray's anxious inquiries, Cecil did in fact give some private written assurances to John Wood in London, to pass on to Moray: whatever Elizabeth might say in public, in order to lure the Scottish queen into accepting her arbitration voluntarily, it was not in fact intended to restore Mary to Scotland if she was found to be guilty. At all events, Moray received some sort of satisfactory answer to his problem at the end of June, for he now began to endorse the plan of an English 'trial' with enthusiasm.

While Mary's emissary in London, Lord Herries, treated with Cecil and Elizabeth over the possibility of the English holding such a 'trial' if Mary would agree to it, Mary herself suffered a change of prison. It was decided to remove her to Bolton Castle in Yorkshire, as Carlisle was dangerously near the Scottish border. The move was complicated by the fact that Mary was still not officially a prisoner. When the suggestion of a change was first broached to Mary she quickly asked whether she was to go as a captive of her own choice. In answer she was told that Elizabeth merely wished to have Mary stationed nearer to herself. To this Mary countered with equal diplomacy that since she was in Elizabeth's hands, she might dispose of her as she willed. But when the actual moment came to leave Carlisle, Mary showed less composure. She began to weep and rage with a temper which was rapidly quickening with the frustrations of her unexpected imprisonment. Knollys had to exercise all his patience to get Mary to agree to proceed, since he did not wish to practise duress. Eventually Mary saw that threats and lamentations were achieving nothing, whereas gentleness might win her some advantage. She therefore withdrew her objections to departure, like a wise woman, said Knollys, and allowed herself to be removed quite placidly.

In spite of her incarceration, Mary had some inkling of the intrigues which were now being spun between Edinburgh and London, and her knowledge of Scotland led her to guess more. The news that some of her own letters were to be used against her reduced her to a state of nervous collapse and the move away from Carlisle proved to be a severe handicap. Carlisle, a frontier town with administrative connections, was easy of access for travellers whereas Bolton was an isolated castle in a remote corner of the North Riding of Yorkshire. The castle itself was comparatively unfurnished on her arrival, and hangings and other furniture had to be borrowed from Sir George Bowes's house some distance away.

Far more serious to Mary's cause than these minor discomforts was the fact that she was from now on placed physically outside the mainstream of political life, although mentally she remained very much part of it. Mary had never been well endowed with advisers, although she was a woman who wished by nature to lean upon others for advice; for the next nineteen years she was deprived of any sort of proper worldly contact by which to judge the situations which were reported to her, and her own counsellors, although loyal, were no match in intelligence for the English politicians with whom they had to deal.

Herries came to Bolton from London at the end of July and put the English proposals to his queen; it is easy to understand how Mary, lit up by false hopes of restoration at Elizabeth's hands, agreed at least to the prospect of an English 'trial'. The fact that the English had no right to try her seemed now less important than the fact that Elizabeth had promised to restore her whatever the outcome. But the climate in the outside world was harsher than Mary remembered. On 20 September Elizabeth wrote privately to Moray promising him what Cecil had already divulged in secret: whatever impression Elizabeth might have given Mary, the Scottish queen would not in fact be restored to her throne if she were found guilty in England. Moray had now every impetus to prepare the blackest possible case against his sister and the queen's 'privy letters' became the central plank of his accusatory edifice.

Under these inauspicious circumstances, the conference of York opened in October 1568. It had been decided that the 'trial' should take the form of examination of the evidence by an English panel, headed by the duke of Norfolk. Both Mary and Moray were allowed commissioners. The conference was remarkable from the first for the confusion of aims among its participants. Elizabeth had already left conflicting impressions upon Mary and the Scottish nobles as to what she regarded as the desirable outcome and their own intentions were equally at variance. Of those present, only Moray was able to show true singleness of purpose, in that he intended to prove the queen of Scotland's guilt up to the hilt in order to prevent her return north; with this object in view he took with him to York the debatable 'privy letters' in their famous silver casket. (The casket, and the documents it contained, had apparently come to light when one of Bothwell's henchmen was apprehended for his part in the Kirk o'Field plot.) The incriminating documents were described as 'missive letters, contracts or obligations for marriage, sonnets or love-ballads, and all other letters contained therein'. In addition Moray had also commissioned George Buchanan to prepare a *Book of Articles* to denounce Mary and this was also to be presented in front of the conference.

Moray's supporters were much less single-minded than their chief in their aims: Maitland, in particular, dangled after a scheme for Anglo-Scottish union, in which a restored Mary could play her part. Nor were Mary's own commissioners, including John Leslie, bishop of Ross, and Lord Herries, as resolute in their determination to prove her innocence as was the queen herself; having lived through the troubled times of the queen's marriage to Bothwell, they conceived their role as rather to secure some sort of compromise by which Mary could be brought back

TOP George Buchanan, who was commissioned by Moray in May 1568 to prepare a 'Book of Articles' to denounce Mary.

ABOVE The silver casket believed to have contained originally the vanished Casket Letters, now in the Museum at Lennoxlove, East Lothian.

LEFT The first page of the contemporary copy of the Fifth Casket Letter, discovered at Hatfield House in 1870: this is the only letter copied in the Italian hand (which Mary used) as opposed to the clerkly hand used by most English and Scots at the same period.

to Scotland than to shout out Queen Mary's freedom from guilt from the house-tops. As for the English 'judges', the earl of Sussex, Sir Ralph Sadler, and the duke of Norfolk, it soon transpired that they too were not immune to private considerations. Norfolk had been recently widowed; he was England's leading noble, and himself a Protestant, although he had many Catholic relations; the queen of Scots was now generally regarded as once more marriageable, despite the fact that divorce from Bothwell was not yet secured, and Norfolk's name had been mentioned in this context, even before the opening of the conference. As a 'judge', therefore, Norfolk might be supposed to be somewhat *parti pris*.

Under these circumstances it was hardly surprising that the

proceedings at York achieved little, and Elizabeth reacted by sending for the whole conference to start again at Westminster. Copies of the so-called 'casket letters' had been secretly shown to the English commissioners. Sussex did not seem to take them particularly seriously but Norfolk was shocked by their contents at first. It seems likely, however, that Maitland revealed to him that they were not all they seemed, and that the allegations against Mary as a murderess were not really to be taken too seriously.

On 29 November Moray presented his 'eik' or list of accusations before the commission at Westminster. Mary protested strongly at not being allowed the right to attend personally on the same footing as Moray, but this Elizabeth could not allow. If Mary appeared before the tribunal she would obviously deny the authenticity of the letters *in toto*, as a result of which she could never be convicted on their evidence; after this Elizabeth would be compelled to acquit her and set her free. If on the other hand, Mary was not allowed to appear personally, the whole matter could probably be 'huddled up' with some show of saving Mary's honour, and yet without exposing the Scottish lords as forgers; after this Mary could still be kept in prison. Elizabeth, therefore, refused Mary's request on the ingenious grounds that no proofs had as yet been shown against her (the casket letters had not yet been produced in court): there was therefore no point in her appearing at this juncture, when as far as Elizabeth knew, it might never be found necessary at all, and Mary might be able to be declared innocent *in absentia*. Winter had come early that year. Thick snow piled the ground between London and distant Bolton, 250 miles and days of hard riding away. Mary's enforced isolation was proving a disastrous hinderance to her cause.

Moray was now asked to produce additional proofs of his eik and he exhibited the December 1567 Act of Parliament and Buchanan's *Book of Articles*. Finally he produced the casket and the letters. The English tribunal duly had the letters copied out for themselves, collated the copies with the originals, and then, at Moray's request, handed him back the originals. Mary's commissioners were not even admitted to the proceedings while the tribunal examined the copies of the letters.

In the meantime Elizabeth gave Mary three choices: she could answer the accusations through her own commissioners, in writing herself, or personally to some English nobles sent expressly to Bolton for the purpose. To all these alternatives Mary returned an indignant negative: she could hardly be expected to answer accusations based on evidence neither she nor her commissioners were allowed to see, or surrender the traditional right of the prisoner to face her accusers. But Elizabeth said that if Mary refused these three alternatives: 'it will be thought as much as she were culpable'.

At last Mary was beginning to have some inkling of the treacherous nature of the quagmire into which she had so unwarily walked. On 19 December she belatedly drew up her own eik for the accusation of Moray. Not surprisingly she waxed especially furious over Moray's accusation that she had planned the death of her own child to follow that of his father, and beyond that she dwelt on her previous troubles with the lords – the murder of Riccio when they would have 'slain the mother

OPPOSITE Mary Queen of Scots, a portrait at Hatfield House.

OVERPAGE
LEFT A detail from a panel of embroidery at Hardwicke House showing Mary's cipher.

RIGHT A contemporary Dutch watercolour showing the beheading of Mary Queen of Scots at Fotheringay.

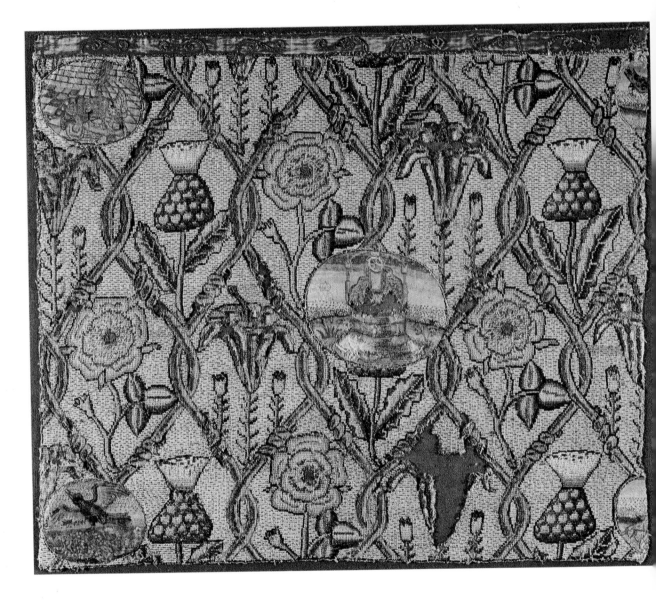

coninginne van schotlant

Den VIII february werde onthalst Maria
Stuart Schots Coninginne s'terwende Roomisch Catho-
lyck Hebbende gesocht veel onrusten aen te richten haer selven
meester te maecken van Engelant t'welck haer vanden staet
ofte te parlement volcomelyck werde vertoont, Anno 1587.
Metren XIII fol. XIII en XIIII. b

and the bairn both when he was in our womb', and the manifest illegality of Moray's regency.

Despite Mary's counter-accusations, and despite her continued requests to be shown the writings which were said to arraign her, the conference at Westminster was officially ended by Elizabeth on 11 January without either Mary or her commissioners being allowed to glimpse these debatable documents. The verdict of the tribunal was indeed as ambivalent as the rest of the proceedings: it was decided that neither party had had anything sufficiently proved against them. Mary had not proved that her nobles had rebelled against her – 'there has been nothing deduced against them as yet that may impair their honour and allegiances'. But, on the other hand, lengthy inspection of the casket letters had not apparently convinced the tribunal of the guilt of the Scottish queen. In short, neither side was adjudged guilty at the end of the 'trial', the only difference being that whereas Moray was now allowed to depart for Scotland, after a personal interview with Elizabeth – and incidentally with a £5,000 subsidy in his pocket – Mary was still held at Bolton, with preparations afoot to move her to a still more secure prison.

As for the casket letters on which Mary's reputation was so thoroughly blasted in later centuries, it is interesting to note that Mary's contemporaries apparently attached a great deal less importance to them than subsequent historians. Queen Elizabeth evidently found nothing in them which was proof against her dearest sister. Compounded of Bothwell's love letters to other women, some textual interpretations from other letters and a certain amount of inexpert forgery, all glossed over by a great deal of optimistic explanation on the part of the lords who presented them, they were certainly never intended to be exposed to the fierce glare of criticism and discussion which has been directed on to them ever since. The intensity of this discussion results from the fact that they are the only direct proof – inadequate as they are – of Mary's adultery with Bothwell before Darnley's death. Yet a rational consideration of the letters, in so far as is possible from mere copies, since the originals disappeared some years after the trial, shows that at most Mary can be accused of two 'crimes', neither of them anything like as serious as the murder of her husband. In the first place, it is likely that she induced Darnley to leave Glasgow for Edinburgh with the promise of resuming physical relations with him once he was cured of his pox; but this does not in itself constitute proof of adultery with Bothwell, and Mary's partisans might even point out in her defence that there was no proof that she would not have implemented her promise if Darnley had lived. Secondly, and much more cogently, she can be accused of foreknowledge of her own abduction by Bothwell. Once more this is not criminal so much as unwise behaviour and has no specific bearing on the death of Darnley six weeks earlier. It reflects much more acutely on Mary's total inability at this point to deal with the internal politics of Scotland without leaning on some sort of support, and in the event she chose the wrong sort of support. These aspects of Mary Stuart's behaviour in the first half of 1567 are certainly not enough to brand her as a murderess or even as a scarlet woman, deserving the vengeance of society.

OPPOSITE A miniature of Mary Queen of Scots, 1575–80.

11 *The Uses of Adversity*

'Tribulation has been to them as a furnace of fine gold – a means of proving their virtue, of opening their so-long-blinded eyes, and of teaching them to know themselves and their own failings.'

MARY QUEEN OF SCOTS *on the lives of rulers,* Essay on Adversity, *1580*

As the last farcical acts of the conference of Westminster were taking place, preparations were already afoot in faraway Yorkshire to move Queen Mary to a more secure prison at Tutbury in Staffordshire. This time Mary could hardly persuade herself that she was no longer a prisoner, or that restoration to her throne was imminent, since the news that Moray had been allowed to return to Scotland unscathed represented an undeniable blight to even her most timid hopes.

The medieval castle of Tutbury was of all her many prisons the one Mary hated most. She always maintained afterwards that she had begun her true imprisonment there, and this in itself was sufficient reason to prejudice her against it; but Tutbury quickly added evil associations of its own to combine with her innate distaste. The castle, which was large enough to be more like a fortified town than a fortress, occupied a hill on the extreme edge of Staffordshire and Derbyshire from which the surrounding country could be easily surveyed. Not only was Tutbury in many parts ruined (as the English government from the vantage point of London never seem to have realized), but it was also extremely damp, its magnificent view of the midlands including a large marsh just underneath it from which malevolent fumes arose, unpleasant enough for anyone and especially so for a woman of Mary Stuart's delicate health. Later on, when Mary had reason to know full well the evils of Tutbury, she wrote of its horrors in winter, and in particular of the ancient structure, mere wood and plaster, which admitted every draught – that *'méchante vieille charpenterie'*, as she put it, through which the wind whistled into every corner of her chamber.

Mary was now in the hands of a new jailer, George Talbot, earl of Shrewsbury, whose wife Elizabeth is known to history as Bess of Hardwicke. Shrewsbury, a man of about forty, was to act as the queen's jailer for the next fifteen and a half years. He was a Protestant and immensely rich; he possessed an enormous range of properties across the centre of England, but like many rich men he was obsessed with the need to preserve his inheritance, so that in the course of his wardship of Queen Mary, his letters to the English court began to sound like one long complaining account book of rising prices, servants' keep and inadequate subsidies. Shrewsbury had long proved his loyalty to Elizabeth, however, and his character, fussy and nervous, constantly worrying about the reactions of the central government to his behaviour or that of his

146

prisoner, made him in many ways an ideal jailer. Moreover, it was felt that Mary would be contained in safety in his string of dwellings across the midlands, equally distant from the London of her desire and the dangerously Catholic northern counties.

The queen and her new captors got on agreeably enough. Mary was allowed to set up her cloth of state to which she attached such importance, and a certain Sir John Morton was introduced into her *ménage*, who was in fact a Catholic priest, a fact of which Shrewsbury was either ignorant or agreed to turn a blind eye. The queen and Bess were described by Shrewsbury as sitting long hours together embroidering in Bess's chamber where they delighted in 'devising' fresh works to carry out.

Embroidery was to prove the great solace of Queen Mary's long years of captivity. It was a taste she had already acquired as a young queen and now, with all too ample leisure at her command, the taste was to become a passion and almost a mania. Pieces of embroidery, lovingly and hopefully done with her own hand as though the needle could pierce the stony heart where the pen could not, were to prove the basis of the gifts which Queen Mary sent to Elizabeth. An inventory of her belongings six months before her death included many items of embroidery not yet finished, including bed hangings and chair covers, as though the captive had set herself the Penelope-like task of ornamenting every object in her daily life. Into her embroidery the queen put much of herself, including

A panel of embroidery now at Oxburgh Hall, Norfolk, believed to have been stitched by Mary Queen of Scots and Bess of Hardwicke, showing the numerous devices and anagrams, often of her own name, which Mary liked to incorporate in her work.

147

TOP George Talbot, Earl of
Shrewsbury, who was
Mary's jailer, with only
short breaks, for fifteen
and a half years.

ABOVE Elizabeth, Countess
of Shrewsbury, second
wife of George Talbot,
also known as Bess of
Hardwicke.

her love of literary devices and allusions, which she had first acquired at the French court. Anagrams of her name and favourite mottoes were often worked into her pieces of embroidery; the now famous motto of Mary Stuart, '*En ma fin mon commencement*', was embroidered on her cloth of state. Quite apart from the contemporary delight in such conceits, they seem to have appealed to the romantic streak in Queen Mary's nature, a child-like love of intrigue and secrecy. This was a strain only encouraged by captivity; it is as though, having been captured at the age of twenty-four and cut off from outside society before she had fully reached maturity, Mary remained in some ways frozen in curiously youthful and even naïve attitudes.

In captivity Mary's health was her most obvious problem, apart from her desire for freedom. It was often the old pain in her side which put a final end to a day's embroidering. Her health was only worsened by the discomfort of Tutbury. In March Shrewsbury noted that she was once more severely ill from what he termed 'grief of the spleen' and which her doctor told him was '*obstructio splenis cum flatu hypochondriaco*'; the queen's symptoms were pains, said to be the result of 'windy matter ascending to the head', strong enough to make her faint. Even a move from the odious Tutbury to the more salubrious Shrewsbury dwelling of Wingfield Manor did not effect the desired cure. Queen Mary's health now became a chronic problem for her and her jailers, and there are few of her letters in the ensuing years which do not refer in some manner to the physical pain she had to endure.

The secret moves to marry Mary to Norfolk, and then presumably restore her to the throne of Scotland, neatly linked to a Protestant English bridegroom, a project first mentioned to Mary before the York conference, now proceeded apace. Mary's captivity in England had after all no legal basis, and her abdication from the throne of Scotland had been made under duress, which robbed it of its validity; in the meantime her blood relationship to Queen Elizabeth, and her possible succession to the English throne made her a rich prize. Elizabeth's disapproval was by no means a foregone conclusion: in fact she herself had suggested Norfolk as a possible bridegroom for Mary before her marriage to Darnley. Many of the Scots were said to look on the scheme with favour, and even Moray himself appeared to play along with the idea of the marriage for the time being. It certainly fitted in with Maitland's plans, and he was involved in the secret manoeuvres. Many of the English nobles, who disliked the dominance of Cecil within the English Privy Council, saw in the elevation of Norfolk as Mary's bridegroom a convenient way of dealing with Cecil's rising influence.

The actual part played by Queen Mary herself in the cobwebs of intrigue and counter-intrigue which followed was negligible, except in so far as her mere existence, for which she could hardly be blamed, made her, as Elizabeth angrily wrote at the end of it all, 'the daughter of debate that eke discord doth sow'. As for her captivity, which made such an apple of discord in the centre of England, there was no one more anxious to end it than Mary herself. In all the first attempts or conspiracies to procure her release, Queen Mary adopted exactly the same attitude: since her imprisonment was illegal, she would consider herself free to try and achieve her liberty by any means in her power. As a 'sovereign princess' over whom Elizabeth had no jurisdiction, she never considered that any schemes, or letters of instruction, however daring from the English point of view, could possibly be fairly held against her by English justice. There were, however, refinements to this attitude: Mary was strongly predisposed towards any scheme that sounded as if it might have the backing of a major power, and strongly disinclined to consider any hare-brained scheme which had exactly the opposite ring. At the head of her list of major powers who she thought might help her was still Elizabeth.

Mary's part in the marriage negotiations – conducted in strict secrecy from Queen Elizabeth whose temper on the subject of any marriage, and especially royal ones, was notoriously uncertain – was confined to writing a series of affectionate and even loving letters to Norfolk; yet since she never met their object, these letters belonged very much to the world of pen-friendship and dreams rather than to that of reality. He was now to Mary 'my Norfolk', to whom she emphasized her unhappiness and the desire for liberty. 'My Norfolk,' she wrote charmingly on occasion, 'you bid me command you, that would be beside my duty many ways, but pray you I will, that you counsel me not to take patiently my griefs ...'

It is clear that, despite these affectionate demonstrations, in the Norfolk negotiations Mary was very much following the line of conduct presented to her by her advisers, rather than leading them forward; this was in part due to the conditions of her captivity which made her dependent on the reports of others to estimate any external situation. It was also due to her natural suspicion of the whole state of marriage: she had believed Bothwell to be the choice of her nobles and he had turned out to be their bane; she had believed Darnley to be the choice of Elizabeth, but she had been rewarded for marrying him by the virulent fury of the English queen. It was hardly surprising that she greeted the first approaches over the Norfolk match with considerable doubt. When she finally gave her consent, it was on the strict understanding that Elizabeth's approval would be secured. It is evident that she was seeking an honourable exit from her cage approved by Elizabeth rather than involvement in a life-and-death conspiracy.

In the summer of 1569 Elizabeth showed encouraging signs of favour to Mary by sounding out the Scots on the subject of restoration again. But the series of proposals, to which Elizabeth herself seems to have been genuinely well disposed, were turned down by the Scots, and six weeks later Elizabeth discovered the Norfolk marriage plot. Her rage was extreme. Mary found herself moved back to the hated Tutbury. Her suite was cut down, her rooms searched, and Elizabeth angrily ordered that Mary should neither give nor receive messages to the outside world. Norfolk was imprisoned in the Tower.

The northern rising in November, under the Catholic earls of Northumberland and Westmorland, did nothing to improve Queen Mary's lot. This rising, ill-prepared and ill-organized, was more in the nature of a separatist movement on the part of the northern Catholics, than a revolt on behalf of Mary Queen of Scots. Mary herself disapproved of it, not only on the grounds that she hated violence and wished to avoid the risk of the slaughter of innocent people, but also on the very sensible grounds that she did not believe it would do her cause any good, since the moment was hardly ripe for such a demonstration. Yet whatever her own wishes, a Catholic queen was the inevitable rallying-point for such an enterprise, and Mary was hastily taken to Coventry for the time being in order to be geographically still farther away from the rebels.

In the meantime events in troubled Scotland were about to take another dramatic turn: on 11 January 1570 Regent Moray fell dead, struck down by the bullets of an assassin in the main street of Linlithgow. It was no coincidence that he was struck down by a Hamilton, a member of a rival family: Scotland was by now a hotbed of warring factions, and continued to be throughout the minority of James. Lennox, Mary's bitterest enemy, now became regent, largely as a result of the favour of Elizabeth, who supported him as being a likely tool of English policy.

Back in England, the papal bull, *Regnans in Excelsis*, which had been promulgated by Pope Pius v, reached London in May. It was to have an enormous effect on Mary's future, since it formally excommunicated Elizabeth and declared that her Catholic subjects were released from their loyalty to her. At the time of the northern rising, Mary had been offered a possible chance of escape, and in the summer of 1570 an ill-conceived plot to rescue her from Chatsworth, where she was now held, was hatched by some local squires. Each time Mary responded unenthusiastically; as John Beaton noted, 'she nothing doubted but that the Queen's Majesty [Elizabeth] at the request of the Kings of Spain and France would restore her to her former dignity hereafter, the which she rather minded to expect, than to adventure upon a mere uncertainty, by such means to work her own delivery which might if the matter miscarried, turn her to confusion and all her partakers'. Mary was by now a woman of nearly thirty, on the verge of middle-age by the standards of the time; the old impetuosity of her youth was gone. She was chronically sick and alone in a country she did not know. Under these circumstances she preferred to pin her hopes to more substantial targets.

In August 1570 Norfolk was released from the Tower. His release proved the signal for a further and much wider conspiracy, in which he was once more involved, under the inspiration of an Italian banker based in London named Roberto Ridolfi. Ridolfi's aim was apparently to secure an invasion of England from the Netherlands, led by Philip ii's general there, the duke of Alva; it was to be supplemented by a rising of native Catholics within England. This combination of invaders and internal rebels would free Mary and, having seized Elizabeth, place Mary on the throne of England, side by side with her consort Norfolk.

Mary's attitude to, and personal involvement in, Ridolfi's schemes is open to question. It is possible that after three years' onerous English captivity, she did allow herself to be persuaded to write the incriminating instructions and letters to Ridolfi quoted against her at Norfolk's trial. Yet she had not despaired of Elizabeth's assistance and in October she wrote to the English queen, stating the full confidence she felt in Elizabeth, and her desire to have her (Mary's) succession rights discussed in the English Parliament. Subsequently Mary did admit to having given some sort of financial commission to Ridolfi, but she always denied that it had been anything so specific and dangerous to England as was suggested.

News of what was afoot began to trickle through to the English government in the late spring and by September the conspirators had been rounded up. Norfolk was arrested once more and in January was tried for treason. He was condemned and finally executed in the following June. When Queen Mary heard of the execution of 'her Norfolk' she cried bitterly and kept to her room.

Following the discovery of the Ridolfi plot and Norfolk's execution, Mary's character underwent a dramatic change in the eyes of the English nobility and the English Parliament. Popular opinion has a loud voice but a short memory. The circumstances of her arrival, now four years away, were quite forgotten in the tide of popular hatred which spread against her – this 'monstrous dragon', as one Member of Parliament termed her. Mary was now seen as a foreign-born Catholic spider, sitting in the centre of England spinning her webs in order to depose the English Protestant queen. The fact that she was an isolated prisoner with very little money was ignored in the light of the dangerous possibilities which the Ridolfi plot seemed to expose. But although Elizabeth did reluctantly agree to the execution of Norfolk, and despite the most ferocious baying for blood on the part of her faithful Commons, she refused to consider the execution of Mary. She personally prevented the Commons from passing a bill of attainder on the Scottish queen; instead a bill was passed merely depriving Mary of her right to succeed to the English throne, and declaring her liable to a trial by peers (peers of the English realm, rather than her own peers, or equals, who would be sovereigns), should she be discovered plotting again.

In the strange tortuous map of her relations with Elizabeth, Mary's feelings are much better charted than those of the English queen. But just as Elizabeth's incarceration of Mary on evidence she herself declared to be insufficient is greatly to her discredit, her preservation of Mary's life in 1572 by personal intervention must be allowed to be to her credit. Elizabeth, like Mary, had a constitutional dislike of spilling blood. Elizabeth was also conscious that Mary was by now by far her closest adult relation, since the death of Catherine Grey; Catherine's sons and Mary's son were still children, and Elizabeth may have had some reluctance to abandon her kingdom to the care of young children (which had proved so fatal in Scotland) if the assassin should find her as he had found Moray. Most of all, however, she was aware that Mary, like herself, was a sovereign princess: the death of one princess might strike at them all.

Too little is known of Elizabeth's inner feelings for Mary, since the English queen had learnt in childhood to hide all inner feelings, those dangerous traitors, within the breast. That closeness which two queens and near cousins should feel for each other, so often chanted by Mary, may have found more echoes in Elizabeth's heart than she ever admitted. In the meantime this merciful strain, this sneaking affection, could not fail to be noticed by Elizabeth's advisers: the point was taken that if ever the execution of Mary Stuart was to be secured, Elizabeth would have to

be thoroughly convinced that her good sister had repaid her clemency with flagrant and harmful ingratitude.

By the summer of 1572 the public cause of Mary Stuart seemed lost indeed; she was left to discover for herself in the private life of captivity the uses of adversity, sweet or otherwise. This outward decline in her circumstances was completed by the turn of events in Scotland. Morton became regent in October 1572, following the death of Lennox. Morton, like Lennox, was no friend of Mary and also an Anglophile. Moreover, the Marian party was by now sadly depleted; leading supporters like Argyll, in despair of her cause, had abandoned it, and Kirkcaldy and Maitland, in the last years of his life a loyal Marian, were dead. Under Morton, the beleagured country enjoyed a period of comparative calm. Its quondam queen, Mary Stuart, also entered a phase of enforced tranquillity, in which the minor pains or pleasures of her prison routine became temporarily more important than European or Scottish politics.

The actual conditions of her captivity were not in themselves particularly rigorous during the 1570s by the standards of a state prisoner, except during moments of national crisis. In the first place Mary was officially allowed a suite of thirty, which was enough to make her adequately comfortable, if not a large number to one who had lived as queen her whole life. At the time of her first committal to Shrewsbury this thirty included Lord and Lady Livingston and their own attendants, Mary Seton, three ladies of the chamber and Jane Kennedy, Mary's favourite bed-chamber woman, John Beaton, her master of the house, her cupbearer and her physician; then there were her grooms of the chamber, Gilbert Curle, her secretary, Willy Douglas, now described as her usher, her chair-bearer, four officers of the pantry and three officers of the kitchen, including a master cook and a pottager. Most of these were Mary's tried and loyal servants who made up the official thirty, but beyond this figure had crept in others, bringing the total up to forty-one. This proliferation, due not only to the infiltration of further aides to the queen such as stable grooms, but also to the introduction of further attendants to look after the attendants, was tolerated by Shrewsbury out of kindness.

ABOVE LEFT Tutbury Castle, situated on a hill overlooking the river Dove, on the borders of Staffordshire and Derbyshire, where Mary was imprisoned for various periods from February 1569 onwards. From a seventeenth-century engraving.

But as the royal suite happily escalated, its increase in numbers inevitably reached the ears of the government in London, who took a much less generous view. In times of danger there would be demands from London that numbers should be cut; this would result in tears and protests from Mary, coupled with guilty denials from Shrewsbury that he had ever allowed the number to rise.

More servants, quite apart from the danger of official complaints from London, meant more mouths to feed. Here Shrewsbury was less indulgent. His allowance from the government for the feeding of the queen was the subject of agonizing solicitude on his part throughout all his long years as her guardian. When Mary was first committed to Shrewsbury, he was allowed £52 a week to maintain her, but in 1575, without any reason being given, this allowance was cut to £30 a week. Shrewsbury squeaked with protest but all to no avail. A later biographer of Shrewsbury estimated that he was actually spending £30 *a day*, and was thus nearly £10,000 a year out of pocket; yet not only were his complaints disregarded, but he frequently had much difficulty in extracting from the government the allowance which remained. Sir Francis Walsingham reflected that cutting Shrewsbury's allowance might turn out to be a false economy if it meant that the queen of Scots was allowed to escape through lack of guards – 'I pray God the abatement of the charges towards the nobleman that hath custody of the bosom serpent hath not lessened his care in keeping her.'

In fact the care which Shrewsbury showed in keeping Queen Mary, like the size of her suite, varied very much with the attitude of the central government, and this in turn depended on the state of national security. Shrewsbury was not a cruel man and strictness generally had to be imposed from above. Even when the government resolved that the queen should be kept more 'straitly', its wishes were not always implemented very speedily; Derbyshire and Staffordshire were a long way from London, and travelling, especially in winter, from houses like Chatsworth set amidst the mountainous area of Derbyshire, represented considerable difficulties. This worked both ways. In the first place, Shrewsbury, like all ambitious Elizabethans, constantly pined for the royal sunshine of the court, and bewailed the duties which kept him so long away from it: he felt he was being excluded from the glorious possibilities of the queen's favour, as well as from an opportunity to make his case about his allowance. But just as Shrewsbury was tortured by the thought of the delights of London and the court, so the government who occupied this delightful city were themselves from time to time agonized at the idea that the Scottish queen in the far-off midlands was enjoying far too much liberty, seeing people, receiving visitors, holding virtual court, riding about on horseback in conditions tantamount to liberty ... such rumours, untrue as they were, caused Elizabeth to choke with fury and fire off indignant reproaches to Shrewsbury for neglecting his duty.

Although Shrewsbury never failed to write in return protesting his extreme loyalty to Elizabeth and his eternal vigilance as a jailer, there was no doubt that he did not always interpret the rules in the harshest possible light. The reason is not hard to find: if Elizabeth died suddenly, who

Arbella Stuart, daughter of Darnley's younger brother, Charles Stuart, and Bess of Hardwicke's daughter, Elizabeth Cavendish, at the age of twenty-three months. Mary Queen of Scots became very attached to her little niece, but this relationship was broken up by the unfortunate quarrel between Mary and Bess of Hardwicke.

knew but that Mary might not be transformed overnight into the queen, and if Mary were to ascend the throne, as would have been a possibility at least, had Elizabeth died while James was still a child, then Shrewsbury could expect much from his former charge if he had shown himself a sympathetic host to her in her times of distress. This consideration died away in the 1580s after James grew to manhood, but it was very much present in the minds of English statesmen – not only Shrewsbury, but also Cecil and Leicester – in the 1570s.

From Mary's own point of view she was of course anxious to be allowed to receive as many local people, and enjoy as much local life as possible. Such visits helped to while away the tedium of her imprisonment: the great families of Staffordshire and Derbyshire, the Manners and the Pagets, far from being Philistines, had the particular enjoyment of music and musical festivities which Mary shared. These visits also provided an excellent cover for messengers and messages to slip by secretly.

Mary's access to the baths at Buxton was the subject of a long-drawn-out three-cornered skirmish between Elizabeth, Shrewsbury and Mary. Buxton, which lay comparatively close to Chatsworth, was endowed with a well, the healing properties of whose waters had been known even to the Romans. The baths enjoyed a considerable vogue, even with Elizabeth's courtiers in far-away London, for their remedial powers which were thought to be particularly helpful in the cure of gout. To visit these baths became Mary's dearest wish; again and again she pleaded the near-breakdown of her health in an effort to secure the desired permission. But every time Elizabeth appeared to be on the point of agreeing, she seemed to hear of some fresh plot to rescue the prisoner. Eventually permission was granted, albeit reluctantly, and Mary paid her first visit to Buxton at the end of August 1573, staying for five weeks. Thereafter it became the outing to which she most keenly looked forward, not only one may suppose for the remedial effects of the waters – considered efficacious for female irregularities as well as gout – but for the unique opportunity which it gave her to mix with court people. Yet so long as Mary's visits there continued they remained a source of apprehension for Elizabeth.

Apart from the visits to Buxton and the demands of safety in time of crisis, Mary's little household found the locality of their prison changing from time to time in any case, owing to the sanitary arrangements of the time: the contemporary method of cleansing large houses such as those inhabited by Shrewsbury was to empty them totally of their inhabitants, who would be transferred to another house, and then clean the dwelling thoroughly from top to bottom. Not all Mary's prisons were as uncomfortable and hateful to her as Tutbury. Wingfield was a great Derbyshire manor house of considerable style and grandeur, and even Mary approvingly called it a palace. Sheffield Castle and Sheffield Manor lay close together, and the propinquity of the two houses made cleaning problems easier, since Mary could be shifted conveniently from one to the other. At Chatsworth Mary could enjoy the beauty of its park and of the wild country in which it was set.

Within the pattern of these moves, the mimic court and household of

the queen had its own tiny excitements and dramas. The queen was allowed to ride when governmental suspicions were not too keen, and even went hawking with Shrewsbury. She was allowed the pleasure of archery, which she had enjoyed in Scotland. Then there were little delights of small dogs, caged birds and lute-playing as in the Scottish days. Nor did the queen lose all her interest in fashion and dress, being prepared to send off for patterns of dresses, such as were then worn at the London court, and cuttings of suitable gold and silver cloth.

A household event of some significance for the future was the appointment of Claude Nau as her secretary in the summer of 1574. Mary's accounts were in chaos and causing her great concern; she needed a secretary with a good business brain. Nau had studied and practised law, he was clever and quick-witted, intelligent and zealous. His abilities impressed Mary and it was to Nau that she now related the important memorials of her personal rule in Scotland.

It will be observed that Mary's day-to-day life during the 1570s and early 1580s was not particularly arduous in itself; but there was one factor which made the whole era intolerably burdensome, her appalling health. This ill-health was grievously exacerbated by the mere fact that she was confined, and few springs, let alone winters, passed without her being subjected to some really violent bout of illness. Her severe illness in the summer of 1569, which she compared later to her near-fatal attack at Jedburgh in 1566, was followed in the autumn by a return of the nagging pain in her side which prevented her sleeping; she also vomited constantly. Norfolk's death brought on a passion of sickness, and in November 1582 the same symptoms led the royal physicians to believe that she was actually dying. Her legs were also extremely painful and by the date of her death she was almost permanently lame.

The miniature of Mary Queen of Scots by Nicholas Hilliard painted, probably from life, during her English captivity about 1578.

Yet apart from the weight of suffering itself, Mary had to endure two additional ordeals with regard to her health. In the first place her captors were extremely reluctant to believe that she was genuinely ill, suspecting that she merely invented her symptoms in order to secure further freedom or privileges, such as visiting Buxton: those symptoms they could not deny they attempted to put down to hysteria. Mary was additionally unfortunate in that her whole being craved fresh air; all her life she had shown a mania for physical exercise, but now she found herself almost totally deprived of it, except when Shrewsbury's regime became lax enough to permit it, and at the same time her health rapidly deteriorated. Her very muscles seemed to seize up with lack of use, and Mary herself attributed her increasing sickness to her deprivation of sufficient exercise and fresh air.

The exact medical causes of Mary's undoubted ill-health have been the subject of several modern investigations. It used to be suggested that her symptoms corresponded most nearly with those of a sufferer from a gastric ulcer. But recent studies on a group of diseases known as the porphyrias have identified the recurrent illness of George III as belonging to it, and similar symptoms have been traced back to his ancestor and ancestress James VI and I and Mary Queen of Scots. The symptoms of porphyria are severe attacks of abdominal 'colicky' pain with vomiting and extreme distress at the time, even transient mental breakdown, which may be interpreted by observers as hysteria. The attacks may occur frequently or at long intervals; and despite the severity of the attack, the patient recovers quickly afterwards. It certainly seems far easier to relate these symptoms than those of a gastric ulcer to the case of Mary; in particular the episodic nature of her sufferings – bouts of severe illness followed by speedy physical recovery – fits better with the known pattern of the porphyria sufferer than that of the ulcer subject. It is clear that Mary, like her descendant George III, underwent genuine rather than hysterical sufferings, which at times amounted to a complete breakdown, indistinguishable from madness.

Sick woman as Mary Stuart might be, she did not abandon hopes of release. Her own correspondence continued to buzz with schemes for assistance from abroad. The fact that she was generally regarded as marriageable meant that despite her captivity she never lost her place as a piece on the complicated chessboard of European politics in the 1570s. A marriage with Philip II's illegitimate brother Don John of Austria was suggested, the event to be preceded by a Spanish invasion of England which would put Mary and her new husband on the throne. Pope Gregory XIII, strongly sympathetic to Mary and her claims to the English throne, was petitioned to nullify the marriage with Bothwell. In the event, the death of Bothwell in April 1578, driven mad by the intolerable conditions of his Danish prison, freed Mary from the bonds of matrimony, just six months before the death of Don John himself put an end forever to Mary's hopes in this direction.

As time and captivity had taken their toll on Bothwell, so they had on the features of the young and beautiful queen he had once served. The 'sweet face', which the good people of Edinburgh had blessed nearly twenty years ago, had altered much as a result of ill-health and confinement. Portraits dating from the later years of her life show a woman with a drawn face, a beaky prominent nose, almost Roman in shape but cut finely at the end, with a small, rather pinched mouth; the smallness of the whole face is in contrast to the fullness of the body, which is now matronly in its proportions.

The outward changes in the appearance of Mary Queen of Scots were paralleled by the inward changes in her character. It would be true to say that the quality of Mary's religious beliefs had never truly been tested up to the present. In France there had been nothing to try and much to encourage them. In Scotland she had insisted on the practice of her own religion, but this minor concession had not been difficult to establish in view of the fact that she was the reigning queen, and was herself prepared to show total tolerance to the official Protestant religion of the country. But now to exercise her religion needed cunning and tenacity; she was living in a country where Catholics were not only not tolerated, but often persecuted, and persecuted with increasing severity after the bull of excommunication towards Elizabeth. Moreover to Mary, as to many others in whom the hectic and heedless blood of youth fades, giving place to a nobler and gentler temperament, her religion itself had come to mean much more to her. It was not only that the Catholic powers abroad represented her best hope of escape from captivity; it was also that she herself had undergone a profound change of attitude to her faith, and indeed to life itself. It is the mark of greatness in a person to be able to develop freely from one phase into another as age demands it. Mary Stuart was capable of this development. Her whole character deepened. Having been above all things a woman of action, she now became, under the influence of the imprisonment which she so much detested, a far more philosophical and contemplative personality. The carefree buoyancy so alluring in the young woman would have been intolerable, even frivolous, in the captive queen. Mary's utterances in her forties show on the one hand an infinitely nobler and deeper spirit, and on the other a serenity and internal repose quite out of keeping with her previous behaviour.

Mary achieved this serenity and this intelligence at the cost of much pain, heart-searching and suffering. She, who had never been known to exist without an adviser, and had never wished to do so, was compelled in the last years of her life to exist without any sort of reliable advice or support from outside. She was now the shoulder on whom her servants leant, and to whom her envoys, many of them of questionable loyalty, looked for direction. She might even secretly write to the outside world for advice, and receive it, but when it came to taking action, actually within the confines of the prison itself, there was Mary and only Mary to make decisions and inspire their implementation. The pretty puppet-queen of France, the spirited but in some ways heedless young ruler of Scotland, could never have carried through the remarkable performance which Mary Stuart was to display in her last years. The uses of adversity for Mary Stuart, bitter-sweet as they might have been, were to teach her that self-control and strength of character which was to enable her to outwit Elizabeth at the last by the heroic quality of her ending.

Mary Queen of Scots and
her son James, painted in
1583, artist unknown. This
is an imaginary portrait as
Mary never saw James
after 1567, when he was
ten months old.

12 Mother and Son

'... nor let thy soul contrive
Against thy mother aught; leave her to heaven
And to those thorns that in her bosom lodge
To prick and sting her ...'

The advice of Hamlet's ghost-father on the subject of his mother Gertrude (the relationship of Hamlet and Gertrude is thought to have been founded by Shakespeare on the story of Mary Queen of Scots and James VI)

While Mary languished in captivity, the child whom she had last seen as a ten-month-old baby at Stirling Castle in 1567 had grown to a precocious adulthood. Mary still pined for James, or the idea of the infant she had lost. In return she genuinely imagined that James also longed for her, prompted by the dictates of natural affection which she believed must always exist between a child and its mother. The reality was very different.

Mary had made frantic efforts to maintain some sort of maternal contact with her son during his childhood. Just before Moray's death, she had sent James a small pony of his own, with a pathetic little note to accompany it: 'Dear Son, I send three bearers to see you and bring me word how ye do, and to remember you that ye have in me a loving mother that wishes you to learn in time to love know and fear God.' Mary wrote in vain, for none of her letters or presents were allowed by Elizabeth to pass to Scotland, to the son who could not remember his mother. James himself, far from being taught to remember his duty 'anent her that has born you in her sides', as his mother hopefully put it, was being instructed by Mary's inveterate enemy, George Buchanan, to regard his mother as the murderess of his father, an adulteress who had deserted him for her lover, and last of all, the protagonist of a wicked and heretical religion.

It was true that James subsequently turned on Buchanan for his libels on his mother; he called Regent Moray that 'bastard who unnaturally rebelled and procured the ruin of his own sovereign and sister'. But the point remained that enough had been done in early childhood to rob James of any natural feeling at all, let alone for his mother, from whose love he was totally cut off. Intellectually he could replace Buchanan's false picture of Mary with one he chose to believe was the true one. But he could never replace in his heart the inborn love of son for mother, since this flickering, newly-lighted flame had been extinguished shortly after his birth by Mary's enemies.

James, like Mary herself, had been brought up to believe himself to be a ruling monarch, despite the fact that his mother was still alive, and Mary's position as queen of Scots threatened his as king. Mary had revoked the abdication she made under duress at Lochleven; in her own mind, therefore, and in those of her supporters, especially the Catholic powers abroad, she was still the true queen of the country, James a usurper. This was Mary's real hold over her son in 1580, rather than the natural ties of affection. There were advantages to James in having his *de facto* kingship recognized as *de jure*: not only would his position with France and Spain be improved, but also his position in the English succession might be better secured. It was under these circumstances that, early in 1581, Mary outlined her own plan for 'Association' – or the joint rule of mother and son – through a Guise emissary: a scheme which naturally involved the restoration of Mary to Scotland.

Mary once more envisaged the prison gates opening and her own return to her throne. James himself was attracted by the idea of the recognition of the Catholic powers. The key to the whole project in James's mind was of course the attitude of Elizabeth: English approval was still in the reign of James, as it had been in the reign of Mary, very much a factor of Scottish politics. But after the trial and execution of the pro-English regent, Morton, for the murder of Darnley (who, like Banquo's ghost, seemed to play a much more effective part in Scottish politics once he was dead), James professed himself to the Guises ready to entertain the notion of the Association, at the sacrifice of Elizabeth's favour.

To promote the idea of the Association, Mary now enlisted Patrick, master of Gray, into her service. Gray, a young man of Lucifer-like beauty, had also all the mingled potentialities of talent and treachery of the former archangel within his breast. Although entrusted by Mary to represent her counsels at the Scottish court, Gray quickly appreciated that it would be far more profitable personally to ally himself with the son, a king on a throne, than the mother, a prisoner without a kingdom. Yet Mary, under the illusion that Gray was her emissary, continued to trust him to work for her, as she continued to believe in the affections of James.

It was now that the attitude of Elizabeth became so vital to the future, if any, of this plan of the Association. On mature reflection, it was only too easy for James to see that the return of Mary to Scotland would be at least a serious nuisance to his own position; they were of different religions, to say nothing of different generations; how much better to secure the benefit of the Association, in the shape of Elizabeth's favour and foreign approval, without the release of Mary. In an extreme case, it would still benefit James more to have an alliance and subsidy from Elizabeth than the official recognition of France. Yet such negotiations had to be conducted with enormous delicacy, since Elizabeth's attitude could only be ascertained by secret probing, and in the meantime Mary had to be encouraged lest after all the Association might turn out to be advantageous to James. In the summer of 1584 it was Gray who was sent down to London to conduct these negotiations on behalf of the king. In the meantime Mary was specifically assured of James's welcoming attitude towards her proposals by a letter in very friendly terms from James himself in July.

Meanwhile Mary showed herself highly conscious of the dangers of her position should James ever try to negotiate separately; with the keen perception of the captive, she saw that her only hope of eluding her prison was if James made her release one of his conditions of treating with Elizabeth. She gave Gray a series of very explicit instructions as to how he was to negotiate while in London, above all stressing the importance of the release and the illegality of her imprisonment in the first place. She begged Gray to make Elizabeth realize that by liberating Mary she would be meriting the approval of James. But even as Mary wrote, it was being made clear to Elizabeth that in fact this was the very last thing that would merit James's approval.

In November, while Gray was busy in London betraying the cause of the mother at the instigation of the son, Nau drew up twenty-eight heads of proposals on the subject of the Association at Mary's request. Mary announced herself ready to stay in England if necessary, prepared to allow an amnesty to be declared over all wrongs she had suffered at the hands of the English, renounce the pope's bull of excommunication, and abandon forever her own pretensions to the English crown over those of Elizabeth. Although confident of French agreement to these proposals, she also offered to join an offensive league against France, so long as an English dowry was assured to her, equivalent to that she would have to abandon in France, in the event of the French not subscribing to the idea of the Association. In Scotland she was also prepared to allow an amnesty, to agree that there should be no upset of the present state of the religion of the country; the only condition she made was that James should marry with Elizabeth's knowledge and 'good counsel', and the only demand the immediate softening of her present harsh conditions of captivity. Such sweeping concessions on the part of Mary made it clear that, sixteen years after her first English imprisonment, she had one aim in view, and one aim only, for which she was prepared to sacrifice all other considerations – her freedom, by any means at all.

By January Gray had successfully concluded his mission in London on James's behalf: he had indicated to Elizabeth that the release of Mary was not necessary to win James's friendship, and he had learnt from Elizabeth also that the friendship could be won for James by a direct channel, without taking into account the claims, rights or, particularly, the desires of the imprisoned queen of Scots. The Association was now doomed; it became stamped merely as the unrealistic scheme of a tiresome middle-aged woman in prison, to whom no further attention need be paid in this context.

It was in March 1585 that the full horrifying truth could no longer be kept from Mary: James formally concluded that the 'Association desired by his mother should neither be granted nor spoken of hereafter'. At first Mary, in her pathetic desire to protect the image of her son in her own mind, tried to persuade herself that the betrayal was all the work of Gray. But her letters reveal the depth of her agitation: 'I am so grievously offended at my heart at the impiety and ingratitude that my child has been constrained to commit against me, by this letter which Gray made him write.' Wildly she threatened to disinherit James and give the crown to the greatest enemy he had, rather than allow this sort of treatment. In letters to Elizabeth, James is referred to as 'this badly brought up child', and she bewails the mischief which has been made recently between herself and James by sinister counsels – unaware of the gristly truth still more unbearable to a mother's heart; that it was not a few months'

ABOVE Mary Stuart and her son James VI from an engraving in 'De origine, moribus, et rebus gestis Scotorum' by John Leslie, Bishop of Ross, 1578.

ABOVE RIGHT Sir Francis Walsingham, Secretary of State to Elizabeth, was responsible for placing spies among those close to Mary. His 'special methods' unravelled many Catholic plots against his queen.

trouble-making by Gray but nearly twenty years of total separation which had led to the breach between mother and son. James had betrayed Mary, and so had Gray. But in the delicate game of Anglo-Scottish relations, James had discovered that whereas he held some of the cards and Elizabeth held some of the others, Mary held none at all. There was nothing Mary, still firmly within the four walls of her prison, could do except rage and weep alternately at the perfidy of her son, and the betrayal of her child.

The effects of the papal bull of excommunication against Elizabeth, promulgated in 1570, had begun to be felt in earnest towards the end of the decade when the reconversion of England was attempted once more from abroad; a trickle and then a faster flow of Jesuit missionaries, many of them Englishmen returning after training abroad, made this cause their own. The appearance of these rekindlers of Catholic flames in English hearts had a two-fold effect: in the first place, the English Catholics themselves became more sanguine and therefore more zealous; secondly, the English government tightened up the laws against the recusants (those who refused to attend the official Protestant services once a week), and using the double-edged weapon of the papal excommunication, began to blur the distinction between recusant and rebel. In view of the delicate situation of England, perpetually facing the prospect of a Spanish invasion, it was a natural act of public relations on the part of the government to seek to present the Catholics from 1580 onwards as

162

dangerous aliens within the state. Similarly, the personal danger of Queen Elizabeth was underlined in order to boost her popularity with her subjects, as a symbol of national solidarity. Both moves – early exercises in the subtle art of propaganda – augured of course extremely ill for the future of the queen of Scots, who was both a Catholic and a rival queen to Elizabeth.

To the forefront of this calculated campaign was the leading secretary of state, Sir Francis Walsingham. Walsingham, a prominent Puritan, combined to a remarkable degree the political abilities of an Italian Renaissance statesman with a very modern conception of the uses of a spy system within the state. He understood to perfection the art not only of forgery but also of permeating his enemies' organizations with his own men. Walsingham now managed to place at least one and probably more spies in the heart of Mary's councils in Paris. In view of this fact, it was not surprising that Mary's reputation became increasingly be-smirched in the English mind and that of Elizabeth, as a result of the plots against the English queen which were uncovered in the 1580s.

The first of these plots, the Throckmorton plot, was apparently Guise-inspired, although right at the centre of it lay one of Walsingham's most successful agents, Charles Paget, who entered Walsingham's ser-vice secretly in 1581 at roughly the same moment as he entered the little Marian embassy of Archbishop Beaton in Paris. The Throckmorton plot, uncovered in November 1583, led to the arrest of Francis Throck-morton, a Catholic cousin of Sir Nicholas, on suspicion of carrying letters to and from Mary. The details of the plot involved once more the invasion of England by Spain, and the release of Mary; Throckmorton, who had acted as messenger throughout, made a full confession before his execution in which he thoroughly implicated the queen of Scots. The discovery of the plot gave Walsingham an excellent opportunity to excite a wave of popular indignation against the Catholics, and their figurehead, Mary.

One of the cruellest aspects of Mary's last years from her own point of view was that while Walsingham was engaged in building up her image as a dangerous conspirator, a spider at the centre of a network of plans with agents at every foreign Catholic court, Mary was in fact no longer in complete sympathy with her Guise relations or indeed with her ambas-sador of so many years, James Beaton, and was actually becoming increasingly alienated from her own organization abroad. She was accused more and more in the popular imagination of crimes in which she was decreasingly involved. In the late 1570s a certain Thomas Mor-gan, a friend of Walsingham's chief agent Phelippes, and most probably a spy himself, became Beaton's chief cipher clerk, a position of enormous trust, since it put him in virtual control of the French correspondence with Mary.

It was tragic that Mary's service should thus be permeated with spies and trouble-makers at this critical moment in her fortunes. From the tone of her own letters, certainly her relations with Beaton seem to have been temporarily impaired, at the very moment when she had most need to be in complete accord with him. Mary's financial affairs were once again in a critical state. The perennial problem of the irregular payment of the income from her French estates was compounded by muddle and maladministration in her organization in France. Mary was compelled to raise loans in London to pay for her necessities in captivity, and her financial embarrassment led to cool relations with Beaton. By the autumn of 1584 Mary was openly accusing him of mishandling her finances. In fact Beaton was probably not to blame; such discord would have been only too easy for Morgan as cipher clerk to whip up. As a result of such trouble-making within Mary's organization her own feelings towards the Guises and Spain became permeated with distrust: she began to be convinced that the Guises were only intending to seize England in order to hand it over to Spain and had no interest in her release. The prospect of losing touch with reality over the years is one which every long-term prisoner has to face. In Mary's case, at the exact moment when her struggles to free herself through the Association were crumbling about her, and the need to concentrate on the aid of Spain and the Guises grew more acute, she became the prey of false notions on the subject and grew to rely more on private schemes than on Beaton.

From June 1584 onwards there had been murmurings in Parliament of a new type of Association – not to be confused with Mary's Association with James – in this case a bond or pledge of allegiance. But it was a pledge with a difference. It was not enough for the signatories of this new bond to swear to bring about the death of all those who might plot against Elizabeth. In addition they also swore – and the inspiration was Walsingham's – to bring about the death of all those in whose favour such plots might be instigated, whether they had personally connived at them or not. In short, if it could be proved that a particular conspiracy had been aimed at the elimination of Elizabeth and the placing of Mary on the throne, Mary herself was as much eligible for execution as any of the plotters, even if she had been in complete ignorance of what was afoot. This bond was formally enacted into a statute by Parliament in the spring of 1585 when the murder of the Prince of Orange brought home still further to the English the constant dangers of assassination to their own queen: in the meantime signatures poured in from loyal subjects, and were presented to Elizabeth in an endless series of documents, from the autumn onwards. Mary, ever conscious of the delicate path she was treading, and the need for Elizabeth's favour, actually offered to sign the bond herself. But her pathetic offer could not gloss over the fact that the enactment of the bond into English law amounted to the drawing up of her own death warrant; it was hardly likely that many years would pass before some conspiracy or other in Mary's favour, to the detriment of Elizabeth, would be brought to book by Walsingham. No one was more conscious of the dangers of the bond to Mary than Elizabeth herself, and the possibility of the trial of a crowned queen was one Elizabeth preferred not to contemplate too closely in advance: she therefore chose to regard the bond of Association, of whose genesis she had been quite ignorant, as a spontaneous act of loyalty on the part of her people.

By the spring of 1585 there was very little that was encouraging to be discerned in the situation of the queen of Scots. Her son had repudiated and betrayed her; her French organization was in administrative chaos, and penetrated by Walsingham's spies; the English Catholics were quarrelling among themselves abroad and increasingly persecuted at home; Mary herself no longer felt complete trust for her erstwhile allies abroad and at times suspected the good faith of the Guises and Spain; in the meantime her position in England may be compared to that of someone tied down unwillingly over a powder keg, which may at any moment be exploded by a match held by an over-enthusiastic friend. To add to Mary's distress, her prison was changed for the worse. In early January 1585 she was once more incarcerated in the loathsome if impregnable fortress of Tutbury. Not only that but at the same time the care of her person was handed over to a new and infinitely more severe jailer, Sir Amyas Paulet, who became in time as odious to her as the masonry of Tutbury itself. Under these doleful circumstances, with very little to cheer her as she surveyed her prospects for the future, Mary Stuart entered on the last and most burdensome phase of her captivity.

The harsh character of Sir Amyas Paulet, Mary's new jailer, was apparent from his very first action. This was to take down from above her head and chair that royal cloth of state by which she set store, since it constituted a proof of her queenship. Paulet's reasoning was that as the cloth of state had never been officially allowed, it must be removed, however long it had been there. Mary first wept and protested vigorously, then retired to her chamber in a mood of great offence; finally she secured the return of the cloth. The incident was typical of the man, who believed profoundly in the letter of the law. Paulet had been specially selected by Walsingham for the task in hand, because, as all his contemporaries agreed, he was not only a prominent Puritan but also a mortal enemy of the queen of Scots and all she stood for. Walsingham understood his man; Paulet was quite immune to the charms of the queen of Scots and, unlike Knollys, found her irritating and even tiresome as a character. Since honour and loyalty were his gods, and these Mary Stuart seemed to offend with every action, Paulet's Puritan conscience allowed him to hate her in advance. When they actually met, Paulet was able to transform charms into wiles of his own mind; like Knox so many years before, he disliked his captive all the more for her possible attractions.

Paulet's instructions from London were clear: Mary's imprisonment was to be transformed into the strictest possible confinement. She was not even to be allowed to take the air, that terrible deprivation which she dreaded. In particular her private letters and messages were to be stopped once and for all. At no point in her captivity so far had Mary been cut off so completely. Her correspondence with Beaton, Morgan and her other foreign agents, had depended on a secret pipeline of letters, without which no foreign plotting could have taken place. During the whole of 1585, under the orders of the Elizabethan government, this pipeline was shut off, and Mary was totally deprived of the news she wanted so much.

Paulet achieved this isolation – which had a calculated position in Walsingham's scheme for Mary Stuart's downfall – by the most rigorous supervision of the Scottish queen's domestic arrangements. There were naturally to be no more visits to Buxton. Not only was Mary herself not allowed to ride abroad but her coachman was not allowed to ride out without permission, and then he had to be accompanied. Paulet also went to great lengths into the difficult and, to him, vexatious subject of the royal laundresses. These elusive maidens, under the pretext of carrying out their work, had carried out a merry trade of message-bearing. Paulet's puritanical brow furrowed over the subject of the laundresses, but, despairing of finding co-operation in their midst, he had to be content with prohibiting all Mary's servants from walking on the thick walls of Tutbury (where they could wave, it was thought, in an enlightening manner to passers-by).

Mary's little private charities in which she had delighted, and by which she endeared herself to the local people, were sternly quelled. Paulet also tried to prevent Mary from making any personal payments to the Tutbury servants, since this would give her an opportunity of secretly bribing them. As a result, his own accounts underwent a financial crisis, augmented by the rocketing food prices in England at the time.

Her renewed sojourn at damp and draughty Tutbury thoroughly broke down Queen Mary's system, and her pleas for a change of air grew pitiful. Yet it is clear from Paulet's letter-books that he felt no sympathy with her ill-health, and seems to have regarded it as just retribution for her sins. In his attitude to her religious beliefs, he showed, to put it at its kindest, the total incomprehension of the bigot.

However, in the autumn of 1585 the protests of the French court to Elizabeth, rather than the compassion of Paulet, led to a search for a new prison for Mary. Not only was her health itself weakened, but the famous middens of Tutbury was stinking to high heaven. Various Staffordshire residences were proposed but in the end the lot fell upon Chartley Hall, an Elizabeth manor house belonging to the young earl of Essex, with a large moat round it, which made it suitable for security

James VI of Scotland as a youth.

reasons. Paulet himself greatly approved of the change, especially as the amount of water round the house meant that the over-spirited laundresses would have less excuse for passing in and out of the gates as they went about their work.

On arrival at Chartley Mary found herself so reduced in health that she fell severely ill, and even Paulet found himself 'for charity's sake' bound to pass on her complaints about her bed which she said was 'stained and ill-favoured'; he recommended the down bed which she herself requested. On this occasion Mary was obliged to keep to her bed for more than four weeks, and it was towards the end of March, eight or nine weeks later, before she felt any real improvement from the 'painful deluxions' which plagued her. It was scarcely to be wondered at that her own servants were gravely worried for her, and feared that the move from Tutbury might have come too late to save her.

While considerations of the queen's health appeared to engross the Chartley household, deep and very different currents were swirling beneath the surface of its domestic pattern. Walsingham took the opportunity of the move from Tutbury to mount a new stage in his campaign to incriminate the queen of Scots. His aim was of course to provide England – and Elizabeth – with sufficient evidence to prove once and for all that it was too dangerous to keep Mary alive. To any plot to rescue the Scottish queen from captivity, foreign aid in the shape of a foreign invasion of England was absolutely essential for success: although Elizabeth might fall a victim of the assassin's dagger, unless these assassins had sufficient resources to rescue Mary immediately, they might find that by the time they reached her place of imprisonment, their candidate for the English throne had either been killed by her captors or else spirited away. In any case the English Catholics could not carry through such a revolution alone. This was a point which was thoroughly appreciated not only by all the level-headed conspirators, but also pre-eminently by Mary herself, who never stopped stressing the danger to her personally of an amateur plan. It was one of Walsingham's most subtle moves to make his agents at all points exaggerate the possibility of this foreign aid, generally supposed to be Spanish. In this way the English conspirators were led to believe that a Spanish invasion was certain, and so travelled even further along the road towards fruition of their plans. The Catholic parties abroad were on the other hand given the impression that the plans and numbers of possible English Catholic insurgents were far more stabilized and numerous than in fact they were.

One false agent in a chain of correspondence can cast a completely different slant on a whole subject: the preliminaries of the Babington plot involved not only Charles Paget and Thomas Morgan, but also a new Walsingham double-agent – Gilbert Gifford – at their very heart. The first time it was known by Mary's supporters that some change in her isolated and news-deprived condition might be expected was when this same Gifford presented himself at the French embassy in London. The secret letters from Morgan which could no longer be smuggled to the Scottish queen had been piling up at the embassy for a whole year. Now Gifford offered to get packets to Mary, and on 16 January 1586, to her unimaginable joy, Mary Stuart received the first secret communication she had had for over a year. Not only that, but she was informed that the same strange pipeline by which the packet had come – the local brewer – could be used to smuggle out her own notes.

The method by which Mary believed she would be contacting the outside world in fact merely signalled her private thoughts and schemes directly to her jailer Paulet and her enemy Walsingham. The letters, taken down and transcribed into code by Nau, were smuggled out of Chartley by the brewer in one of his casks and handed to Gifford. He passed them to Walsingham, who having deciphered and noted the contents, returned them to Gifford for delivery. On the return journey the process was merely reversed. In the spring of 1586 all those concerned in the conspiracy, from whatever angle, felt something like happiness. Mary was intoxicated by the pleasure of renewed communications. Gifford enjoyed the luxurious god-like superiority of the spy, who can observe the whole battlefield from above. Paulet had the grim satisfaction of watching this woman he had never for a moment trusted reveal herself to be every bit as deceitful as he had suspected. As for the brewer, he was happy enough, since he was being paid twice over, once by Mary, and once by Paulet.

It was at this point that the conspiracy of a number of young English Catholic gentlemen under the leadership of Anthony Babington, emerged. These young men showed a very different attitude to the imprisoned queen of Scots from that of the previous generation: indeed the Babington plot may perhaps be regarded as the first manifestation of that romantic approach to the beleaguered Stuart dynasty which was afterwards to play such a part in British history. In recent years Mary had come to symbolize the martyrdom of the Catholic faith in England. Gone were the days when she had represented the spirit of religious compromise in Scotland. A whole generation had grown up in England since those far-off days at Kirk o'Field and the shameful, hasty Bothwell marriage: to these young men Mary was a Catholic princess in an English Protestant tower; to them Elizabeth was the monstrous dragon who held Mary in thrall.

Spurred on by lavish promises of foreign aid and encouraged by Gifford, Babington concocted a plan to rescue the queen of Scots. In July his letter to Mary outlining the main points of the conspiracy was duly delivered by the brewer, by which time of course it had been thoroughly scrutinized by Walsingham. It was Mary's reaction which was crucial: for although she was already doomed by the terms of the Act of Association, it would have been far more difficult for Walsingham to work up Elizabeth's odium against her if Mary had shown the Babington plot the cool reception she had displayed to other would-be rescuers in the past. While Mary pondered, the English gloatingly attended her reply: 'We await her very heart in the next', commented Phelippes. Finally on 17 July she wrote back to Babington an extremely long, full letter in principle approving his schemes. There was no wonder that Phelippes drew a gallows mark on the outside of this letter when he passed it on to Walsingham. Mary had fallen plumb into the trap which had been laid for her.

It is important to judge Mary's acceptance in principle of the Babing-

An anti-catholic print of 1580.

ton conspiracy against the background of her own mood in the course of the late summer of 1586, and how it developed up till July. Her mental state was by now very different from what it had once been; the old notion of establishing her on the throne of England, however much it appealed to her youthful champions, was not uppermost in the mind of the middle-aged woman, by now quite out of touch with Europe, let alone England. Mary herself was beginning to feel weary of the prolonged battle for some sort of decent existence in which she had now been involved for eighteen years, and the constant strain of being ever on her guard, ever plotting, ever hoping, ever planning. The period in which she was perforce cut off from her secret post contributed much to this feeling of melancholy and lassitude. She began to speak of liberty in terms of retirement rather than government. In July this abandoned and exhausted frame of mind received a terrible fillip from the news that

James and Elizabeth had actually signed a treaty of alliance. The maternal heart-break Mary had suffered in the spring of 1585 was now spiked with fearful bitterness. It was one thing to repudiate the idea of the Association but at Berwick on 6 July, only eleven days before Mary's vital answer to Babington, a proper treaty was signed between the English and Scottish sovereigns, a treaty from which Mary and her interests were totally excluded. There was no doubt that the publication of the treaty sent her temporarily off her balance, and robbed her of the sustained powers of calm reason which might have led her to act far more cautiously over the Babington plot. Even the fact that her health – for so long enfeebled – was now somewhat restored by the better conditions of Chartley contributed towards her downfall. With renewed health came greater energy to escape, a prospect impossible to contemplate for an invalid endlessly confined to her chamber and her bed. It was against this background that Mary tacitly acceded to – for her letter came to no more than that – a conspiracy involving the assassination of Elizabeth.

With the gallows letter in his hands, Walsingham now rounded up the conspirators; Babington confessed every detail of the conspiracy and the queen of Scots, as well as all his fellow-conspirators, was fatally incriminated.

In the meantime Mary herself, cut off at Chartley, had absolutely no inkling of the dramatic turn which events had taken. Her spirits were high at the beginning of August: she felt she might even hope again. On 11 August, when the dour Paulet suggested that she might like a ride out of Chartley in the direction of Tixall in order to enjoy a buck hunt, this seemed yet another favourable omen of future happiness, since such manifestations of goodwill from her jailer were rare indeed. Mary took particular trouble with her costume under the impression that she might be meeting some of the local gentry at the hunt. Her secretaries, Nau and Curle and Bourgoing, her personal physician, accompanied her. It was a fine August day. The queen's mood was so gay and so gentle that when she noticed Paulet lagging behind, she remembered that he had recently been ill, and stopped her horse to let him catch her up.

As the little procession wound its way across the moors, the queen suddenly spied some horsemen coming fast towards her. They were strangers. For one wild moment her heart leapt and she actually believed that these apocalyptic horsemen were the Babington plotters, their plans more advanced than she supposed, coming to rescue her. The first words of their leader speedily undeceived her: this was Sir Thomas Gorges, Queen Elizabeth's emissary. As Paulet introduced him, Gorges dismounted from his horse and strode over towards Mary. 'Madame, the Queen my mistress, find it very strange that you, contrary to the pact and engagement made between you, should have conspired against her and her State, a thing which she could not have believed had she not seen proofs of it with her own eyes and known it for certain.' As Mary, taken off her guard and flustered, protested, turned this way and that, explained that she had always shown herself a good sister and friend of Elizabeth, Gorges told her that her own servants were immediately to be taken away from her, since it was known that they too were guilty. From Gorges's tone, Mary even imagined that she might be now taken summarily to execution. She turned to Nau and Curle and begged them not to allow her to be snatched away without some defence. But there was little the wretched secretaries could do: they were dragged from her side – in fact she never saw either of them again – and taken to prison in London. Mary herself, with her physician, was conducted directly to Tixall in the pretty riding clothes she had donned to impress the 'pleasant company' she expected to find there.

Tixall was an Elizabethan house built about thirty years earlier. But its beauties must have been fairly lost on the distraught and anguished woman who was now imprisoned there. Mary did not leave her chambers for the entire fortnight which she spent in the house. Meanwhile Mary's apartments at Chartley were thoroughly searched: her letters and ciphers were taken away to London. After a fortnight at Tixall, in which anguish for the past mingled with apprehension for the future, Mary was conducted back to Chartley by Paulet.

In the meantime the revelations which Walsingham was able to make to Elizabeth concerning the abominable perfidy of her good friend and sister Mary were eminently satisfactory from his own point of view. Elizabeth was plunged into a panic of acute physical fear, unaware how much of the assassination plot had in fact been elaborated by Walsingham's own agents. In a letter to Paulet, the English queen was ecstatic with relief; Mary was now 'your wicked murderess' and any future fate, however rigorous, no more than 'her vile deserts'. It was understandable that Elizabeth should feel a mixture of keen fear at the danger to her personal safety and righteous horror at Mary's ingratitude: the confessions of the Babington conspirators, arrested and examined in turn, did nothing to reassure her. In mid-September they were tried, condemned and then executed.

There was now little left for Mary to hope for. But there was one terrible thing left for her to dread: the secret death, the slow drip of poison, the assassin's knife, all the fates by which she would be deprived of the public martyrdom by which she now hoped to proclaim the Catholic faith at her death. From now on, she deliberately played every scene with this climax in view. Her hope was to triumph at the moment of her death, her fear was to be extinguished meaninglessly without an opportunity of bearing witness to the truths in which she believed. In September she managed to write to this effect to her cousin, Henry, duke of Guise: 'For myself, I am resolute to die for my religion ... With God's help, I shall die in the Catholic faith and to maintain it constantly ... My heart does not fail me ... *Adieu, mon bon cousin.*' It was in this heroic frame of mind that Queen Mary allowed herself to be taken without protest out of Chartley on 21 September and began her last journey towards Fotheringhay. It was Mary's triumph that by her deliberate behaviour in the last months of her existence, she managed to convert a life story which had hitherto shown all the elements of a Greek tragedy – disaster leading ineluctably to disaster – into something which ended instead in the classic Christian martyrdom and triumph through death. This transfiguration in the last months of her life, which has the effect of altering the whole balance of her story, was no fortunate accident. The design was hers.

13 The Trial

'As a sinner I am truly conscious of having often offended my Creator and I beg him to forgive me, but as a Queen and Sovereign, I am aware of no fault or offence for which I have to render account to anyone here below.'

MARY QUEEN OF SCOTS *to Sir Amyas Paulet, October 1586*

On 25 September Mary Stuart first sighted the ancient towers of Fotheringhay Castle. Quite apart from its heavy, brooding appearance, Fotheringhay had a stark history. It had been built in the time of the Conqueror and rebuilt in the reign of Edward III. Here in 1452, Richard III, that sad and twisted king, had been born. It was now used entirely as a state prison, but was considered of sufficiently bleak reputation for the wretched Catherine of Aragon to refuse to go there unless, as she said, she were dragged thither. The front of the castle and the enormous gateway faced north, the mighty keep rose to the north-west; a large courtyard filled the interior of the building, which included a chapel and a great hall. There was a double moat system along three sides and the River Nene winding along the very edge of the castle made up the fourth side of the defences. Around its grim towers stretched the flat Northamptonshire countryside.

Despite the size of Fotheringhay, Mary found herself incarcerated in comparatively mean apartments and her servants reported that many of the state rooms had been left empty. From this Mary drew the correct conclusion that she was about to be tried, and that the rooms were awaiting the arrival of dignitaries from London. At this evidence that she was about to undergo the public martyrdom she sought, as Bourgoing reported: 'Her heart beat faster and she was more cheerful and she was in better health than ever before.'

In London commissioners were appointed to judge the Scottish queen under the Act of Association enacted in 1585. It had been made quite clear at the time that this Act had been especially framed in order to be able to try and execute the queen of Scots: now it was coming into its own. The provisions of the Act of Association were so heavily weighted against Mary that she stood absolutely no chance of acquittal. At the forthcoming trial she was to be allowed neither counsel nor witnesses in her defence; she was not even to be allowed a secretary to help her prepare her own case. She was left quite alone, a sick woman and a foreigner, who knew nothing of England, its laws, or customs, to conduct and manage her own defence against the best legal brains in the country.

Yet, curiously enough, by the standards of the sixteenth century the innate injustice of the trial of Mary Stuart lay not so much in its arrangements – the accused was never allowed counsel at an English treason trial at this date – as in the fact that the trial took place at all. How, indeed, could it ever be legal for Mary as sovereign, the queen of a foreign

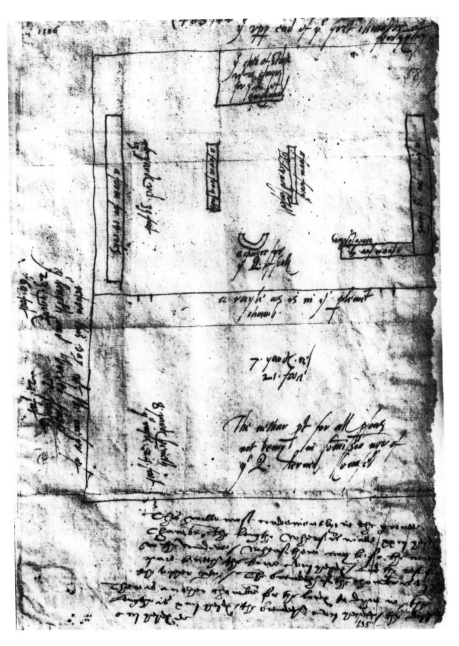

A contemporary plan, with modern key, of the layout at the trial of Mary Queen of Scots. The commission of twenty-four peers and Privy Councillors appointed to investigate Mary's guilt included her jailer, Shrewsbury.

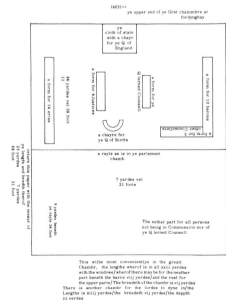

(463)++
ye upper end of ye Gret chammbre at fordynghay

ye cloth of state with a chayr for ye Q of England

a form for 14 erles

46 yardes vel 39 foot
13

a form for 4 Justices

Q lerned Counsell

a form for ye

a chayre for ye Q of Scotts

a form for 4 Justices

a form for 13 barons

a form for 5 other Counsellers

a rayle as is in ye parlement chamb

7 yardes vel 21 foote

return this paper with the mesur of
23 yardes 7 yardes
69 foot 21 foot

ye length and bredth therof

8 yardes beneth
ye rayle 24 foot

The nethar part for all persons not being in Commission nor of ye Q lerned Counsell

This wilbe most convenientlye in the greatt Chambr, the lengthe wherof is in all xxiii yerdes with the windowe/wherof there may be for the neathar part beneth the barre viij yerdes/and the rest for the upper parte/The breadeth of the chambr is vij yerdes There is another chambr for the lordes to dyne in/the Lengthe is xiiij yardes/the breadeth vij yerdes/the deppth iiij yerdes country, to be tried for treason, when she was in no sense one of Elizabeth's subjects? In 1586 the sovereignty of a ruler was taken extremely seriously with regard to his own subjects – how much more difficult then was it to try and execute one who was actually or had been the sovereign of another country? Elizabeth herself was the first to perceive the dangers for the future of pulling down any monarch to the rank where he or she could be punished like any other subject – let alone the monarch of another country. If Mary had partaken in treasonable activities in England where in any case she was a prisoner, held against her will, the correct remedy (although of course it was never considered) was surely to expel her from the country. The mere judicial proceedings for trying a sovereign presented enormous difficulties by English common law. In England it was the foundation-stone of justice that every man had a right to be tried by his peers; Mary being a queen had no peers in England except Elizabeth herself. The only possible justification for what was in fact unjustifiable was the Act of Association itself, which by defining the commission which was to try anyone found coming within the terms of the act, disposed of such knotty problems as sovereignty and a queen's peers by merely cutting through them and all the laws, both national and international, of the time.

On Saturday 11 October, the commissioners began to arrive at Fotheringhay. Mary was given a copy of the commission which had summoned them and the next day a deputation of lords waited on her. The object of this mission was to get Mary to consent to appear in person at the trial and thus acknowledge its legality. To this Mary replied in fine style:

I am myself a Queen, the daughter of a King, a stranger, and the true Kinswoman of the Queen of England. I came to England on my cousin's promise of assistance against my enemies and rebel subjects and was at once imprisoned ... As an absolute Queen, I cannot submit to orders, nor can I submit to the laws of the land without injury to myself, the King my son and all other sovereign princes ... For myself I do not recognize the laws of England nor do I know or understand them as I have often asserted. I am alone, without counsel, or anyone to speak on my behalf. My papers and notes have been taken from me, so that I am destitute of all aid, taken at a disadvantage.

On the subject of her actual guilt, whereas Mary admitted that she had thrown herself under the protection of Catholic kings and princes, she denied any knowledge of an actual attempt against Elizabeth.

The next morning Mary received another less courteous deputation. She was told that whatever she might protest, she was subject to the laws of England, whether as a sovereign or as a captive, and that if she did not appear in person at her trial she would merely be condemned *in absentia*. Mary shed a few tears at such brusqueness and exclaimed that she was no subject, and she would rather die a thousand deaths than acknowledge herself one, since she would both betray the majesty of kings, and virtually admit that she was bound to submit to the laws of England even over religion. During the prolonged discussions which followed between Mary and her would-be judges, Mary continually reiterated her sovereign status. It was not until 14 October that she finally succumbed and agreed to appear in order to answer the single charge that she had plotted the assassination of Elizabeth.

Mary has been criticized for rescinding her determination never to appear before this illegal court; but there can be no doubt that her noble bearing at this trial, and the magnificent speeches she made there, all directed towards showing her in the light of the martyr queen, did much to enhance this picture when they gradually became known after her death. Furthermore, the full publicity she was able to give at it to her wrongs also distracted attention from points on which she might be held considerably more vulnerable, such as the letter she had written to Babington. The queen of Scots was clever to see this when she agreed to appear before the judges – intuition in this case being more potent than legal knowledge. Even so, the stress of making this critical decision reduced Mary to faintness, and she had to be revived with wine before her resolve could be committed to writing.

The trial of Mary Queen of Scots began the next day, Wednesday, 15 October, in a room directly above the great hall of Fotheringhay Castle. Queen Mary entered at nine o'clock, with an escort of soldiers. She wore her chosen garb of the sad years of captivity – a dress and mantle of flowing black velvet, her traditional white head-dress with its widow's peak, and a long white gauzy veil. Queen Mary was now so lame with rheumatism that she could scarcely walk or even limp along, and she had to be supported by Melville and Bourgoing. The queen sat down quietly in the chair allotted to her and observed to Melville as she scanned the faces of the English peers: 'Ah! here are many counsellors, but not one for me.'

The trial was opened by a speech from the Lord Chancellor, Sir Thomas Bromley, in which he explained the motives which had impelled Queen Elizabeth to institute these proceedings – how she had been informed that the queen of Scots had planned her fall and was therefore bound to convoke a public assembly to examine the accusation – and ended by stating that Queen Mary would have every opportunity of declaring her own innocence. To all this Mary replied in terms very much as before, not only denying the jurisdiction of the court over a queen, but also laying great stress on the conditions under which she had first arrived in England. She also emphasized that the only reason she had condescended to appear before the commission was in order to show that she was not guilty of the particular crime of conspiring against Elizabeth's life. In answer the Lord Chancellor utterly denied that Mary had arrived in England under promise of assistance from Elizabeth, as also he declared futile her protests against the jurisdiction of the court itself over her. The commission to try the Scottish queen was then read aloud in Latin: at which Mary made a further protest against the laws on which it was based, which she said had been expressly framed to destroy her.

Letters said to have been dictated by Babington before his death were then read aloud, and copies of the correspondence between Mary and Babington passed round, together with the confessions of the other conspirators. Mary strongly protested against this second-hand evidence and refused to admit anything at all on such indirect proofs, suggesting that her own ciphers could all too easily have been tampered with. Despite her lonely position without counsel, Mary never for a moment lost her head: she continued to draw a sharp distinction between the

The trial of Mary Queen of Scots from a contemporary drawing. The trial took place in the hall of Fotheringhay Castle in October 1586.

actions which she as a prisoner had inevitably taken to try and secure her own rescue ('I do not deny that I have earnestly wished for liberty and done my utmost to produce it for myself. In this I acted from a very natural wish') and actual connivance at the death of Elizabeth, which she strongly denied.

Mary was now reproached with having assumed the English royal arms at the time of her French marriage and of aggravating the offence by refusing to ratify the Treaty of Edinburgh, in which her pretensions to the English throne were formally abandoned. Cecil accused her of having personally coveted Elizabeth's throne, and Mary responded with a long and closely argued speech on the subject of the English royal succession. She made two main points; firstly, she had never at any time wished to usurp the English throne while Elizabeth lived; secondly, and in no way contradicting her previous point, she had 'no scruple of conscience in desiring the second rank as being the legitimate and nearest heir'. It was the right to inherit at the proper time, rather than the right to reign immediately, which Mary was not prepared to surrender.

The queen now went on to declare that although she knew that her enemies wished to compass her death by unlawful means, yet with God's help she would still manage to meet her end publicly as a witness to the faith in which she believed. In a moving passage, which marked her out as far more tolerant than the age in which she lived, Mary gave her own philosophy of life, in which there was no place for revenge: 'I do not desire vengeance. I leave it to Him who is the just Avenger of the innocent and of those who suffer for His Name under whose power I will take shelter. I would rather pray with Esther than take the sword with Judith.'

According to the physician Bourgoing's account, the whole trial now broke down into a bedlam of accusations on the part of Mary's judges: these *chicaneurs* (as he persistently termed them – pettifogging lawyers) attacked her like furies, sometimes one by one, sometimes all together, all shouting that she was guilty. When Mary returned to her own apartments, she was utterly exhausted.

As she entered the hall on the second morning of her ordeal, it was noticed that the queen was extremely pale. But she immediately made it known that she wished to address the assembly personally. Mary's first point was to protest strongly and movingly against the manner in which she had been treated on the previous day, being attacked on every issue, although she had only consented to answer accusations specifically related to the assassination plot against Elizabeth. Weak and ill as she was, she was alone among them, with no papers, no notes and no secretary, taken by surprise by a commission which had long been preparing such charges against her: under such circumstances she concluded 'there is not one, I think, among you, let him be the cleverest man you will, but would be incapable of resisting or defending himself were he in my place.'

Strangely enough this speech met with a moderate reply from Cecil, and Bourgoing noted that the whole behaviour of the judges was now more courteous. Not only that, but Mary's servants noticed that many of the nobles had come to the assembly in riding-dress and boots, from which they deduced that the proceedings were already designed, willy-nilly, to end that day. Accusations were now piled on Mary's head from the intended murder of the queen, to the prayers said at Rome for Mary as the true queen of England. Throughout all these speeches, Mary adhered steadfastly to the statement that she had neither planned nor known of any lethal enterprise. She appealed to her own reputation for mercy, how in Scotland she had always been blamed for being so tolerant to the Protestants, and she took her stand on the two things which she had always desired and freely admitted to having done so – her own deliverance and the support of the Catholic cause in England. Beyond these aims, she no longer wished for anything, neither honours nor king-doms; and in defence of this last aim she was prepared to die. The queen's last demand was to be granted a full hearing in front of Parliament, and to be permitted to confer personally with Queen Elizabeth. Mary then rose. As she proceeded from her chair, she regarded the assembly, and most regally declared that she pardoned them for what they had done: 'My lords and gentlemen, I place my cause in the hands of God.'

In answer to the express wish of Elizabeth who wanted no sentence pronounced before she herself had considered the proceedings, the court

The white gauze veil traditionally said to have been worn by Mary at her trial, which came into the possession of her Stuart descendant, the Cardinal of York; its history is recorded in the legend embroidered round the edge in Latin.

was now prorogued, and as the noblemen, booted and spurred in advance, rode away from Fotheringhay, Mary was left to go back once more to the little round of captivity. Her tranquillity was not in the slightest disturbed by the harrowing ordeal through which she had just passed. It was as though she had predicted long ago in her own mind the course which events were likely to take and had even found in the working out of her prophecies, melancholy as they were, a source of strength.

The next few weeks represented a strangely serene interlude in Mary's life, the Indian summer of her captivity, when she was able to add to the self-discipline of the long-held prisoner the peace of mind of one who knew her confinement was rapidly moving towards its finish. Bourgoing found her so far from being troubled by what had passed that 'I had not seen her so joyous, nor so constantly at her ease for the last seven years.'

On 25 October the commissioners met again in London and found Mary guilty of 'compassing and imagining ... matters tending to the death and destruction of the Queen of England'. The two Houses of Parliament now presented an address to Queen Elizabeth in which they prayed fervently for the execution of the Scottish queen for the sake of Elizabeth's own safety. Elizabeth replied in a long and ambivalent speech in which she showed how much she personally was aware, even if her Commons were not, that 'we princes are set as it were upon stages, in the sight and view of all the world', and that the execution of Mary was one thing for the Commons to demand, quite another for Elizabeth, a fellow-queen, to confirm.

Mary herself was not immediately informed that the sentence of death had been passed against her. In the meantime Paulet was instructed to secure a full confession from her on Elizabeth's express orders. On the evening of 19 November Paulet and Lord Buckhurst visited Mary. Buckhurst warned her that it was considered impossible that both she and Elizabeth should continue to live. Although Elizabeth had not given her consent to the execution, Buckhurst solemnly called on Mary to repent. Mary afterwards described the whole interview in a letter to Beaton in Paris. 'I thanked God and them for the honour they did me in considering me to be such a necessary instrument of the re-establishing of religion in this island ... In confirmation of all this as I had protested before, I offered willingly to shed my blood in the quarrel of the Catholic Church.' This was of course the very last answer which Paulet and Buckhurst wanted; they told Mary roughly that as she was to die for the intended murder of Elizabeth, she would certainly not be regarded as either a saint or a martyr. But Mary was quite intelligent enough to see that, despite Paulet's protests, matters were going in the direction she hoped. It was no wonder the historian Camden heard that her face was now illumined with extraordinary joy at the thought that God had thus chosen her to be a martyr. It was left to Paulet to castigate her speeches angrily in his report to London as 'superfluous and idle'.

Such pieces of oratory might be superfluous and idle to Paulet but to Mary they were essential planks in the platform from which she intended to undergo her martyrdom for the Catholic faith: Paulet's opinion was a matter of indifference to her, so long as her words would one day echo forth in the theatre of the world. But Paulet's next action, the removal of the royal cloth of state over Mary's chair, offended her in the vital matter of her queenship. However, the next day Paulet repented his hasty action and offered to write to London for leave to restore the canopy. This merely gave Mary the opportunity to point sublimely to the symbol which she had already hung in the place of the vanished cloth of state – a crucifix.

It was now the end of November. Mary imagined that her days were truly numbered. She spent two days writing her farewell letters to her friends on the Continent. Religious rather than dynastic interests were now paramount in her mind, and it was the Catholic faith, rather than maternal feelings, which now swayed Mary in the dispositions she laid down for the English throne after her death: in her letter to the pope she begged him to let the Catholic king of Spain secure her rights to the crown of England, in place of James if he remained obstinately outside the Catholic Church. To Mendoza, the former Spanish ambassador to London, Mary repeated solemnly her bestowal of her rights to the English throne on the Spanish king. As she wrote, Mary could hear the banging of workmen in the great hall of the castle. She imagined quite genuinely that she was listening to the sound of her own scaffold being erected. In fact it was to be over two months before this final scene was actually played.

The reason of course was that Elizabeth obstinately hesitated to confirm the sentence. The English people might rejoice and ring their bells at the news of the sentence on the Scottish queen, but their queen was still very far from resolving her own dilemma. Quite apart from the fact that Mary was an anointed queen and her own cousin, there were the problems of foreign relations to consider. How would France, where Mary had once been queen, react to the news of her death – still more Scotland, where she had actually reigned and her own son now ruled. As the prospect of war with Spain loomed nearer, the goodwill of France and the continuance of the alliance with Scotland became more important than mere diplomatic friendship. Were such benevolences really worth sacrificing for the death of an old and sick woman, who had been a prisoner for nearly twenty years? While Mary the prisoner was calm and tranquil, Elizabeth the jailer suffered the torments of indecision.

14 The Dolorous Stroke

'Rue not my death, rejoice at my repose
It was no death to me but to my woes:
The bud was opened to let out the rose,
The chain was loosed to let the captive go.'

From Decease, release, *ode by* ROBERT SOUTHWELL, S.J.,
on the death of Mary Queen of Scots

When King James first heard the news of his mother's arrest at Chartley, he contented himself with observing that she should 'drink the ale she had brewed' and in future be allowed to meddle with nothing except prayer and the service of God. It was not until after the trial and death sentence that it was made clear to James that he might shortly have to choose between his mother's life and the continuation of the newly formed Anglo-Scottish alliance, which in turn involved his hopes of inheriting the English throne.

But James's dilemma did not cause him the human anguish which Elizabeth in her reluctance to confirm the death sentence was undergoing. She told the French ambassador at the beginning of December that she had never shed so many tears over anything as at what she termed this 'unfortunate affair', and whether her grief was at her own indecision or at the prospect of shedding Mary's blood, there is no reason to doubt the genuineness of her emotion. James, on the other hand, felt considerable perplexity as to what course to take, but no purely personal feelings; the chief concern of the Scottish mission to Elizabeth in November was to ensure that nothing would be done against Mary 'to the prejudice of any title of the King's'. In the meantime Scottish public opinion was reacting most strongly to the idea that their former sovereign should be executed in a foreign country. As Gray noted in November, James would find it hard to keep the peace if her life were touched. 'I never saw all the people so willing to concur in anything as in this. They that hated most her prosperity regret her adversity.' James himself pointed out his invidious position to Elizabeth, in language which made clear that it was fear of a national outcry which animated him, rather than some more personal emotion: 'Guess ye in what strait my honour will be, this disaster being perfected,' he wrote, 'since before God I already scarce dare go abroad, for crying out of the whole people.'

Despite these fears, the one sanction which James had it in his power to invoke to save his mother's life was never made. At no point did he say that he would break the Anglo-Scottish league if his mother's death was brought about by England. A series of dire but meaningless threats, intended to save his face in Scotland, were not intended to save his mother's life in England. Once it became apparent to the English that despite all James's protests the league was to be considered inviolable whatever action they took against Mary, the date of the Scottish queen's death drew appreciably nearer.

OPPOSITE A contemporary sketch of the scene at the execution of Mary Queen of Scots in the Great Hall of Fotheringhay on 8 February 1587: the Queen is seen entering (*left*) and being disrobed by her ladies (*centre*).

The protests made by the French were more authentically passionate, but proved in the end equally ineffective: a special ambassador was sent by King Henry III to plead with Elizabeth and was answered, in Cecil's words, 'that if the French king understood her Majesty's peril, if he loveth her as he pretendeth, he would not press her Majesty to hazard her life'. The resident French ambassador, Châteauneuf, continued to make valiant efforts to save Mary, but in January his attempts were sharply curtailed by the fortunate discovery by Walsingham of yet another plot against Elizabeth's life. This providential coincidence led to Châteauneuf's house arrest, and rendered him impotent to help Mary further during the last crucial weeks.

There was certainly to be no question of the captive eluding her fate: at Paulet's request the garrison at Fotheringhay was strengthened. In mid-December Mary asked Paulet to dispatch on her behalf a farewell letter to Elizabeth, in which she requested that after her death her servants should be allowed to convey her body to France, rather than Scotland, where the Protestant burial rites would constitute a profanation by her standards. She also asked to be allowed to send a jewel and last farewell to her son James. She concluded on a magisterial note of warning to Elizabeth: 'Do not accuse me of presumption if, on the eve of leaving this world and preparing myself for a better one, I remind you that one day you will have to answer for your charge, as well as those that are sent before ...' Mary signed the letter: 'Your sister and cousin, wrongfully imprisoned.'

Slowly the winter days passed by. It was now over three months since those booted and spurred judges had galloped away from Fotheringhay and there was still no news from London that the end was even near. Although Mary had no doubts that sooner or later she would die, when Christmas had passed, the long delay encouraged her servants to begin to hope on her behalf. Then, in the middle of January, Paulet informed Melville and the queen's chaplain de Préau that, although they were to continue in residence in Fotheringhay, henceforth they were to be parted from their mistress. The removal of these loyal servants lowered Mary's spirits; her old fears of secret death were revived. When Mary expressed these fears to Paulet through the medium of Bourgoing, he fell into a rage and told Bourgoing that 'he was a man of honour and a gentleman, and he would not so dishonour himself as to wish to exercise such cruelty or to conduct himself like a Turk'. Man of honour as he professed himself – and time was to prove the truth of his claim – Paulet had no objections to imposing a series of further petty humiliations on his prisoner. Her butler was forbidden to carry the rod before her meat dishes, a service usually performed by Melville. Once again Mary jumped to the conclusion that this regal dignity was being stripped from her in order to kill her secretly. In answer to her protest she received the chilling reply from Paulet that her priest, her steward, her canopy and her rod had all been taken from her for the same reason: because she was no longer a queen but 'an attainted, convicted and condemned woman'.

Attainted, convicted, and condemned Mary might be, yet there was still no official word concerning her execution. But it was said afterwards that on the Sunday, 29 January, between midnight and one o'clock in the morning, the heavens gave their own portent that the end was not far off: a great flame of fire illuminated the windows of the queen's room three times, blinding the guards stationed beneath, but was seen nowhere else in the castle. This supernatural warning, if warning it was, was certainly borne out by events. Three days later, at her court at Greenwich, Queen Elizabeth at last sent for Davison, the secretary of the Council, to bring the warrant for the execution, which for so long had lacked her own signature. Davison discreetly placed the warrant in the middle of a pile of other papers which the queen was due to sign. The ruse – for Elizabeth had made it clear to her anxious ministers that she must be the subject of a ruse – was successful. It was thus, in the midst of an innocuous conversation on the subject of the weather, that Elizabeth finally signed the warrant with all her other papers, and having done so, threw them idly down on the table.

Elizabeth did, however, stipulate that the execution was under no circumstances to be held in public. Then she laid it down that she personally was to be told no more on the subject until the execution was successfully completed. Despite this Pilate-like observation, Elizabeth still did not totally wash her hands of the matter. Having signed the warrant, she murmured wistfully to Davison that if a loyal subject were to save her from embarrassment by dealing the blow, the resentment of France and Scotland might be disarmed. The obvious loyal subject to assume this helpful role was Paulet, and a letter was duly sent expressing regret at this oversight.

Now the issue which Mary had so long dreaded was squarely placed before her jailer: and it is one of the ironies of history that Paulet, the man whom Mary had for so long both disliked and feared, seized his pen and wrote back to his royal mistress in the most trenchant language refusing the odious commission: 'God forbid that I should make so foul a shipwreck of my conscience, or leave so great a blot on my poor posterity, to shed blood without law or warrant.' Paradoxically, Mary was saved from the private extinction which she dreaded by the action of the Puritan who had done so much to make her last months uncomfortable and humiliating. It was left to Elizabeth, on whom the course of action reflects no credit, to exclaim furiously at the 'niceness' of those 'precise fellows' who professed great zeal for her safety but would perform nothing.

Elizabeth's Council, experienced in the ways of their mistress, did not wait for Paulet's answer before acting. With the warrant in their possession, it was unanimously decided to set proceedings in hand immediately. The warrant was handed to Beale, the clerk of the Council, who was instructed to set forth immediately for Fotheringhay, accompanied by Shrewsbury and the earl of Kent.

The sadly depleted royal household at Fotheringhay had no inkling of what was afoot. On Saturday, 4 February, Bourgoing asked Paulet if he might visit the neighbouring villages and search for certain herbal remedies which might help the queen against her rheumatism. Paulet was evasive, and said he could take no decision until the Monday. On Sunday, however, Mary learnt that Beale had arrived at Fotheringhay and, interpreting the significance of his arrival correctly, told Bourgoing he might cease searching for a cure since she would now have no need of it. But no authoritative intimation was given to the queen concerning her fate until the Tuesday, and the official time given to the queen to prepare for death was of a minimum.

It was not until after dinner that a deputation of Paulet, Beale and the two earls asked to see the queen. It was Shrewsbury who told Mary that she had been found guilty and condemned to death, and Beale read aloud the warrant. Mary received the news with absolute calm. When Beale had done, she replied with great dignity and no show of emotion: 'I thank you for such welcome news. You will do me great good in withdrawing me from this world out of which I am very glad to go.' She touched on her queenly position and royal blood, adding that in spite of this 'all my life I have had only sorrow', and saying that she was now overjoyed to have the opportunity at the end to shed her blood for the Catholic Church. Mary then placed her hand on the New Testament and solemnly protested herself to be innocent of all the crimes imputed to her. When Kent objected that it was a Catholic version of the Bible, Mary answered: 'If I swear on the book which I believe to be the true version, will your lordship not believe my oath more than if I were to swear on a translation in which I do not believe?'

But Mary's captors were not prepared to concede either the sincerity of her religious convictions or the need to display a certain tolerance towards a woman *in extremis*. They offered her the services of a Protestant minister but Mary refused to consider it. When Mary asked for her own chaplain to be readmitted to her presence, in order to make ready her soul, in Paulet's words, 'we utterly denied that unto her'. This was a serious blow to Mary, who had not anticipated this final in-humanity. However, when Kent exclaimed: 'Your life would be the death of our religion, your death would be its life,' her face lit up. At least his words revealed that already in the opinion of the world her death was linked with the survival of the Catholic Church in England.

When the queen asked at what hour she was to die, Shrewsbury replied in a faltering voice: 'Tomorrow morning, at eight o'clock.' Mary remarked that the time was very short since it was already late. She then made a series of requests, all of which were denied to her: she applied for her papers and account books which had been taken from her; once more she begged vainly for her chaplain; thirdly she asked that her body might be interred in France, only to be told that Elizabeth had ruled against it. Mary's servants, in a state of hysteria, tried to get some sort of reprieve or at least a stay of execution, weeping and crying and protesting that the time was too short, to no avail. There was to be no delay.

The queen of Scots was left alone to spend the last evening of her life with her servants, some of whom, like Jane Kennedy, had spent a whole generation in her service. She tried to rally them. 'Well, Jane Kennedy,' said the queen. 'Did I not tell you this would happen? ... I knew they would never allow me to live, I was too great an obstacle to their religion.' Mary then asked for her supper to be served as speedily as possible, in order that she might have time to put her affairs in order. It was a heart-breaking meal, the servants outdoing themselves in the assiduousness of their service, as though there was some comfort to be had in making each little gesture as perfect as possible; Bourgoing acting as steward in Melville's absence, presented the dishes to his mistress and, as he did so, he could not prevent the tears from pouring down his cheeks. The queen herself ate little. She sat in a sort of dream, from time to time referring to Kent's outburst on the subject of her death and her religion: 'Oh how happy these words make me,' she murmured. 'Here at last is the truth.' When the meal was over, the queen asked her servants to drink to her, and as they did so, kneeling before her, their tears mingled with the wine.

Mary now seated herself and went through the contents of her wardrobe in detail. Her money she sorted personally into little portions, and placed in packets, on which she wrote the name of the servant for whom they were destined. From her belongings she divided off certain mementoes for royalties and her relations abroad, such as the king and queen of France, Queen Catherine, and the Guises; from the rest she bestowed numerous little personal objects on all her servants; Bourgoing received rings, silver boxes, her music book bound in velvet to remind him of the many musical evenings of the captivity, as well as the red hangings of Mary's bed; Elizabeth Curle received miniatures set in gold and enamelled tablets of Mary, Francis II and James. Melville received a little tablet of gold set with another portrait of James. Having thus disposed of those actual physical possessions which remained within her sphere, the queen drew up an elaborate testament of which Henry, duke of Guise, Beaton, the bishop of Ross, and du Ruisseau, her chancellor in France, were to be executors. She asked for Requiem Masses to be held in France, and made detailed financial arrangements for the benefit of her servants. Beyond that, there were charitable requests for the poor children and friars of Rheims, and instructions that her coach was to be used to convey her women to London, where the horses were to be sold to defray their expenses, and her furniture likewise, that they might be able to afford to return to their countries of origin.

Having completed these detailed dispositions for the welfare of those she would leave behind, Mary considered her own spiritual welfare in the shape of a farewell letter to be handed to the chaplain de Préau. Deprived of his physical presence, she used the medium of the letter as a general confession of her sins, in which she asked him to spend the night in prayer for her. Mary's last letter of all was to her brother-in-law, King Henry of France; she related the abrupt circumstance in which her sentence had been broken to her, and her conviction that it was her religion, coupled with her place in the English succession, which was the true cause of her death. She begged him to listen to the personal testimony concerning her execution which her physician should give to him so soon as he could reach France, and her last thoughts were for the faithful servants who had served her so long – she asked that their pensions and wages might be paid throughout their lives, and in particular that de Préau, her chaplain, might be awarded some little benefice in France from which he could spend the rest of his days in prayer for his dead mistress. When these elaborate dispositions were finally completed, it was two o'clock in the morning. Mary's letter to the king of France was thus dated Wednesday, 8 February 1587, the day of her execution.

The golden rosary and prayer-book carried by Mary at her execution; the rosary was bequeathed to Anne, wife of Philip Earl of Arundel.

The traveller was now ready for her last journey on earth. The queen lay down on her bed without undressing. She did not try to sleep. Her women gathered round her already wearing their black garments of mourning, and Mary asked Jane Kennedy to read aloud the life of some great sinner. The life of the good thief was chosen, and as the story reached its climax on the cross, Mary observed aloud: 'In truth he was a great sinner, but not so great as I have been.' She then closed her eyes and said nothing further. Throughout the night the sound of hammering came from the great hall where the scaffold was being erected. The boots of the soldiers could be heard ceaselessly tramping up and down outside

186

the queen's room, for Paulet had ordered them to watch with special vigilance in these final hours, lest their victim escape her captors at the last. The queen lay on her bed without sleeping, eyes closed and a half smile on her face.

So the short night passed. At six o'clock, long before light, the queen rose, handed over the will, distributed her purses, and gave her women a farewell embrace. Her men servants were given her hand to kiss. Then she went into her little oratory and prayed alone. She was extremely pale but quite composed. Bourgoing handed her a little bread and wine to sustain her. The day now dawned fine and sunny; it was one of those unexpected early February days when it suddenly seems possible that spring will come. It was between eight and nine when a loud knocking was heard at the door, and a messenger shouted through it that the lords were waiting for the queen. Mary asked for a moment to finish her prayers, at which the lords outside in a moment of panic feared some sort of last-minute resistance might be planned, unable to believe in the courage of their captive. But when they entered, they found Mary kneeling quietly in prayer in front of the crucifix which hung above her altar.

It was this crucifix which her groom Hannibal Stuart now bore before her as she was escorted towards the great hall. The queen was totally calm, and showed no signs of fear or distress. Her bearing was regal, and some of the contemporary observers afterwards even described her as cheerful and smiling. The last moment of agony came in the entry chamber to the hall, when her servants were held back from following her and the queen was told that she was to die quite alone, by the orders of Elizabeth. Melville, distracted at this unlooked-for blow, fell on his knees in tears. The queen dashed away her own tears and said gently: 'You ought to rejoice and not to weep for that the end of Mary Stuart's troubles is now done. Thou knowest, Melville, that all this world is but vanity and full of troubles and sorrows. Carry this message from me and tell my friends that I died a true woman to my religion, and like a true Scottish woman and a true French woman ...' And commending Melville to go to her son, and tell him that her dearest wish had always been to see England and Scotland united, that she had never done anything to prejudice the welfare of the kingdom of Scotland, she embraced her steward and bade him farewell.

Mary now turned to Paulet and the lords and pleaded with them to allow at least some of her servants to be with her at the death, so that they could later report the manner of her death in other countries. Kent replied that her wish could not well be granted for before the execution her servants were sure to cry out and upset the queen herself, as well as disquieting the company, while afterwards they might easily attempt to dip their napkins in her blood for relics which, said Kent grimly, 'were not convenient'. 'My Lord,' replied Mary, 'I will give my word and promise for them that they shall not do any such thing as your Lordship hath named. Alas poor souls, it would do them good to bid me farewell.' After hurried whispered consultations, the lords relented and Melville, Bourgoing, Jane Kennedy, Elizabeth Curle and two others were allowed to go forward with the queen.

Mary now entered the great hall in silence. The spectators gathered there – about 300 of them by one account – gazed with awe and apprehension at this legendary figure whose dramatic career was about to be ended before their eyes. They saw a tall and gracious woman, dressed in black, save for the long white lace-edged veil which flowed down her back to the ground like a bride's, and the white stiffened and peaked head-dress, that too edged with lace, below which gleamed her auburn hair. Her satin dress of black was embroidered with black velvet, with black acorn buttons of jet trimmed with pearl; through the slashed sleeves could be seen inner sleeves of purple. She held a crucifix and a prayer book in her hand, and two rosaries hung down from her waist; round her neck was a pomander chain and an *Agnus Dei*. Despite the fact that Mary's shoulders were now bowed and stooping with illness, and her figure grown full with the years, she walked with immense dignity. Time and suffering had long ago rubbed away the delicate youthful charm of her face, but to many of the spectators her extraordinary composure and serenity had its own beauty. Above all, her courage was matchless, and this alone in many people's minds, whatever honours and dignities had been stripped from her by Paulet, still gave her the right to be called a queen.

In the centre of the great hall was set a wooden stage, all hung with black. On it were two stools for Shrewsbury and Kent and beside them, also draped in black, the block, and a little cushioned stool on which it was intended the queen should sit while she was disrobed. The great axe was already lying there.

Once led up the three steps to the stage, the queen listened patiently while the commission for her execution was read aloud. Her expression never changed. Cecil's own official observer, Robert Wise, commented later that from her detached regard, she might even have been listening to a pardon, rather than a warrant for her own death. The first sign of emotion was wrung from her when the Protestant dean of Peterborough stepped forward and proposed to harangue the queen according to the rites of the Protestant religion. 'Mr Dean,' said the queen firmly, 'I am settled in the ancient Catholic Roman religion, and mind to spend my blood in defence of it.' Shrewsbury and Kent both exhorted her to listen to him, and even offered to pray with the queen, but all these proposals Mary resolutely rejected. 'If you will pray with me, my lords,' she said to the two earls, 'I will thank you, but to join in prayer I will not, for that you and I are not of one religion.' And when the dean, in answer to the earls' direction, finally knelt down on the scaffold steps and started to pray out loud and at length, in a prolonged and rhetorical style as though determined to force his way into the pages of history, Mary still paid no attention but turned away, and started to pray aloud out of her own book in Latin, in the midst of these prayers sliding off her stool on to her knees. When the dean was at last finished, the queen changed her prayers, and began to pray out loud in English for the afflicted English Catholic Church, for her son, and for Elizabeth, that she might serve God in the years to come. Kent remonstrated with her: 'Madam, settle Christ Jesus in your heart and leave those trumperies.' But the queen prayed on, asking God to avert his wrath from England, and calling on the Saints to

intercede for her; and so she kissed the crucifix she held, and crossing herself, ended: 'Even as Thy arms, O Jesus, were spread here upon the cross, so receive me into Thy arms of mercy, and forgive me all my sins.'

When the queen's prayers were finished, the executioners asked her, as was customary, to forgive them in advance for bringing about her death. Mary answered immediately: 'I forgive you with all my heart, for now I hope you shall make an end of all my troubles.' Then the executioners, helped by Jane Kennedy and Elizabeth Curle, assisted the queen to undress – Robert Wise noticed that she undressed so quickly that it seemed as if she was in haste to be gone out of the world. Stripped of her black, she stood in a red velvet petticoat and it was seen that above it she wore a red satin bodice, trimmed with lace; one of her women handed her a pair of red sleeves, and it was thus wearing all red, the colour of blood, and the liturgical colour of martyrdom in the Catholic Church, that the queen of Scots died. According to their usual practice, the executioners stretched forth their hands for the queen's ornaments which were their perquisites. When they touched the long golden rosary, Jane Kennedy protested, and the queen herself intervened and said that they would be compensated with money in its place, and the same promise had to be made regarding the *Agnus Dei*. Yet all the time her belongings were being stripped from her, it was notable that the queen neither wept nor changed her calm and almost happy expression of what one observer called 'smiling cheer'; she even retained her composure sufficiently to remark wryly of the executioners that she had never before had such grooms of the chamber to make her ready. It was the queen's women who could not contain their lamentations as they wept and crossed themselves and muttered snatches of Latin prayers. Finally Mary had to turn to them and, mindful of her promise to Shrewsbury, she admonished them softly: '*Ne crie point pour moi. J'ai promis pour vous . . .*' Once more she bade them not mourn but rejoice, for they were soon to see the end of all her troubles.

The time had come for Jane Kennedy to bind the queen's eyes with the white cloth embroidered in gold which Mary had herself chosen for the purpose the night before. Jane first kissed the cloth and then wrapped it gently round her mistress's eyes, and over her head so that her hair was covered as by a white turban and only the neck left completely bare. The two women then withdrew from the stage. The queen without even now the faintest sign of fear, knelt down once more on the cushion in front of the block. She recited aloud in Latin the psalm *In te Domino confido, non confundar in aeternum* – In you Lord is my trust, let me never be confounded – and then feeling for the block, she laid her head down upon it, placing her chin carefully with both hands, so that if one of the executioners had not moved them back they too would have lain in the direct line of the axe. The queen stretched out her arms and legs and cried: '*In manus tuas, Domine, confide spiritum meum*' – 'Into your hand, O Lord, I commend my spirit' – three or four times. When the queen was lying there quite motionless, the executioner's assistant put his hand on her body to steady it for the blow. Even so, the first blow, as it fell, missed the neck and cut into the back of the head. The queen's lips moved, and her servants thought they heard the whispered words: 'Sweet Jesus.' The second blow severed the neck, all but the smallest sinew, and this was severed by using the axe as a saw. It was about ten o'clock in the morning of Wednesday, 8 February, the queen of Scots being then aged forty-four years old and in the nineteenth year of her English captivity.

In the great hall of Fotheringhay, before the wondering eyes of the crowd, the executioner now held aloft the dead woman's head, crying out as he did so: 'God save the Queen.' The lips still moved and continued to do so for a quarter of an hour after the death. But at this moment, weird and moving spectacle, the auburn tresses in his hand came apart from the skull and the head itself fell to the ground. It was seen that Mary Stuart's own hair had in fact been quite grey, and very short at the time of her death: for her execution she had chosen to wear a wig. The spectators were stunned by the unexpected sight and remained silent. It was left to the dean of Peterborough to call out strongly: 'So perish all the Queen's enemies,' and for Kent, standing over the corpse to echo: 'Such be the end of all the Queen's, and all the Gospel's enemies.' But Shrewsbury could not speak, and his face was wet with tears.

It was now time for the executioners to strip the body of its remaining adornments before handing it over to the embalmers. But at this point a strange and pathetic memorial to that devotion which Mary Stuart had always aroused in those who knew her intimately was discovered: her little lap dog, traditionally a Skye terrier, which had managed to accompany her into the hall under her long skirts, where her servants had been turned away, now crept out from beneath her petticoat, and in its distress stationed itself piteously beneath the severed head and the shoulders of the body. Nor would it be coaxed away, but steadfastly and uncomprehendingly clung to the solitary thing it could find which still reminded it of its mistress. To all others save this poor animal, the sad corpse lying so still on the floor of the stage, in its red clothes against which the blood stains scarcely showed, with its face now sunken to that of an old woman in the harsh disguise of death, bore little resemblance to her whom they had known only a short while before as Mary Queen of Scots. The spirit had fled the body. The chain was loosed to let the captive go.

At Fotheringhay now it was as if a murder had taken place. The weeping women in the hall were pushed away and locked in their rooms. The castle gates were locked, so that no one could leave and break the news to the outside world. The body was lain unceremoniously in the presence chamber, wrapped in a coarse woollen covering. The blood-stained block was burnt. Every other particle of clothing or object of devotion which might be associated with the queen of Scots was burnt, scoured or washed, so that not a trace of her blood might remain to create a holy relic to inspire devotion in years to come. The little dog was washed and washed again, although it subsequently refused to eat and so pined away. At about four o'clock in the afternoon the body was further stripped, the organs were removed and buried in a secret spot deep within the castle; the body was then wrapped in a wax winding sheet and incarcerated in a heavy lead coffin.

Only one messenger was allowed to gallop forth from the castle hard towards London, to break the news of what had taken place that morning to Elizabeth. He reached the capital the next morning. When Elizabeth was told the news, she received it at first with great indignation, and then with terrible distress: 'her countenance changed, her words faltered, and with excessive sorrow she was in a manner astonished, insomuch as she gave herself over to grief, putting herself into mourning weeds and shedding abundance of tears'. In the meantime, before grief could over-come her altogether, she turned like an angry snake on the secretary Davison, and had him thrown into prison for daring to use the warrant for the execution which she herself had signed. She now maintained that she had only signed it for 'safety's sake' and had merely given it to Davison to keep, not to use. Further ostentatious manifestations of her displeasure might have followed, had not Cecil himself felt obliged to remonstrate with Elizabeth. He pointed out that such theatricals, even if they salved her own conscience, would cut little ice with the outside world. On the other hand, the papists and the queen's enemies might all too easily be encouraged, if it was suggested that the queen of Scots had been killed unlawfully. Unlike the queen, London itself suffered from no such doubts: the bells were rung, fires were lighted in the streets and there was much merry-making and banqueting to celebrate the death of her whom they had been trained to regard as a public enemy.

But at Fotheringhay itself nothing was changed. It was as though the castle, cut off from the rest of the world, had fallen asleep for a thousand years under an enchantment, as a result of the dolorous stroke which had there slain Mary Queen of Scots. Her attendants were still kept in prison within the castle, and none of them was allowed to return to their native lands of France and Scotland as Mary had so urgently stipulated at the last. Paulet remained in charge of arrangements at Fotheringhay and continued to complain over the excessive expenses of his prisoners' diet. Spring turned to summer. The snowdrops which had scattered the green meadows round the River Nene on the day of her death gave place to purple thistles, sometimes romantically called Queen Mary's Tears. Still the body of the dead queen, embalmed and wrapped in its heavy lead coffin, was given no burial, but remained walled up within the precincts of the castle where she had died.

Epilogue: The Theatre of the World

'Remember that the theatre of the world is wider than the realm of England.'
MARY QUEEN OF SCOTS *before her judges, October 1586*

As the gates of Fotheringhay were locked, so were the English ports closed immediately after the death of the queen of Scots. It was three weeks before the French ambassador Châteauneuf could write back to his master in Paris with tidings of the calamity. The news of the death of Mary Stuart, their own queen dowager, was received in France with national and solemn mourning. On 12 March a Requiem Mass was held in the black-draped cathedral of Notre Dame, where nearly thirty years before Mary had married Francis amid so much magnificence.

Despite the sorrow of the French nation and in spite of Mary's own desire to be buried in France, her wishes in this respect were never fulfilled. However, in other ways, Mary's last wishes were being met. By 7 March Mendoza, who was in Paris, was able to spread the tale of her heroic death to Spain for, despite all the English precautions, news of her bravery during the last hours leaked out. Not only her courage but even her sanctity were discussed. Paris was the scene of mass demonstrations, as well as sermons that virtually canonized Mary as a saint who had died in the cause of the Catholic faith. The woman who deliberately chose the story of the good thief to be read aloud to her on the eve of her death because she considered herself in all humility to be a great sinner would he viewed this popular canonization with detachment; on the other hand Mary would undoubtedly have been pleased at the way the Catholic League and Philip II were galvanized by her death as by a Catholic rallying cry; even the French king, who generally viewed the Guise-inspired Catholic League with suspicion, gave vent to some newly bellicose sentiments towards the Protestants, on receiving the news of Mary's death.

The grief of the Scottish court was more difficult to estimate and contemporary accounts differ radically in their reports of how James received the news of his mother's execution. According to one story, he shammed sorrow in public, but observed to his courtiers gleefully in secret: 'Now I am sole King.' Another story told how the 'King moved never his countenance at the rehearsal of his mother's execution, nor leaves not his pastimes more than of before.' Still other reports spoke of his evident grief, how he became very sad and pensive when the intelligence reached him, and went to bed without eating. Whatever James's outward show of lamentation, it is difficult to believe that the news of his mother's death aroused at long last the filial passion of which he had

OPPOSITE The tomb and effigy of Mary Queen of Scots in Westminster Abbey, sculpted by Cornelius and William Cure and erected in 1612 by her son James VI and I.

shown so little evidence during her life. His conduct subsequently showed that so long as the English crown still dangled within his reach, he was prepared to swallow the insult to his family and his nation. The Scottish people as a whole showed more spirit than their king, and seemed to evince both humiliation and anger at the killing of one who had once sat on the throne of Scotland. When James ordered the Scottish court into mourning as a formal gesture, according to one tradition the earl of Sinclair appeared before him dressed in steel armour in place of black. When James asked him whether he had not seen the general order for mourning, Sinclair replied sternly: 'This *is* the proper mourning for the Queen of Scotland.' Prayers were said for the defunct queen in a form specially prescribed by the Council. Some of Mary's former subjects discussed plans for reprisals, posters appeared in the streets against England and James, and there was a general clamour for war. James did make the formal gesture of breaking off formal communications with England for a time, but James finally accepted Elizabeth's explanation of her own 'unspotted' part in the execution, and by mid-March the English were confident that James would not fight to avenge his mother's death. The Anglo–Scottish alliance remained unsevered by the axe of Fotheringhay.

It was, however, in deference to James's feelings, or the sort of appropriate feelings he might be supposed to cherish for his mother, that the subject of the burial of the queen of Scots was raised again in the summer after her death. The coffin had remained unburied, like the corpse of Achilles, within Fotheringhay itself. Now it was planned to give the coffin an honourable burial in Peterborough Cathedral. So far as anything explained this curious ceremony, the line adopted seemed to be that Mary had been a revered dowager queen of Scotland who happened to die in England of natural causes. Under the auspices of Garter King of Arms, heralds, nobles and mourners were imported from London to give the occasion the right degree of solemnity due to the mother of the king of Scotland. But no Scots were present: and although the cathedral was hung with black, paid for by the master of the wardrobe, and the arms of Scotland, as well as those of Mary's first two husbands, nowhere was there any mention of Bothwell, to the events leading to her imprisonment in England, let alone the manner of her death. Elizabeth's personal friend, the countess of Bedford, acted the role of chief mourner with due gravity, while the procession was headed with one hundred poor widows also dressed for the occasion in black at the government's expense; yet the dichotomy at the heart of this strange apologetic ceremony was revealed by the fact that the coffin was actually transported from Fotheringhay to Peterborough at dead of night for fear of demonstrations. The whole ceremony was of course Protestant and thus sung in English. But the late queen's servants, who had been allowed out of their seclusion at Fotheringhay to attend the service, were nearly all pious Catholics. They, therefore, withdrew from the body of the church once the procession was over.

The coffin was placed in a vault in the south aisle of the cathedral and when the service was completed, the courtiers and the ecclesiastics adjourned to the Bishop's Palace for a funeral banquet of considerable

festivity: but Mary's former servitors were not so easily transferred from tears into laughter; what to the worshipful company from London was only a ritual proceeding to round off a distasteful incident in English history, was to them the last obsequies of their beloved mistress. Thus, while the English caroused, Mary's servants gathered in another room and wept bitter tears.

The most passionate desire left to these poor people was that they should now be released from their melancholy prison and allowed to go their several ways. Despite the completion of the interment, there was a further delay of two months before they were allowed to depart. At last in October, the ordeal of the little royal household was at an end. Bourgoing went to King Henry III, as he had been instructed, and told his tale of the uplifting last months and hours of the late queen of Scots. Gorion went to Mendoza and he too related the story. The farewell letters written nearly a year before reached their destinations at last, and King Philip, moved by this reminder from beyond the grave of the woman who had once been his sister-in-law, and long his Catholic confederate, honoured Mary's last requests for payments of her servants' wages, and her debts in France. He also pursued in correspondence with Mendoza the subject of what he believed to be Mary's last gift to him in her will – the reversion of the English crown. In the interests of his own foreign policy, Philip conveniently allowed himself to credit the story that Mary had finally disinherited James altogether on the eve of her execution, and had consequently ceded to Philip directly her own claims to the English throne. It was now late in 1587. It was in the next year,

The memorial portrait commissioned by Mary's lady-in-waiting Elizabeth Curle, now in Blairs College, Aberdeen: to the left of the figure of the queen can be seen the execution scene, and to the right the figures of Elizabeth Curle and Jane Kennedy.

ABOVE Peterborough Cathedral, where Mary was given an 'honorable burial' until, in 1612, her son had her body exhumed and brought to Westminster Abbey.

195

1588, that Philip took the momentous decision to pursue his supposed English inheritance with the great force of the Spanish Armada. Ironically enough, therefore, the mighty Spanish fleet of rescue, for which Mary had waited so long and so hopefully, only sailed towards England after, and as a direct result of, her death.

Even now with the burial at Peterborough, the earthly peregrinations of the queen of Scots were not at an end. After James had ascended the English throne in 1603 and had erected a large and handsome monument to Queen Elizabeth in Westminster Abbey, it was generally felt that something should be done for his mother's memory. Thus it was that the queen of Scots' body found its final resting-place in Westminster Abbey. The tomb, commissioned by James, is magnificent, a monument to James's taste if not to filial piety. By the white marble of which it is composed, Mary Stuart becomes once more 'la reine blanche' of her first widowhood. It shows her lying full-length beneath a great ornamental canopy, her face serene and noble, her eyes closed, her long fingers stretched out in an attitude of prayer; she wears the simple peaked head-dress in which she died, but a royal cloak edged with ermine stretches around her body; at her feet rests the lion of Scotland. Altogether the whole impression of this awe-inspiring catafalque is of beauty – beauty which is made up of both majesty and repose.

So the queen of Scots found peace at last. There can be little doubt that Mary, who cared so much and so prolongedly for the English succession, would have been satisfied at the last with her burial place among the kings and queens of England. Her rights as a queen, to which she attached such importance to the end, had thus been respected. Viewing that splendid edifice in marble, white in the darkness of the Henry VII Chapel, the last of the royal monuments and the most imposing of them all, she would surely have felt that the cruelty of Elizabeth in denying her the French burial she craved had been atoned for in an unlooked-for and glorious manner. Nor was the significance of her tomb entirely royal: a few years after her interment there, pious Catholics were spreading the news that holy benefits could be gained from a visit to the tomb as to a shrine.

Once more, however, the repose of the queen of Scots was destined to be disturbed. In 1867 a search was instituted by the dean within the royal tombs of the abbey for the body of James I, whose position was unrecorded. Among the places it was thought he might have appropriately chosen for his own sepulchre was the tomb of his mother. When the vault was opened a startling and harrowing sight greeted the gaze of the Victorian searchers: the queen of Scots was far from lying alone in her tomb. A vast pile of lead coffins rose upwards from the floor, some of them obviously children and babies, all heaped together in confusion, amid urns of many different shapes, which were scattered all through the vault.

It was discovered that Mary shared her catacomb with numbers of her descendants, including her grandson Henry, Prince of Wales, her granddaughter Elizabeth of Bohemia, the Winter Queen, and her great-grandson Prince Rupert of the Rhine, among the most romantic of all the offshoots of the Stuart dynasty. Most poignant of all were the endless

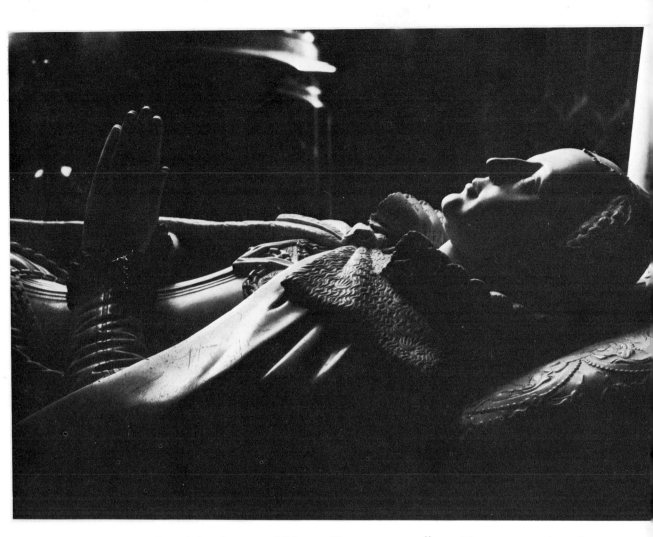

The monument above the tomb of Mary Queen of Scots in Westminster Abbey.

tiny coffins: here were found the first ten children of James II as well as the eighteen pathetic babies born dead to Queen Anne. Finally the great lead coffin of the queen of Scots herself was found, against the north wall of the vault. No attempt was made to open it: 'The presence of the fatal coffin which had received the headless corpse at Fotheringhay', wrote the dean, 'was sufficiently affecting without endeavouring to penetrate further into its mournful contents.' The vault was thus reverently tidied, the urns rearranged, but the queen's coffin was left untouched, and the little children who surrounded her were not removed.

Meanwhile in the opposite chapel, during the same search, beneath the monument to Queen Elizabeth I, were found together in one grave the two daughters of Henry VIII, Mary Tudor and Elizabeth. Barren in life, they had been left to lie alone together in death. Mary, however, lies amid her Stuart posterity, her face locked in the marble of repose on the monument above and her hands clasped in prayer, her body in the vault below which harbours so many of her descendants. She who never reigned in England, who was born a queen of Scotland, and who died at the orders of an English queen, lies now in Westminster Abbey where every sovereign of Britain since her death has been crowned; from her down to the present queen. As Mary herself embroidered so long ago on the royal cloth of state which was destined to hang over the head of a captive queen: *In my end is my Beginning.*

197

The Scottish

Royal Stewarts, Lennox Stewarts, Hamiltons, showin

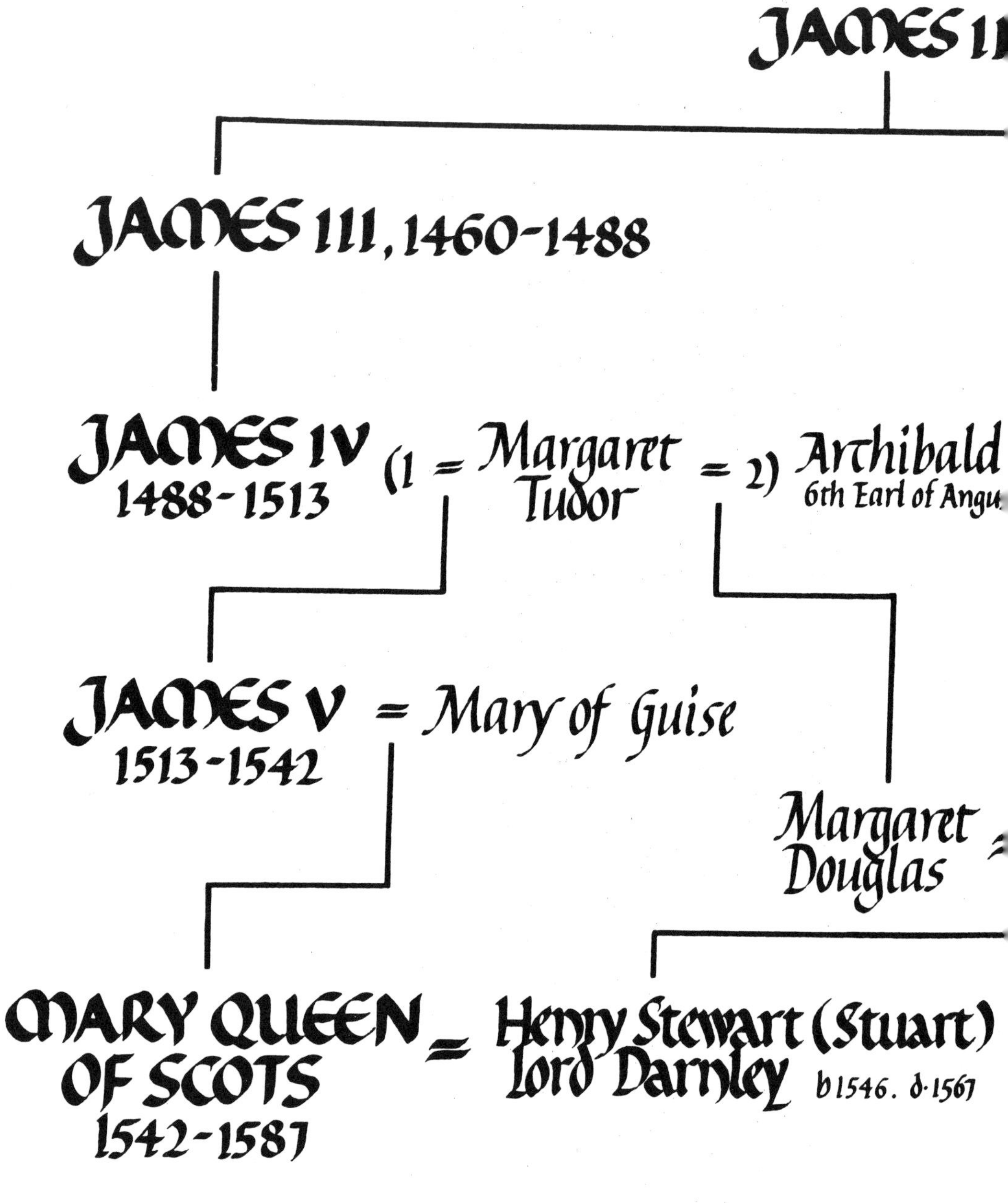

JAMES II

JAMES III, 1460-1488

JAMES IV (1 = Margaret = 2) Arthibald
1488-1513   Tudor   6th Earl of Angu

JAMES V = Mary of Guise
1513-1542

Margaret
Douglas

MARY QUEEN OF SCOTS = Henry Stewart (Stuart)
1542-1587   Lord Darnley b 1546. d·1567

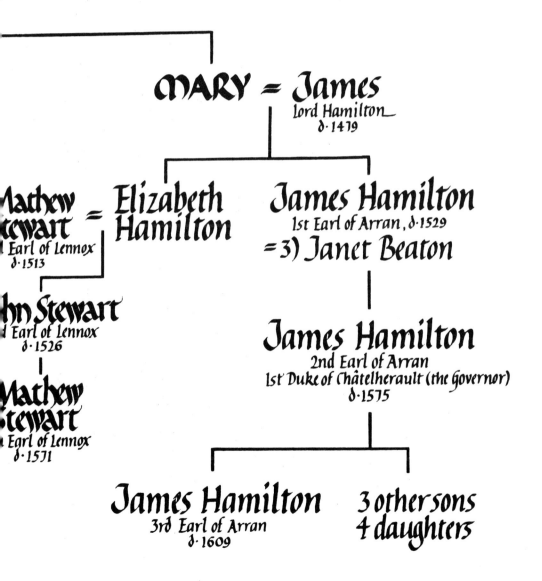

MARY = James
Lord Hamilton
d · 1479

Mathew Stewart = Elizabeth Hamilton

1 Earl of Lennox
d · 1513

James Hamilton
1st Earl of Arran, d · 1529
= 3) Janet Beaton

hn Stewart

1 Earl of Lennox
d · 1526

James Hamilton
2nd Earl of Arran
1st Duke of Châtelherault (the Governor)
d · 1575

Mathew Stewart

1 Earl of Lennox
d · 1571

James Hamilton
3rd Earl of Arran
d · 1609

3 other sons
4 daughters

The English

showing the position of Mary Queen of Scots a[n]

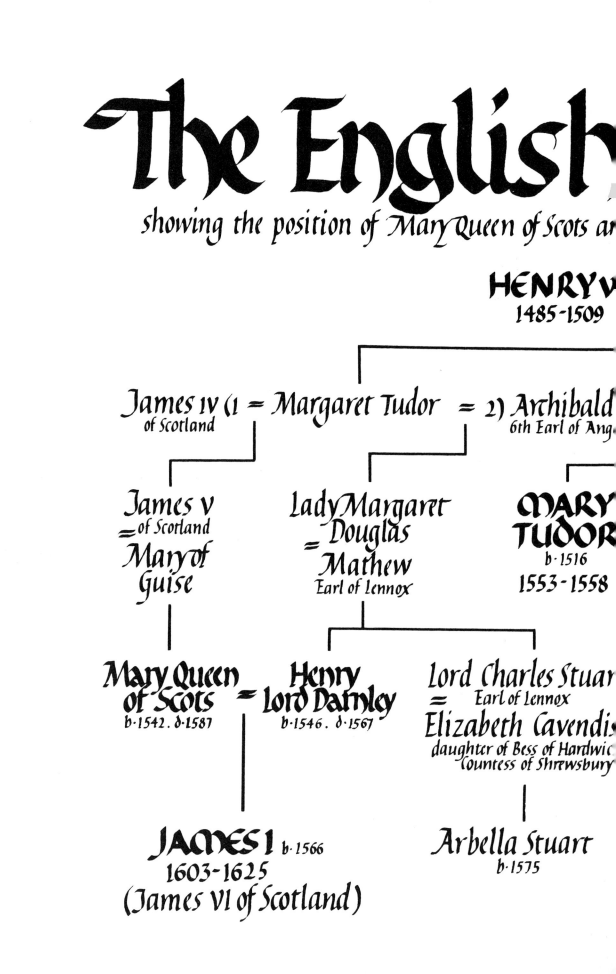

HENRY V[I]
1485-1509

James IV (1 = Margaret Tudor = 2) Archibald
of Scotland   6th Earl of Ang[us]

James V
= of Scotland
**Mary of
Guise**

Lady Margaret
Douglas
= Mathew
Earl of Lennox

**MARY
TUDOR**
b·1516
1553-1558

**Mary Queen
of Scots**
b·1542. d·1587

= **Henry
Lord Darnley**
b·1546. d·1567

Lord Charles Stuar[t]
= Earl of Lennox
Elizabeth Cavendi[sh]
daughter of Bess of Hardwic[k]
Countess of Shrewsbury

JAMES I b·1566
1603-1625
(James VI of Scotland)

Arbella Stuart
b·1575

succession

...ord Darnley, in relation to the English throne

...lizabeth of York

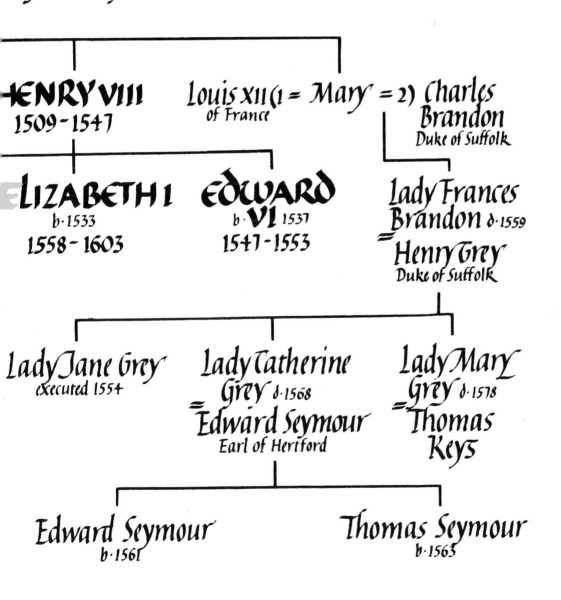

HENRY VIII 1509-1547	**Louis XII** (1 = Mary = 2) of France	**Charles Brandon** Duke of Suffolk
ELIZABETH 1 b·1533 1558-1603	**EDWARD VI** b·1537 1547-1553	**Lady Frances Brandon** d·1559 = **Henry Grey** Duke of Suffolk

Lady Jane Grey executed 1554

Lady Catherine Grey d·1568 = **Edward Seymour** Earl of Hertford

Lady Mary Grey d·1578 = **Thomas Keys**

Edward Seymour b·1561

Thomas Seymour b·1563

Acknowledgments

Photographs were supplied or are reproduced by kind permission of the following:

By gracious permission of Her Majesty the Queen: *49*, *52*, 66 (right), *70*, *122–3*, *166*

The Duke of Atholl: 158–9

John Bethell: *51*, 106, 112–13, *121* (above)

Bibliothèque Nationale: 21, 29

The Trustees of the Blair Collection (Robert Harding): *144*

Bodleian Library, Oxford: 134 (left)

British Museum: 9, 18, 78, 97, 100, 126, 169, 176, 181, 189 (right)

The Duke of Buccleuch and Queensberry: 17

Bulloz: 32–3, 38

Central Public Library, Edinburgh: 85

Department of the Environment, Edinburgh: 88–9, 90, 125, 129

Dixon Compton: 80

Lady Antonia Fraser: 13, 93, 115 (above and below), 132–3 (below)

John Freeman: 48

Gordon Fraser Gallery: 197

The Duke of Hamilton and Brandon: 57, 139 (below right)

Hatfield House: *124* (John Freeman), *141* (John Freeman)

The Controller, Her Majesty's Stationery Office: 60–1, 98, 103, 112

Mrs D. Herschorn: 156

Hunterian Museum, University of Glasgow: 54 (left)

A. F. Kersting: 36, *72*, 134 (right), 195 (right)

Kunstsammlungen, Kassel: 73

Louvre, Paris: 34

Mansell Collection: 2, 20, 40–1 (below), 162 (left)

The Marquess of Salisbury: 132–3 (above), 139 (left)

Metropolitan Museum of Art, Washington: Gift of J. P. Morgan, 1917: *71*

Musée Condé, Chantilly: 7

National Gallery of Art, Washington: 15

National Galleries of Scotland: 10, 37, 58, 68, 84, 101, 109, 118, 120, *121* (below), 139 (above right), *143*, 155 (right)

National Monument Record of Scotland: 61

National Museum of Antiquities of Scotland: 127

National Portrait Gallery, London: 66 (left), *69*, 117, 148 (above), 162 (right), 189 (left)

National Trust: *50–1* (John Bethell), 74–5, *142* (Country Life), 152–3

The Duke of Norfolk: 186

The Duke of Northumberland: 54 (right)

Sir David Ogilivy: 65

The Earl of Oxford and Asquith: 178

Private Collection: 155

Radio Times Hulton Picture Library: 173 (above and below)

Royal College of Music, London: 77

St Mary's College, Blairs, Aberdeen: 195 (left)

Scottish Record Office: 24–5

Baron H. H. Thyssen-Bornemisea: 14

Versailles: 41

Select Bibliography

Unless otherwise specified, the place of publication of the following books is London, and in the case of a series, published over a number of years, only the earliest publication date is given.

C. Ainsworth Mitchell, *The Evidence of the Casket Letters*. Historical Association Pamphlets. 1927.

J. W. Allen, *History of Political Thought in the 16th Century*. 1941.

James Anderson, *Collections relating to the history of Mary Queen of Scotland*. 4 vols. 1727.

M. H. Armstrong-Davison, *The Casket Letters*. 1965.

Balcarres Paper: *Foreign correspondence with Marie de Lorraine Queen of Scotland, from Balcarres Papers*. Vol. I, 1537–48. Vol. II, 1548–57. Ed. Marguerite Wood. Scot. Hist. Soc. 3rd series. IV. Edinburgh. 1923 and 1925.

Lacey Baldwin Smith, *The Elizabethan Epic*. 1966.

J. B. Black, *Andrew Lang and the Casket Letter Controversy*. Edinburgh. 1951.

J. B. Black, *The Reign of Elizabeth*. 1959.

Collection Blis, *Manuscrits, Livres, Estampes et Objets d'Art relatys a Marie Stuart*. Bibliothèque Nationale, Paris.

George Buchanan, *The Tyrannous Reign of Mary Stewart*. See W. A. Catherer.

Lionel Cust, *Authentic Portraits of Mary Queen of Scots*. 1903.

W. Croft Dickinson, *History of Scotland*. Vol. I. 1961.

Gordon Donaldson, *Scotland: James V–James VI*. Edinburgh. 1965.

Gordon Donaldson, *The Scottish Reformation*. 1960.

Francis Edwards, S.J., *The Dangerous Queen*. 1964.

Francis Edwards, S.J., *The Marvellous Chance*. 1968.

Sir James Fergusson, *The White Hind*. 1963.

J. A. Froude, *History of England from the Fall of Wolsey to the Defeat of the Spanish Armada*. 1862.

W. A. Gatherer, trans. and ed., *The Tyrannous Reign of Mary Stewart by George Buchanan*. Edinburgh. 1958.

R. Gore-Browne, *Lord Bothwell*. 1935.

P. M. Handover, *Arbella Stuart*. 1957.

T. F. Henderson, *Mary Queen of Scots*. 2 vols. 1905.

John Maxwell, Baron Herries, *Historical memoirs of the reign of Mary Queen of Scots*. Abbotsford Club. Ed. R. Pitcairn. Edinburgh. 1836.

J. Hosack, *Mary Queen of Scots and her Accusers*. Edinburgh. 1969.

P. Hume Brown, *Scotland in the Time of Queen Mary*. 1904.

John Knox, *History of the Reformation in Scotland*. Trans. and ed. by W. Croft Dickinson. 1949.

Prince Labanoff (A. I. Lobanov-Rostovosky), *Lettres et Mémoires de Marie, Reine d'Ecosse*. 7 vols. 1844.

Andrew Lang, *Portraits and Jewels of Mary Queen of Scots*. 1906.

D. Macgibbon and T. Ross, *The castellated and domestic architecture of Scotland*. 5 vols. Edinburgh. 1887.

J. D. Mackie, *The Earlier Tudors*. 1966 edition.

Sir Arthur Salusbury MacNalty, *Mary Queen of Scots: the daughter of debate*. 1960.

R. H. Mahon, *The Tragedy of Kirk o'Field*. 1930.

J. E. Neale, *The Elizabethan House of Commons*. 1949.

J. E. Neale, *Queen Elizabeth I and her Parliaments*. 1953.

Sir Charles Oman, *History of the Art of War in the 16th Century*. 1937.

Painted Ceilings of Scotland. M. R. Apted. HMSO. Edinburgh. 1966.

J. E. Phillips, *Images of a Queen: Mary Stuart in 16th century literature*. California. 1964.

J. H. Pollen, S.J., *Letters from Mary Queen of Scots to the Duke of Guise*. Scottish History Society. 1st series. 1904.

Conyers Read, *Bibliography of British History*. Tudor period, 1485–1603.

A. L. Rowse, *The England of Elizabeth*. 1950.

I. M. Stewart, *Scottish coinage*. 1955.

Jane T. Stoddart, *The Girlhood of Mary Queen of Scots*. 1908.

A. Teulet, *Lettres inédites de Marie Stuart*. Paris. 1859.

Marcel Thomas, *Le procès de Marie Stuart. Documents originaux présentes par Marcel Thomas*. Paris. 1956.

George Malcolm Thomson, *The Crime of Mary Stuart*. 1967.

Tudor and Jacobean Portraits. National Portrait Gallery Catalogue, Roy Strong. 1969.

Neville Williams, *Elizabeth Queen of England*. 1967.

Francis du Zulueta, *Embroideries by Mary Stuart and Elizabeth Talbot at Oxburgh Hall*. 1923.

Index